THE
CAMBRIDGE EDITION OF
THE LETTERS AND WORKS OF
D. H. LAWRENCE

THE WORKS OF D. H. LAWRENCE

APOCALYPSE
AND THE WRITINGS ON
REVELATION

D. H. LAWRENCE

EDITED BY
MARA KALNINS

CAMBRIDGE UNIVERSITY PRESS

CAMBRIDGE

LONDON   NEW YORK   NEW ROCHELLE

MELBOURNE   SYDNEY

Published by the Press Syndicate of the University of Cambridge
The Pitt Building, Trumpington Street, Cambridge CB2 1RP
32 East 57th Street, New York, NY 10022, USA
296 Beaconsfield Parade, Middle Park, Melbourne 3206, Australia

Printed in Great Britain at the University Press, Cambridge

British Library Cataloguing in Publication Data
Lawrence, David Herbert
Apocalypse and the writings on Revelation.
(Cambridge edition of the letters and works of
D. H. Lawrence).
1. Bible. New Testament Revelation – Commentaries
I. Title   II. Kalnins, Mara   III. Series
228'.06   BS2825.3   79-41417
ISBN 0 521 22407 1

CONTENTS

GENERAL EDITORS' PREFACE

D. H. Lawrence is one of the great writers of the twentieth century – yet the texts of his writings, whether published during his life-time or since, are, for the most part, textually corrupt. The extent of the corruption is remarkable; it can derive from every stage of composition and publication. We know from study of his MSS that Lawrence was a careful writer, though not rigidly consistent in matters of minor convention. We know also that he revised at every possible stage. Yet he rarely if ever compared one stage with the previous one, and overlooked the errors of typists or copyists. He was forced to accept, as most authors are, the often stringent house-styling of his printers, which overrode his punctuation and even his sentence-structure and paragraphing. He sometimes overlooked plausible printing errors. More important, as a professional author living by his pen, he had to accept, with more or less good will, stringent editing by a publisher's reader in his early days, and at all times the results of his publishers' timidity. So the fear of Grundyish disapproval, or actual legal action, led to bowdlerisation or censorship from the very beginning of his career. Threats of libel suits produced other changes. Sometimes a publisher made more changes than he admitted to Lawrence. On a number of occasions in dealing with American and British publishers Lawrence produced texts for both which were not identical. Then there were extraordinary lapses like the occasion when a compositor turned over two pages of MS at once, and the result happened to make sense. This whole story can be reconstructed from the introductions to the volumes in this edition; cumulatively they will form a history of Lawrence's writing career.

The Cambridge edition aims to provide texts which are as close as can now be determined to those he would have wished to see printed. They have been established by a rigorous collation of extant manuscripts and typescripts, proofs and early printed versions; they restore the words, sentences, even whole pages omitted or falsified by editors or compositors; they are freed from printing-house conventions which were imposed on Lawrence's style; and interference on the part of frightened publishers has been eliminated. Far from doing violence to the texts Lawrence would have wished to see published, editorial intervention is essential to recover them. Though we have to accept that some cannot now be recovered in their entirety because early states have not survived, we must be glad that so much evidence remains. Paradoxical as it may seem, the outcome of this recension will be texts which differ, often radically and certainly frequently, from those seen by the author himself.

Editors have adopted the principle that the most authoritative form of the text is to be followed, even if this leads sometimes to a 'spoken' or a 'manuscript' rather than a 'printed' style. We have not wanted to strip off one house-styling in order to impose another. Editorial discretion has been allowed in order to regularise Lawrence's sometimes wayward spelling and punctuation in accordance with his most frequent practice in a particular text. A detailed record of these and other decisions on textual matters, together with the evidence on which they are based, will be found in the textual apparatus. This gives significant deleted readings in manuscripts, typescripts and proofs; and printed variants in forms of the text published in Lawrence's lifetime. We do not record posthumous corruptions, except where first publication was posthumous.

In each volume, the editor's introduction relates the contents to Lawrence's life and to his other writings; it gives the history of composition of the text in some detail, for its intrinsic interest, and because this history is essential to the statement of editorial principles followed. It provides an account of publication and reception which will be found to contain a good deal of hitherto unknown information. Where appropriate, appendixes make available extended draft manuscript readings of significance, or important material, sometimes unpublished, associated with a particular work.

Though Lawrence is a twentieth-century writer and in many respects remains our contemporary, the idiom of his day is not invariably intelligible now, especially to the many readers who are not native speakers of British English. His use of dialect is another difficulty, and further barriers to full understanding are created by now obscure literary, historical, political or other references and allusions. On these occasions explanatory notes are supplied by the editor; it is assumed that the reader has access to a good general dictionary and that the editor need not gloss words or expressions that may be found in it. Where Lawrence's letters are quoted in editorial matter, the reader should assume that his manuscript is alone the source of eccentricities of phrase or spelling. An edition of the letters is still in course of publication: for this reason only the date and recipient of a letter will be given if it has not so far been printed in the Cambridge edition.

ACKNOWLEDGEMENTS

I would like to thank Mr T. R. M. Creighton and Mrs Lindeth Vasey for their invaluable help in reading and criticising the introduction; the Reverend Donald Whittle for assistance in finding several obscure references; and Mr W. Forster, Mr George Lazarus and Mrs Edna Whiteson for kind permission to consult the manuscripts and books in their collections. I also wish to thank the staff of the Humanities Research Center at the University of Texas for their help and Mr Michael Black and the staff of Cambridge University Press, in particular Dr Andrew Brown and Miss Maureen Leach, for their unfailing patience and assistance in producing this volume. My special thanks must go to Professor James Boulton, general editor of the edition, for his generous advice and encouragement throughout.

M.K.

July 1980

CHRONOLOGY

11 September 1885	Born in Eastwood, Nottinghamshire
September 1898–July 1901	Pupil at Nottingham High School
1902–1908	Pupil teacher; student at University College, Nottingham
7 December 1907	First publication: 'A Prelude', in *Nottinghamshire Guardian*
October 1908	Appointed as teacher at Davidson Road School, Croydon
November 1909	Publishes five poems in *English Review*
3 December 1910	Engagement to Louie Burrows; broken off on 4 February 1912
9 December 1910	Death of his mother, Lydia Lawrence
19 January 1911	*The White Peacock* published in New York (20 January in London)
19 November 1911	Ill with pneumonia; resigns his teaching post on 28 February 1912
March 1912	Meets Frieda Weekley; they elope to Germany on 3 May
23 May 1912	*The Trespasser*
September 1912–March 1913	At Gargnano, Lago di Garda, Italy
February 1913	*Love Poems and Others*
29 May 1913	*Sons and Lovers*
June–August 1913	In England
August 1913–June 1914	In Germany, Switzerland and Italy
13 July 1914	Marries Frieda Weekley in London
July 1914–December 1915	In London, Buckinghamshire and Sussex
26 November 1914	*The Prussian Officer*
30 September 1915	*The Rainbow*; suppressed by court order on 13 November
June 1916	*Twilight in Italy*
July 1916	*Amores*
15 October 1917	After twenty-one months' residence in Cornwall, ordered to leave by military authorities
October 1917–November 1919	In London, Berkshire and Derbyshire
December 1917	*Look! We Have Come Through!*
October 1918	*New Poems*
November 1919–February 1922	To Italy, then Capri and Sicily
20 November 1919	*Bay*

November 1920	Private publication of *Women in Love* (New York), *The Lost Girl*
10 May 1921	*Psychoanalysis and the Unconscious* (New York)
12 December 1921	*Sea and Sardinia* (New York)
March–August 1922	In Ceylon and Australia
14 April 1922	*Aaron's Rod* (New York)
September 1922–March 1923	In New Mexico
23 October 1922	*Fantasia of the Unconscious* (New York)
24 October 1922	*England, My England* (New York)
December 1922	Correspondence between D. H. Lawrence and Frederick Carter begins
March 1923	*The Ladybird, The Fox, The Captain's Doll*
March–November 1923	In Mexico and USA
15 June 1923	Receives Carter's MS 'The Dragon of the Apocalypse'
27 August 1923	*Studies in Classic American Literature* (New York)
September 1923	*Kangaroo*
9 October 1923	*Birds, Beasts and Flowers* (New York)
December 1923–March 1924	In England, France and Germany
3–5 January 1924	Stays with Carter in Shropshire
February 1924	'On Being Religious' published in *Adelphi*
c. 15 February 1924	Writes 'A Review of *The Book of Revelation* by Dr. John Oman' and sends it to Middleton Murry
March 1924	'On Human Destiny' published in *Adelphi*
March 1924–September 1925	In New Mexico and Mexico
April 1924	'A Review of *The Book of Revelation* by Dr. John Oman' published in *Adelphi*
August 1924	*The Boy in the Bush* (with Mollie Skinner)
10 September 1924	Death of his father, John Arthur Lawrence
14 May 1925	*St Mawr together with The Princess*
September 1925–June 1928	In England and mainly Italy
7 December 1925	*Reflections on the Death of a Porcupine* (Philadelphia)
January 1926	*The Plumed Serpent*
June 1927	*Mornings in Mexico*
24 May 1928	*The Woman Who Rode Away and Other Stories*
June 1928–March 1930	In Switzerland and, principally, in France
July 1928	*Lady Chatterley's Lover* privately published (Florence)
September 1928	*Collected Poems*
July 1929	Exhibition of paintings in London raided by police. *Pansies* (manuscript earlier seized in the mail)
23 August 1929	Resumes correspondence with Carter
September 1929	*The Escaped Cock* (Paris)
October 1929	Writes most of the *Last Poems*

1 October 1929	Work on Revelation begins
by 12? November 1929	Wrote the mystical notes to *Birds, Beasts and Flowers*
30 November 1929	'Nearly 20,000 words' of *Apocalypse* written
15 December 1929	*Apocalypse* 'roughly finished'; revision continues
by end December 1929	*Apocalypse* typed
by 6 January 1930	'Introduction to *The Dragon of the Apocalypse* by Frederick Carter' finished
by 9 January 1930	*Apocalypse* typescript corrected and the ending revised
by 25? January 1930	Wrote his 'Introduction' to Koteliansky's translation of Dostoyevsky's 'The Grand Inquisitor' from *The Brothers Karamazov*
2 March 1930	Dies at Vence, Alpes Maritimes, France
July 1930	'Introduction to *The Dragon of the Apocalypse* by Frederick Carter' published in *The London Mercury*
early January 1931	*Apocalypse* sent to Curtis Brown, London
21 January 1931	Orioli, Frieda Lawrence and George Lawrence sign a contract for the publication of *Apocalypse* in a limited edition
3 June 1931	First edition of *Apocalypse*, Orioli, Florence
27 November 1931	First American edition of *Apocalypse*, Viking, New York
13 February 1932	First American edition of *Apocalypse* with Richard Aldington's 'Introduction', Viking, New York
May 1932	First English edition of *Apocalypse* with Richard Aldington's 'Introduction', Secker
Autumn 1932	First continental edition of *Apocalypse* with Richard Aldington's 'Introduction', Albatross, Hamburg

CUE-TITLES

(The place of publication is London unless otherwise stated.)

Burnet
John Burnet. *Early Greek Philosophy*. Edinburgh: Black, 1892

Carter
Frederick Carter. *D. H. Lawrence and the Body Mystical*. Denis Archer, 1932

Charles
R. H. Charles. *A Critical and Exegetical Commentary on the Revelation of St. John*. 2 volumes. Heinemann, 1964

Complete Poems
Vivian de Sola Pinto and Warren Roberts, eds. *The Complete Poems of D. H. Lawrence*. 2 volumes. Heinemann, 1964

Letters
James T. Boulton, ed. *The Letters of D. H. Lawrence*. Volume 1. Cambridge: Cambridge University Press, 1979

Murray
Gilbert Murray. *Five Stages of Greek Religion*. Oxford University Press, 1925

Nehls
Edward Nehls, ed. *D. H. Lawrence: A Composite Biography*. 3 volumes. Madison: University of Wisconsin Press, 1957–9

Phoenix
Edward D. McDonald, ed. *Phoenix: The Posthumous Papers of D. H. Lawrence*. Heinemann, 1936

Phoenix II
Warren Roberts and Harry T. Moore, eds. *Phoenix II: Uncollected, Unpublished and other Prose Works by D. H. Lawrence*. Heinemann, 1968

Roberts
Warren Roberts. *A Bibliography of D. H. Lawrence*. Rupert Hart-Davis, 1963

INTRODUCTION

INTRODUCTION

Apocalypse and the Writings on Revelation

This volume contains Lawrence's writings on the Book of Revelation: namely the short review of John Oman's *Book of Revelation* published in *Adelphi*, April 1924; and two works he wrote in 1929–30 shortly before his death: 'Introduction to *The Dragon of the Apocalypse* by Frederick Carter', and *Apocalypse*. The Appendixes present for the first time previously unpublished material on Revelation.

Lawrence's familiarity with the Book of Revelation dates from his youth, when he attended the Congregationalist chapel in Eastwood – 'From early childhood I have been familiar with Apocalyptic language and Apocalyptic image'[1] – and the influence of the Bible, its imagery, language and symbolism, did much to form his style and to shape his vision of man and the cosmos. But it was not until 1923 when he began corresponding with Frederick Carter,[2] an English painter and a mystic, that Lawrence thought of writing about the Book of Revelation. Carter was impelled by his interest in astrology and the occult and by his liking for Lawrence's work to write to him in December 1922 asking for his opinion of a manuscript and drawings on the symbolism of Revelation. Lawrence, then living at Taos, New Mexico, agreed to read the manuscript,[3] although his own interests at the time lay in the psychological revelation, rather than the astrological symbolism, of St John's apocalyptic writing: 'Your letter interests me, and makes me want to read your whole MS. Myself I am more interested in the *micro*cosm than in the macrocosm, and in the gates to the psyche rather than the astrological houses. But one gets such rare hints from astrology.'[4]

[1] 'Introduction to *The Dragon of the Apocalypse*', p. 54.
[2] Frederick Carter (1883–1967), painter and etcher, studied in Paris and Antwerp and on his return to England took up book illustrating. The MS he sent DHL in 1923 was eventually revised and published as *The Dragon of the Alchemists* (1926). Carter is the author of *D. H. Lawrence and the Body Mystical* (1932), which tells of his association with DHL, and *Gold Like Glass* (1932). His second book on apocalyptic symbols, for which DHL wrote his 'Introduction', was originally entitled *The Dragon of the Apocalypse* but the title was later changed by Carter to *The Dragon of Revelation* (1931) and the book as a whole was still later revised and published as *Symbols of Revelation* (1934).
[3] Letter to Carter, 31 December 1922.
[4] Letter to Carter, 8 March 1923.

3

In the previous year Lawrence had completed *Fantasia of the Unconscious*, where he had explored his ideas about the psyche, and in March 1923 he left Taos and moved to Mexico where he began work on 'Quetzalcoatl', the novel that was to become *The Plumed Serpent*. From here he wrote to Carter offering to help him find a publisher and to write a foreword to the manuscript if he liked it: 'If I find myself capable, I will gladly do a brief foreword for the drawings: when I get them.'[5] But it was not until 15 June 1923 that Carter's astrological drawings and the text of *The Dragon of the Apocalypse* as it was then called, finally arrived.[6] Lawrence's reaction was enthusiastic, and in an important letter dated 18 June 1923, he explained his own theories about St John's Revelation:

It's a revelation of Initiation experience, and the clue is in the microcosm, in the human body itself, I believe, and the Zodiac is only used from the table of the Zodiacal Man, and the Man in the Zodiac has his clue in the man of flesh and blood...The subtle thing is the relation between the microcosm and the macrocosm. Get that relation – the Zodiac man to me – and you've got a straight clue to Apocalypsis.[7]

Lawrence interpreted the astrological scheme of Revelation that Carter had sent him as an attempt to narrate a profound psychical experience in man, an experience too fundamental for rational explanation or scientific description. For him, St John's book was a 'revelation of Initiation experience', a manual of esoteric lore derived from the ancient pagans, corrupted by later Jewish and Christian editors, but nevertheless showing the way to mystic liberation of the self. A clue to this process, he argued, lay in the ancient symbol of the Zodiacal Man, the starry figure of the heavens whose body was composed of the twelve signs of the Zodiac, symbols of the powers ruling the various parts of man. This great figure was an emblem of that mystic correspondence between microcosm and macrocosm, the individual and the universe. Lawrence had assimilated these esoteric ideas from his extensive reading during the war years of writers on the occult and especially of Helena Blavatsky, the Russian-born theosophist. Though his critical sense made him doubtful of the value of her theosophical books *Isis Unveiled* and *The Secret Doctrine* – 'they're not *very* much good'[8] – he

---

[5] Letter to Carter, 23 April 1923.
[6] Letter to Carter, 15 June 1923. The revised version of this MS was later published as *The Dragon of the Alchemists* (1926).
[7] Letter to Carter, 18 June 1923.
[8] Letter to Nancy Henry, 13 November 1918. See also letter to Mark Gertler on DHL's occult readings, 28 April 1918.
    Helena Blavatsky (1831–91) was a Russian-born spiritualist who became involved in spiritualist research in New York as well as in Europe and, with Col. H. S. Olcott and W. Q. Judge, founded the Theosophical Society. She wrote *Isis Unveiled* (1877), *The Secret*

believed in the existence of true and ancient knowledge which had been repressed by Christianity with its doctrine of a spiritual salvation which must be attained in another world: 'The religious systems of the pagan world did what Christianity has never tried to do: they gave the true correspondence between the material cosmos and the human soul. The ancient cosmic theories were exact, and apparently perfect. In them science and religion were in accord.'[9] However, 'the early Christian world...rejected every trace of the old true science – every trace save, perhaps, the unreadable riddle of the Apocalypse'.[10] With the decline of Christianity in our century we needed to regain 'the old true science', to find a way of releasing the potential for a richer and fuller life in the here and now. 'The Resurrection is to life, not to death'[11] wrote Lawrence as early as *The Rainbow*. Increasingly he turned away from Christianity (with its emphasis on the crucifixion and the hereafter) to the pagan religions of re-birth and the occult theories of revivifying descent into the self, for the symbols with which to express his belief: 'Man wants his physical fulfilment first and foremost, since now, once and once only, he is in the flesh and potent. For man, the vast marvel is to be alive. For man, as for flower and beast and bird, the supreme triumph is to be most vividly, most perfectly alive.'[12]

Lawrence had been particularly influenced by the Dublin theosophist James Pryse, whose *The Apocalypse Unsealed* he had read.[13] He liked Pryse's notion of a latent power within man that could be liberated through the controlled awakening of the seven principal nerve centres or 'chakras' along the spine. The 'chakra' – generally translated as 'plexus', a term Lawrence used in *Fantasia of the Unconscious* though elsewhere he also calls it a 'primary affective centre' – is a vortex or centre of psychic energy. In yoga this power is called *kundalini* and is symbolically represented as a dragon or a serpent coiled at the base of the spine; it is that 'startled life which runs through us like a serpent, or coils within us potent and waiting, like a

Doctrine (1888), *The Key to Theosophy* (1889) and *The Voice of Silence* (1889).

9   'The Two Principles', *Phoenix II* 227.
10 'Fenimore Cooper's Anglo-American Novels', *The Symbolic Meaning*, ed. A. Arnold (New York, 1962), p. 76.
11 *The Rainbow* (1915), chapter 10.
12 *Apocalypse* p. 149.
13 Letter to David Eder, 25 August 1917.

Have you read Blavatsky's *Secret Doctrine*? In many ways a bore, and not quite real. Yet one can glean a marvellous lot from it, enlarge the understanding immensely. Do you know the physical–physiological–interpretations of the esoteric doctrine? – the *chakras* and dualism in experience?...Did you get Pryce's *Apocalypse Unsealed*?

James Pryse, author of *The Apocalypse Unsealed* (1910) and friend of Helena Blavatsky, had also introduced A. E. and W. B. Yeats to magic and initiation rites.

serpent'.[14] When awakened this serpent releases a life-giving force by moving
upward and gaining power with the '.conquest' of each 'chakra'. According
to Pryse the opening of the seven seals in Revelation represents this
movement, 'the opening, and conquest of the great psychic centres of the
body' as Lawrence phrased it,[15] and the New Jerusalem is the newly
regenerated spirit. Lawrence's letter to Carter continues with an interpretation of St John's imagery in Revelation as precisely this process of willed
self-liberation.

I believe...his imagery started primarily from the physical psyche, the organic and
the nervous and cerebral psyche, and expanded into the stars. That I believe. He
was seeking to project the spinal chord into the Galactic Way. The Seals are ganglia
of nerve-consciousness, projected into zodiacal signs and star-constellations. The
Dragon is the Will and Desire. The riders are the energetic messages, releases of
consciousness and energy, resultant on the conquest by mind and will of one after
the other of the primary affective centres...The revelation is a conquest, one by one,
of the lower affective centres by the mind, and the New Jerusalem is the mind
enthroned.[16]

Lawrence had already explored some of these ideas in *Fantasia of the
Unconscious* and in the early versions of *Studies in Classic American
Literature*, re-written in the winter of 1922–3,[17] where he expresses his
conviction:

It is quite certain that the pre-Christian priesthoods understood the process of
dynamic consciousness, which is pre-cerebral consciousness. It is certain that St. John
gives us in the Apocalypse a cypher-account of the process of the conquest of the
lower or sensual dynamic centres by the upper or spiritual dynamic consciousness,
a conquest affected centre by centre, towards a culmination in the *actual* experience
of spiritual infinitude.[18]

This redeeming conquest however was not a subjugation of the physical to
the cerebral, a notion that Lawrence with his belief in the primacy of instinct
and passion over intellect would have detested, but the release of power latent
in the dark lower centres. This meant a fresh start away from intellect, as
he wrote to Carter, 'in the first great direction, with the polarity downwards,
as it was in the great pre-Greek Æons, all Egypt and Chaldea. Greece
changed the direction, the Latins went it full tilt. The great *down* direction,

[14] *Apocalypse* p. 123.
[15] Ibid., p. 101.
[16] Letter to Carter, 18 June 1923.
[17] Letter to Carter, 8 March 1923 which reads: 'I am publishing *Studies in Classic American Literature* this spring, but I have taken out all the esoteric stuff. Best keep it esoteric.'
[18] 'Fenimore Cooper's Anglo-American Novels', *The Symbolic Meaning*, 75.

away from mind, to power, that was old Egypt. The sceptre, not the logos.'[19] Lawrence believed that the movement in 'the great *down* direction' would end the domination of the Logos, the Word, and would restore the balance between the spiritual and sensual planes of existence that Greece, Rome and Christianity, with their emphasis on the spirit and the mind, had destroyed. Man need not wait for a postponed spiritual salvation – he held the key to fulfilment within himself, bound in the 'physical psyche'. Lawrence resolved the logical and semantic contradiction inherent in this term by defining the 'physical psyche' as the inseparable union of soul and body through the life-force informing both: 'the psyche comprising our whole consciousness, physical, sensual, spiritual, pre-cerebral as well as cerebral'.[20] The initiation process depicted in Revelation was 'the rise of pre-cerebral consciousness in the great plexuses, and the movement of passional or dynamic cognition from one centre, towards culmination or consummation in what we may call whole-experience or whole consciousness'.[21] This 'whole consciousness', what Jung termed 'integration', was the attainment of inner harmony and balance and a sense of living connection with the greater universe. Like Jung, Lawrence saw the human psyche poised between two worlds – the objective material universe, and the subjective inner world – with an equal need to relate to both, to integrate them for the enrichment and development of the psyche. 'What man most passionately wants is his living wholeness and his living unison'[22] he later wrote in his *Apocalypse*. Only by recognising the duality inherent in the cosmos and in man's being and by transcending it, could that 'living wholeness', the aim of human existence, be achieved. To this state of wholeness and to the power that creates it Lawrence gave many names – the Crown, the Rainbow, the Holy Ghost, the New Jerusalem are some of them – but it was always in essence a religious experience, a fulfilling of the human potential, of God incarnate in man: 'the clue or quick of the universe lies in the creative mystery...in the human psyche...the only form of worship is *to be*'.[23]

Lawrence adopted ideas and images from many myths and religions in his search to discover the means of achieving this wholeness, but he always returned to the Bible and finally to the Book of Revelation, in whose vision of the opening of the seven seals and the re-birth of the soul, he found a symbolically dramatic account of that quest. He recognised that the

[19] Letter to Carter, 18 June 1923.
[20] 'Fenimore Cooper's Anglo-American Novels', *The Symbolic Meaning*, 75.
[21] Ibid., 75.   [22] *Apocalypse* p. 149.
[23] 'Nathaniel Hawthorne I', *The Symbolic Meaning*, 137.

importance of his extensive reading in anthropology and the esoteric as well as his liking for Carter's astrological schemes lay in the stimulus they offered to his imagination and he did not seek for any ultimate validity in the doctrines he found there. Indeed he acknowledged in the 'Foreword' to *Fantasia*:

I am not a proper archaeologist nor an anthropologist nor an ethnologist. I am no "scholar" of any sort. But I am very grateful to scholars for their sound work. I have found hints, suggestions for what I say here in all kinds of scholarly books, from the Yoga and Plato and St. John the Evangel and the early Greek philosophers like Herakleitos down to Frazer and his "Golden Bough," and even Freud and Frobenius. Even then I only remember hints – and I proceed by intuition.[24]

Lawrence corresponded with Carter over the summer of 1923 about the publication of the *Dragon*, and in the autumn converted his original offer of a brief foreword into the possibility of writing an introduction.[25] His subsequent travels to California, Mexico and then England temporarily disrupted plans for the *Dragon* but in December 1923 Lawrence was again writing to Carter, and from 3–5 January 1924, he stayed with him in Shropshire,[26] drawn by the prospect of discussing the dragon emblem which was to become the central symbol of *The Plumed Serpent*. Carter recalls the visit.

At different periods I had occasion to discuss his theories upon the psyche with him and compare opinions upon the significance of old myths and traditions. And whilst he was staying with me for a little while in Shropshire, we considered means for the development of a certain line of research in symbolism, and the publication of some essays and a book or two about ancient ideas on the soul and their permanent validity, and of the problem of the last end of the world.

The first fruit of our conversation – an essay preliminary – was an article, written by me, on 'The Antique Science of Astrology' and one or two articles on man and cosmos by Lawrence, all published in the *Adelphi Magazine* in the early part of 1924. More would have followed – for example one on the Sacred Art of Alchemy – but serious business difficulties in America called him back there. And so fell through the whole scheme which he had in mind for a publishing office of books to be

---

[24] 'Foreword' to *Fantasia of the Unconscious* (1922).

[25] Letter to Carter [15? September 1923]

I got the new MS. of the *Dragon* from Seltzer today. So long these things take! I am going through it carefully. I think you'll have to give me permission to punctuate a little more, and sometimes to re-arrange your words a trifle, where you are a bit obscure. Will you do this? Because I am going to do my best to get Seltzer to publish the book. And perhaps I will write an introduction.

Thomas Seltzer (1873–1943) publisher and translator, was DHL's chief American publisher in the early 1920s.

[26] See letters to Carter [1? January 1924] and [6? January 1924].

established in London and, beyond that, a society of students to live and work in New Mexico, on the farm at Questa, near Taos.[27]

Carter's article was to be the first of 'a series of articles on...the astronomical symbolism that conditioned the religious writings of the beginning of this era'.[28] It undoubtedly owed something to Lawrence, who revised it – 'I made a few slight alterations only to your style, which is sometimes odd and obscure...and the title I think shall be *The Ancient Science of Astrology*'[29] – and several passages bear an unmistakably Lawrentian stamp for, as Carter observed, Lawrence 'had an insistent desire to amend, enhance and colour anything that deeply moved his interest'.[30] Carter's article did not appear until the April issue of the *Adelphi* and he never wrote another,[31] but Lawrence's two essays, 'On Being Religious' and 'On Human Destiny', came out in the February and March 1924 issues respectively. They contain Lawrence's thoughts on the universal nature of religion, for which St Augustine's words (also quoted by Carter in 'The Ancient Science of Astrology') are an epitome: 'There never has been but one religion, nor has it ever been absent from the world. It commenced to call itself Christian in apostolic times.'[32] It is in this spirit that Lawrence felt that today 'the long light of Christianity is guttering to go out and we have to get at new resources in ourselves'.[33] These essays pose what was always for Lawrence the central question facing humanity in every age: 'How shall Man put himself into relation to God, into a living relation?'[34]

Lawrence's interest in apocalyptic symbols prompted him to read a new interpretation of St John, *Book of Revelation* by John Oman, published in

27 Carter 5–6. The two articles were 'On Being Religious' and 'On Human Destiny' published in the *Adelphi* for February and March 1924, respectively. In March 1924 the Lawrences moved to The Flying Heart ranch, seventeen miles from Taos, New Mexico, which had been presented to them by Mrs Mabel Dodge Luhan. DHL first re-named the ranch Lobo and later Kiowa. However the Lawrences continued to receive their post at nearby Del Monte ranch, Questa, Taos.
28 Carter 32.
29 Letter to Carter [11? January 1924].
30 Carter 34.
    We made a synopsis of the first article which I wrote out and sent to him in town. Lawrence read it and inserted a few passages before the typescript was made. Some of these it was necessary to delete for his notions of the interrelation of parts in the astrological heavens and their stars was hazardous, but even yet some hints of the Laurentian purple may there be discovered by the perspicuous reader. Carter 32.
31 Ibid., 32.
32 These words were quoted by Carter in his article 'The Ancient Science of Astrology', *Adelphi*, i (April 1924) 1005, but they also reveal the direction of DHL's thinking at this time.
33 'On Human Destiny', *Phoenix II* 628.
34 'On Being Religious', *Phoenix* 726–7.

1923, which he thought 'fairly sound'.[35] On [15? February 1924] he wrote to John Middleton Murry, then editor of the *Adelphi*, enclosing a short review: 'I send you a little review of Oman's book, which you print if you like or throw away if you like...Don't put my name on the review if you use it.'[36] This appeared under his pseudonym 'L. H. Davidson' in the April 1924 issue. Middleton Murry may have altered the text but there is no surviving manuscript or typescript of this review and in the absence of any subsequent correspondence the published version is assumed to have had Lawrence's sanction. (It is therefore the *Adelphi* text which is printed in this volume.)

In this short review the lines on the apocalyptist of Revelation are an equally telling comment on Lawrence's feeling about and commitment to our century: 'John's passionate and mystic hatred of the civilization of his day, a hatred so intense only because he knew that the living realities of men's being were displaced by it, is something to which the soul answers now again.'[37] His own 'passionate and mystic hatred of the civilization of his day', a civilisation which he saw as progressively dehumanising the individual, was to express itself in the bitter and misanthropic aspects of his writings in the years to come, but the need to search for 'the living realities of men's being' was the primary force in the development of his thought and art. It was a search that was to lead him back to old pagan religions and myths in the quest for symbols that would refresh the springs of religious experience in modern man.

The attraction of Revelation was inexhaustible, as Lawrence acknowledged,[38] and its symbols, imagery and myth continued to fascinate him; but for the moment his correspondence with Carter lapsed, and with it the particular desire to write on Revelation itself. It was not until the end of his life that he returned to the idea of writing about St John's apocalyptic

---

[35] Letter to Carter [14? February 1924]. Dr John Wood Oman (1860–1939) was a Presbyterian theologian. From 1907 to 1935 he was professor at, and from 1925 to 1935 principal of, Westminster College, Cambridge. He published his *Book of Revelation* in 1923 (DHL, however, refers to it as *The Book of Revelation*). His other writings include a translation of F. D. E. Schleiermacher's *Speeches on Religion* (1893), *Vision and Authority* (1902), *The Church and the Divine Order* (1911), *Grace and Personality* (1917).

[36] Letter to John Middleton Murry [15? February 1924]. John Middleton Murry (1889–1957), author, editor and critic, met DHL in 1913, whereupon began a long, although erratic and tempestuous, friendship. Murry married Katherine Mansfield in 1918. He edited the *Athenaeum* (1919–21) and wrote two books on DHL: *Son of Woman* (1931) and *Reminiscences of D. H. Lawrence* (1933).

   DHL's review was published in the *Adelphi*, i (April 1924) 1011–13 under a version of his pseudonym 'L. H. Davison', here 'L. H. Davidson'. See Nehls, i. 471.

[37] 'A Review of *The Book of Revelation* by Dr. John Oman' p. 41.

[38] Ibid., p. 42.

work. Carter recalls the disappointing end to their correspondence soon after Lawrence's visit in January 1924:

When he left it was settled that he was to be back again in March from Germany, and with all the schemes discussed in working order – even started. But by that time difficulties in business had called him away to New York. Nothing was done and my MSS came back from London, the matter seemed to have ended. A rare postcard from a discouraged Lawrence and another. Away in that far corner of the country I heard nothing except rumours sufficiently vague, until, once more residing in London, Lawrence's venture into painting came under discussion.[39]

In the intervening years Lawrence had travelled back to Mexico where he finished *The Plumed Serpent*, and then returned to Taos again. Finally in September 1925 he left America for good and sailed for Europe. Between 1925 and 1929 he spent much of his time in Italy, at the Villa Mirenda near Florence, where he wrote *Lady Chatterley's Lover*; and he travelled to Austria, England, Germany, Majorca, Switzerland and France. But his health, never robust, was failing, and at the end of September 1929 the Lawrences decided to return to Bandol in the south of France, where they moved into the Villa Beau Soleil. There Lawrence was to write his last poems, a few late reviews and essays, and his last book, *Apocalypse*.

News that Lawrence's paintings had been seized from the Warren Gallery in London and impounded for obscenity in the summer of 1929[40] had reached Frederick Carter and, hearing that Lawrence was again on the continent, he contacted his agent and their correspondence resumed.[41] Lawrence's interest in Revelation revived and on 30 August 1929 he wrote to Carter enquiring after the old manuscript of the *Dragon* and again offering to help with publication and with a foreword.[42] The original *Dragon*, however, no longer existed. A much reduced and revised version had been published as *The Dragon of the Alchemists* in 1926 and the remaining

[39] Carter 41–2.

[40] The Warren Gallery at 39a Maddox St, London, was owned by Mrs Dorothy Trotter (née Warren), a friend of DHL's since 1915. DHL's pictures were exhibited at the gallery from June to September 1929. For the story of their impounding see Nehls, iii. 327–89.

[41] See Carter 42. DHL replied to Carter on 23 August asking where he might get a copy of *The Dragon of the Alchemists*. See also letter to Edward Titus, 19 August 1929 and letter to Charles Lahr [23? August 1929]. Edward Titus had published the 'Paris Popular Edition' of *Lady Chatterley's Lover* which included 'My Skirmish with Jolly Roger' in May 1929.

[42] Letter to Carter, 30 August 1929.

I should really like to read the whole thing again, and see if my first impression holds good. I should like to read the second version too. And if I like the *Dragon* as much as I originally did – though I admit it was a bit tough and tangled – I'm sure we can find a way of printing it complete, even if I have to write a real spangled foreword to it (perhaps you would refuse to let me)...

manuscript 'had been reconsidered, rewritten in parts, rejected in others as too complicated and esoteric, too occult'.[43] During the autumn of 1929 Carter agreed to work on its reconstruction. He sent portions of manuscript to Lawrence, and on 1 October Lawrence mentioned that he had undertaken 'to do some work on the Apocalypse, more or less in conjunction with Frederick Carter'.[44] With characteristic enthusiasm he wrote to Charles Lahr, the London bookseller, ordering a formidable reading list that included 'a good annotated edition of *Revelations* – or of New Testament', a copy of Carter's published book, and 'any books, really good, on civilisation in the Eastern Mediterranean, before the rise of Athens – on Tree and Pillar cult – on the Chaldean and Babylonian myths – Sir Arthur Evans on Crete is so huge and expensive'.[45] On the same date he wrote to Carter acknowledging that he had received his last manuscript.

The "Apocalypse" came yesterday, and I have read it. And again I get a peculiar pleasure and liberation out of it. It is very fragmentary – I suppose it is natural to you to be fragmentary. But in fragments fascinating. . .Send me whatever remaining MS. there is, and we will see how we can arrange. We'll get it published. What I shall have to do is to write a comment on the Apocalypse also, from my point of view – and touching on yours – and try to give some sort of complete idea. . .We will make a joint book. I very much want to put into the world again the big old pagan vision, before the *idea* and the concept of personality made everything so small and tight as it is now.[46]

Lawrence was reading portions of Carter's manuscript, including an essay entitled 'Apocalyptic Images' and *The Dragon of the Alchemists* around 10 October[47] and beginning to tackle Archdeacon Charles' scholarly books on Revelation: 'I have got "Charles" from Lahr – two fat vols – and have ordered Moret and Loisy in Paris.'[48] He wrote to his friend Koteliansky asking for John Burnet's *Early Greek Philosophy* which he used extensively

[43]   Carter 42.
[44]   Letter to Lahr, 1 October 1929.
[45]   Ibid. Sir Arthur John Evans (1851–1941), the famous archaeologist whose excavations in Crete uncovered the prehistoric Palace of Knossos, had written *The Mycenaean Tree and Pillar Cult* (1901).
[46]   Letter to Carter, 1 October 1929.
[47]   See letter to Carter, 10 October 1929.
[48]   Ibid. 'Charles' refers to the two-volume *A Critical and Exegetical Commentary on The Revelation of St. John* (1920) by R. H. Charles (1855–1931), Archdeacon of Westminster from 1919. Archdeacon Charles was a distinguished biblical scholar, author of many translations of and works about the Old and New Testaments. DHL consulted his *Commentary* for his own work on Revelation. The two French books (see also letter to Carter, 1 October 1929) were *Rituel journalier en Egypte* by A. Moret and *L'Apocalypse de Jean* by A. Loisy (see also letter to Titus, 7 October 1929). DHL never received the Moret book, however (see letter to Titus, 20 November 1929).

for the late poems and essays. 'Do you still have that book *Early Greek Philosophers* which I bought when I was last in London? if so, would you send it me, I want to do some work on the Apocalypse and consult it.'[49] Lawrence had read and re-read Burnet over the years and had been profoundly influenced by his account of early Greek science, religion and philosophy. As early as July 1915 he had written: 'I shall write all my philosophy again. Last time I came out of the Christian Camp. This time I must come out of these early Greek philosophers'[50] and 'I shall write out Herakleitos, on tablets of bronze.'[51] In his search to define his cosmology and to understand the manifestations of God as he saw them revealed in the phenomenal universe, Lawrence found the pre-Socratic vision of the cosmos – 'All things are full of Gods'[52] – naturally congenial: 'We want to realise the tremendous *non-human* quality of life... the tremendous unknown forces of life.'[53] Two of Heraclitus' ideas in particular had a lasting influence on Lawrence and are present in most of his writing after 1915. First, the notion of the duality inherent in the universe and the concept of the 'Boundless' – the primary absolute out of which all duality emerges to form the universe but which itself transcends these contraries: 'All existence is dual, and surging towards consummation into being'[54] and 'the Infinite, the Boundless, the Eternal... [is] the real starting point'.[55] And second, Heraclitus' belief that 'strife' or conflict is the power which causes all things to rise into being.

There are the two eternities fighting the fight of Creation, the light projecting itself into the darkness, the darkness enveloping herself within the embrace of light. And then there is the consummation of each in the other, the consummation of light in darkness and darkness in light, which is absolute: our bodies cast up like foam of two meeting waves, but foam which is absolute, complete, beyond the limitation of either infinity, consummate over both eternities. The direct opposites of the

49 Letter to Koteliansky, 10 October 1929. DHL had read John Burnet's *Early Greek Philosophy* (Edinburgh, 1892) several times over the years, though he mistakes the title here. He first mentions the book by title in a letter to Dollie Radford on 5 September 1916 although it is probable that he had read it the previous year (see letter to Bertrand Russell [21? July 1915]. John Burnet (1863–1928), Professor of Greek at the University of St Andrews, wrote several books on Plato and Greek philosophy. Samuel Solomonovich Koteliansky ('Kot') (1882–1955) was a Ukrainian-born translator who came to England in 1911 where he met DHL, whose life-long friend he became. He collaborated with Katherine Mansfield, Virginia Woolf, Leonard Woolf and DHL in translating Tolstoy, Dostoyevsky, Chekhov, Gorky, Bunin, etc.
50 Letter to Lady Ottoline Morrell, [19 July 1915]. The 'philosophy' refers to an early version of 'The Crown' entitled 'Morgenrot'.
51 Letter to Bertrand Russell, [21? July 1915].
52 Burnet 48. This is a quotation from Thales.
53 Letter to Gordon Campbell, 21 September 1914.
54 'Reflections on the Death of a Porcupine', *Phoenix II* 470.
55 Letter to Morrell [12? July 1915].

Beginning and the End, by their very directness, imply their own supreme relation. And this supreme relation is made absolute in the clash and the foam of the meeting waves. And the clash and the foam are the Crown, the Absolute.[56]

Lawrence first explored Heraclitus' doctrines in 'The Crown', written in 1915, and the ideas he adopted are found in nearly all his subsequent writing, not only in the non-fiction but also in the novels, for Lawrence's concept of character is based on Heraclitus' notion of creation through conflict. Rarely seen as 'stable egos', in the sense of concrete personalities whose motivations and behaviour can be analysed, Lawrence's characters are depicted as beings in a continual flux of opposition, evolving themselves through the conflict of deep pressures from within and without, destroying or creating themselves into new being: 'And there is no rest, no cessation from the conflict. For we are two opposites which exist by virtue of our inter-opposition. Remove the opposition and there is collapse, a sudden crumbling into universal nothingness.'[57] John Burnet's book was therefore immensely important in shaping Lawrence's thoughts about humanity and the universe. His indebtedness is particularly striking in the late works and the *Last Poems*, and indeed in a rare acknowledgement he mentions that the prefaces written in the autumn of 1929 for a new edition of his *Birds, Beasts and Flowers* poems 'are part original and sometimes quotations from the fragments of Xenophanes and Empedocles and others, but I should like it all put in inverted commas, and let them crack their wits (the public) to find out what is ancient quotation and what isn't (It is nearly all of it me)'.[58]

On 29 October Lawrence wrote to Carter that he was still trying 'to make a book for the public'[59] out of Carter's various manuscripts, but his letter already contains the firm outlines of the ideas about Revelation which he was to expand later.

Personally, I don't care much about the bloody Revelations, and whether they have any order or not – or even any meaning. But they are a very useful start for other excursions. I love the pre-Christian heavens – the planets that become such a prison of the consciousness – and the ritual year of the Zodiac. But I like the heavens best *pre-Orphic, before* there was any "fall" of the soul, and any redemption. The soul only "fell" about 500 B.C. or thereabouts with the Orphics and late Egypt. Isn't that

[56] 'The Crown', *Phoenix II* 371.
[57] Ibid., 368.
[58] Letter to Laurence Pollinger, 25 November 1929. Laurence Pollinger (1899–1976) was at this time working for Curtis Brown, Ltd, DHL's literary agent in England from 1921 and in America from 1923. The new edition of *Birds, Beasts and Flowers* was published by the Cresset Press (1930) with wood-engravings by Blair Hughes-Stanton.
[59] Letter to Carter, 29 October 1929.

so? Isn't "fall" and "redemption" quite a late and new departure in religion and in myth: about Homer's time? Aren't the great heavens of the true pagans – I call all these orphicising "redemption" mysteries half-Christian – aren't they clean of the "Salvation" idea, though they have the re-birth idea? and aren't they clean of the "fall", though they have the descent of the soul? The two things are quite different. In my opinion the great pagan religions of the Aegean, and Egypt and Babylon, must have conceived of the "descent" as a great triumph, and each Easter of the clothing in flesh as a supreme glory, and the Mother Moon who gives us our body as the supreme giver of the great gift, hence the very ancient Magna Mater in the East. This "fall" into Matter (matter wasn't even conceived in 600 B.C. – no such idea) this "entombment" in the "envelope of flesh" is a new and pernicious idea arising about 500 B.C. into distinct cult-consciousness – and destined to kill the grandeur of the heavens altogether at last. The Jews were particularly pernicious, for them regeneration, instead of being vital and hyacinthine, was always moral and through the nose. So I wish you would always look for the great heavens, and damn the candlesticks.[60]

The letter summarises Lawrence's belief in the wisdom of the ancient pagans whose myths contained a lost 'science' as he was fond of calling it, that showed the way to that state of harmony and spontaneity when man still lived 'breast to breast with the cosmos'.[61] The Orphic religion which arose in Greece between the sixth and third centuries B.C. saw the soul as a fallen god, and sought to release it from the 'wheel of birth', from further reincarnation in a physical form, and thus enable it to become once more a god living in eternal bliss. For Lawrence, however, this division of soul and body was a pernicious falsehood. He argued that the physical and the spiritual, the phenomenal and the imaginative must be fused for the greater life. The pagan religions had created their resurrection rituals as symbols of the heavenly interfusing the earthly to the enrichment of the human soul. But today 'we have lost the art of living',[62] of achieving that state when body and soul were in balanced harmony. The clue to regeneration lay in understanding that the soul – 'that forever unknowable reality which causes us to rise into being'[63] – is indeed inseparable from the body: 'the body is the flame of the soul',[64] a notion very close to Blake's: 'Man has no Body distinct from his Soul; for that call'd Body is a portion of Soul discern'd by the five Senses, the chief inlets of Soul in this age.'[65] Even God is 'our experience of the senses'[66] and can be apprehended through what Lawrence

[60] Ibid.   [61] *Apocalypse*, p. 130.
[62] *Etruscan Places* (1932), chapter 4.
[63] *Fantasia of the Unconscious*, chapter 11.
[64] *The Plumed Serpent* (1926), chapter 19.
[65] 'The Marriage of Heaven and Hell', *Blake: The Complete Writings*, ed. Geoffrey Keynes (1966), p. 149.
[66] *Apocalypsis II*, Appendix III, p. 197.

called 'the *natural* religious sense':[67] 'Whenever the soul is moved to a certain fulness of experience, that is religion.'[68]

Lawrence railed against St John and the smug morality of much of Revelation with its power lust for the end of the world and the reign of martyrs and its doctrine of salvation for the 'elect':

I do hate John's Jewish nasal sort of style – so uglily moral, condemning other people – prefer the way Osiris rises, or Adonis or Dionysus – not as Messiahs giving "heaven" to the "good" – but life-bringers for the good and bad alike – like the falling rain – on the just and unjust – who gives a damn? – like the sun.[69]

As for my soul, I simply don't and never did understand how I could "save" it. One can save one's pennies. But how can one save one's soul? One can only *live* one's soul. The business is to live, really alive. And this needs wonder.[70]

Much of his feeling against the Old and New Testaments – 'My very instincts *resent* the Bible'[71] – came from the memory of his strict Congregationalist upbringing, 'that stiff, null "propriety" which used to come over us, like a sort of deliberate and self-inflicted cramp, on Sundays'.[72] Yet looking back in 1929 he acknowledged that this training had given him that intimate knowledge of the Bible and its poetry which so deeply influenced his writing: 'I think it was good to be brought up a Protestant: and among Protestants, a Nonconformist, and among Nonconformists, a Congregationalist. Which sounds pharisaic. But I should have missed bitterly a direct knowledge of the Bible,...'[73]

Lawrence had lost his faith in Christianity during his student years, and he never regained any belief in the anthropomorphic deity of his childhood. But his rejection of Christian doctrine never diminished his faith in a God, though he often refused to call him by that name,[74] nor shook his reverence

---

[67] 'Hymns in a Man's Life', *Phoenix II* 599.
[68] *Apocalypse*, Fragment 1, Appendix I, p. 155.
[69] Letter to Carter, 10 October 1929.
[70] 'Hymns in a Man's Life', *Phoenix II* 599.
[71] *Apocalypse*, p. 59.
[72] 'The Return Journey', *Twilight in Italy* (1916). Also see Carter 26.
[73] 'Hymns in a Man's Life', *Phoenix II* 600. DHL continues: 'The Congregationalists are the oldest Nonconformists, descendents of the Oliver Cromwell Independents. They still had the Puritan tradition of no ritual. But they avoided the personal emotionalism which one found among the Methodists when I was a boy.'
Nonconformist is a term generally used of all dissenters but especially those of Protestant sympathies such as the Presbyterians (in England), Congregationalists, Methodists, Quakers and Baptists. Congregationalism believes in the principle of democracy in Church government; every local church is fully independent, acknowledging only Christ as its head.
[74] See Earl Brewster and Achsah Brewster, *D. H. Lawrence: Reminiscences and Correspondence* (1934), p. 224. Earl Brewster, the American painter and student of oriental philosophy, and his wife Achsah, knew DHL at Capri (1921–2) and continued their friendship upon his return from the United States in 1925.

for the mystery and beauty of the created world. In 1911 he had written: 'There still remains a God, but not a personal God: a vast, shimmering impulse which wavers on towards some end, I don't know what – '[75] and in 1929 he wrote: 'There is Almighty God...there must be that in the cosmos which contains the essence, at least, or the potentiality, of all things, known and unknown...And this terrific and frightening and delighted potency I call Almighty God.'[76] The crucial question was always how to come into living contact with God and how to live to the fullest of one's capacity by awakening 'the religious element inherent in all life...the sense of wonder'.[77]

His own sense of wonder never diminished even in these last months of his life, although encroaching ill-health progressively limited his ability to read and to work. Early in November 1929 Lawrence confessed to his friend Brewster Ghiselin, 'I'm doing nothing at the moment'[78] and to his publisher Secker, 'as for work, I haven't felt like doing anything at all and am still that way. I neither write nor paint – which I suppose is best for my health.'[79] Then his letter to Carter of 7 November betrays a growing frustration with the latter's manuscripts and an indecision about their publication.

The last batch of Apocalypse – and the last chapter of it very interesting. I think you are right, not to do any more of this MS. We must try and put a book together out of these four MSS. The difficulty is, you see, that for the general reader nothing hangs together, and many chapters are absolutely dry and without live interest – you have got much drier and colder than you were some years ago – whereas for the scholar there is not enough developed argument and scholarship. We must see what we can do – it will be difficult to get a publisher.[80]

But his reading for the projected study of Revelation continued. He admired Moffatt's translation of the Bible which he was using;[81] he asked Charles

[75] Letter to Ada Lawrence, 9 April 1911. *Letters*, i. 256.
[76] *Apocalypse*, Fragment 1, Appendix I, p. 155.
[77] 'Hymns in a Man's Life', *Phoenix II* 599.
[78] Letter to Brewster Ghiselin, 3 November 1929.
[79] Letter to Martin Secker, 3 November 1929. Martin Secker (1882–1978) was DHL's principal publisher in England from 1921 until the 1930s when the English rights to his books were bought by Heinemann.
[80] Letter to Carter, 7 November 1929. Mandrake Press had actually announced a forthcoming book, 'The Revelation of St John the Divine' with an introduction by D. H. Lawrence and illustrations by Frederick Carter, but the Press was suspended shortly after its announcement and the project came to nothing. See also Carter's letter to the Editor of *The London Mercury*, xxii (September 1930), 451.
[81] Letter to Lahr [2? November 1929]. 'Did I thank you for the Bible and Testament? I like that Moffatt translation.' James Moffatt, *The New Testament: A New Translation* (1913).

Lahr to find him copies of Hesiod and Plutarch[82] which he read for their accounts of ancient cosmogony and cosmology; and the Brewsters recall that he was reading Dean Inge's lectures on Plotinus and Gilbert Murray's *Five Stages of Greek Religion*[83] which provided him with many of the ideas on ancient Greek religion that he explored in the *Apocalypse* essays. Despite poor health he was also doing some writing. On 12 November he wrote to Blair Hughes-Stanton, the engraver, enclosing the prefaces to *Birds, Beasts and Flowers*,[84] and he still occasionally produced an article.[85]

Carter visited Lawrence in mid-November: 'Carter is here, looking a good bit older – I haven't seen him for six years. We are talking about his Apocalyptic work.'[86] He stayed until the end of the month.[87] By the time he left, Lawrence had already written about 20,000 words on the Book of Revelation, as Carter remembers: 'However, before I left to return to London in order to prepare the last chapters of the book – the *Dragon of Revelation* as it was to be called – our joint book, he let me know that he had already written nearly twenty thousand words of introduction.'[88] But it was the imaginative value of Frederick Carter's manuscripts, not his visit in particular[89] nor his theories about Revelation, which in any case Lawrence

[82] See letter to Lahr [9? November 1929]. DHL had received Hesiod by [27? November 1929] and Plutarch by 9 December 1929 (letters to Lahr).

[83] Brewster, *D. H. Lawrence: Reminiscences and Correspondence*, p. 305. William Ralph Inge (1860–1954), Dean of St Paul's (1911–34) gave the Gifford lectures at St Andrews University in 1917–18 on 'The Philosophy of Plotinus' (these were published in 1918).
      Gilbert Murray (1866–1957), Regius Professor of Greek at Oxford University (1908–36), translated many ancient Greek plays and poems and wrote several books on Greek classical literature, philosophy and religion. His *Four Stages of Greek Religion* (Columbia University Press, New York, 1912) was revised and became *Five Stages of Greek Religion* (1925). DHL read the later version.

[84] Letter to Hughes-Stanton [12? November 1929].

[85] Letter to Nancy Pearn, 7 November 1929. 'Here is an article on Rosanov's *Fallen Leaves* and I wish you would find somebody to publish it, for the book's sake.
      Hope you got the MS of the other three articles'.
      The 'other three articles' were: 'Nobody Loves Me', 'We Need One Another', and 'The Real Thing' (unpublished letter from Pearn to DHL dated 22 November 1929, in the Curtis Brown correspondence at the University of Texas, Austin). Nancy Pearn worked in the magazine department of DHL's agent Curtis Brown. DHL had read and admired Rozanov's *Solitaria and the Apocalypse of Our Times* (translated by Koteliansky, 1927) which he had also reviewed in the summer of 1927. He agreed with some of Rozanov's ideas about the Book of Revelation and found his phallic mysticism congenial.

[86] Letter to Titus, 20 November 1929.

[87] Letter to Titus, 30 November 1929. 'Frederick Carter leaves today and will call in to see you.'

[88] Carter 61.

[89] See letter to Giuseppe Orioli [27? November 1929]. 'Frederick Carter is here – the Apocalypse man – another quite clever ineffectual blighter – no fire, no courage, no spunk – It drives me mad.'

disputed, that stimulated him to write *Apocalypse*. Looking back to the time when he first read Carter's work in 1923, Lawrence recalls:

The *Dragon* as it exists now is no longer the *Dragon* which I read in Mexico. It has been made more – more argumentative, shall we say. Give me the old manuscript and let me write an introduction to that! I urge. But: No, says Carter. It isn't *sound*.

Sound what? He means his old astrological theory of the Apocalypse was not sound, as it was exposed in the old manuscript. But who cares? We do not care, vitally, about theories of the Apocalypse: what the Apocalypse means. What we care about is the release of the imagination.[90]

Who cares about explaining the Apocalypse, either allegorically or astrologically or historically or any other way. All one cares about is the lead, the lead that the symbolic figures give us, and their dramatic movement...If it leads to a release of the imagination into some sort of new world, then let us be thankful, for that is what we want. It matters so little to us who care more about life than about scholarship, what is correct or what is not correct...What we want is *complete* imaginative experience, which goes through the whole soul and body. Even at the expense of reason we want imaginative experience. For reason is certainly not the final judge of life.[91]

This 'release of the imagination' was central to Lawrence's ideas about art and religion. Man is 'related to the universe in some "religious" way'[92] and seeks to give form to that sense of vital connection through art. Through the act of imagining reality the psyche is released and can create those moments of intuitive apprehension that are its closest connection with the cosmos and with God: 'essentially the feeling in every real work of art is religious in its quality, because it links us up or connects us with life'.[93] As early as 1915 Lawrence had seen the purpose of human existence in terms of artistic creation: 'to create oneself, *in fact, be the artist creating a man in living fact*...[to] create that work of art, the living man, achieve that piece of supreme art, a man's life'.[94] In order to achieve this creation of self by self, 'men must develop their poetic intelligence if they are ever going to be men'[95] and the poetic intelligence is developed through art and its symbols which 'stand for units of human *feeling*, human experience'.[96] Any expansion of the awareness is therefore both a religious and a poetic action. Lawrence called it 'the essential act of attention, the essential poetic and vital act'[97]

---

90 'Introduction to *The Dragon of the Apocalypse*', p. 47.
91 Ibid., p. 50.
92 Letter to Trigant Burrow, 3 August 1927.
93 *Apocalypse*, Fragment 1, Appendix I, p. 155.
94 Letter to Morrell [1? March 1915].
95 Letter to Charles Wilson, 2 February 1928.
96 'Introduction to *The Dragon of the Apocalypse*', p. 49.
97 '*Chariot of the Sun*, by Harry Crosby', *Phoenix* 261.

which puts us in touch with the heart of all things, which '"discovers" a new world within the known world'.[98] Some of these ideas are developments of notions Lawrence had suggested earlier, but they find their final expression in the essays and poems of 1929 and in the *Apocalypse* writings.

Lawrence continued to work on Revelation after Carter's departure on 30 November, and on 15 December he wrote: 'I have roughly finished my introduction, and am going over it, working it a bit into shape. I'm hoping I can get Brewster's daughter to type it – she comes this week.'[99] Lawrence was still 'working it a bit into shape' as late as 26 December when he mentions: 'I am working on a little book about the Apocalypse – Offenbarung Johannis – which I suppose will annoy everybody who reads me.'[100] Between then and 6 January 1930, however, he gave up the idea of making what was now nearly 25,000 words (with another 20,000 words in deleted and cancelled portions, some of which are in the Appendixes to this volume) into an introduction for Carter's *Dragon*. Instead he wrote a completely new and much shorter introduction for it.

I meant to write before – but I waited, getting bothered by my Introduction. It became so long and somehow unsuitable to go in front of your essays. So at last I laid it aside, and have written you now a proper introduction, about 5,000 words, I think, which is really quite good and to the point, I feel. So I shall send it tomorrow or the next day to Curtis Brown to be typed, and they will send you a typescript copy. I shall not say anything to them about placing the book: then if you can do it yourself, well and good. – For such an introduction I usually get £20 or £25, as outright payment, with right to include the introd. in a book of collected essays later on: which is quite simple, and leaves you free to arrange all terms yourself; the publisher merely paying me the £20 down for his right to use the introd. for, say, a term of two years. – Probably I shall publish my first Introd., which grew to 25,000 words nearly, later on, as a small book. But I am in no hurry, and hope you'll have yours out first. I too thought of *Dragon of Revelation*: it seems to me a good title. If the publishers don't like it, we can think of another.[101]

Lawrence sent this new introduction to Nancy Pearn at Curtis Brown, his agent, to be typed, with instructions to forward a copy to Carter[102] who received it but did not include it in his book. Instead the essay was published shortly after Lawrence's death in *The London Mercury*, July 1930.[103] In this

[98]   Ibid., 255.
[99]   Letter to Carter, 15 December 1929.
[100] Letter to H. E. Herlitschka, 26 December 1929. 'Offenbarung Johannis' is St John's Book of Revelation.
[101] Letter to Carter, 6 January 1930.
[102] Letter to Pearn [6? January 1930]. The letter bears a pencilled note at the top (not in DHL's hand): 'Handed to Carter [illegible] Jan. 20 '30.'
[103] *The London Mercury*, xxii (July 1930), 217–26.

new introduction Lawrence remembers his first delighted reaction to Carter's original manuscript which he had read in Mexico in 1923, and his disappointment with the later version, but the essay is also a radical criticism of the limitations of science and a plea for the recognition of the imaginative values in life. Here, as in so many of his writings, Lawrence argues for the integration of science and poetry, of intellect and feeling through greater imaginative awareness: 'What we want is *complete* imaginative experience which goes through the whole soul and body.'[104]

The long 'first Introduction which grew to 25,000 words nearly', originally intended for Carter's *Dragon*, became Lawrence's last book, *Apocalypse*. This was entirely written in a notebook presented to Lawrence by the Brewsters' daughter, Harwood, for his birthday in September 1929. Although the page numbering is erratic, with many deleted, re-written and re-numbered pages, a careful reading of the directions included in the manuscript makes it possible to trace a text that is consistent and coherent. This manuscript forms the basis for the typescript made by Harwood Brewster over the Christmas holidays of December 1929.[105] The surviving typed carbon copy bears Lawrence's extensive interlinear revisions and corrections, and a complete revision of the conclusion in ink on both sides of the last page. The writing of *Apocalypse* can therefore be dated with reasonable precision. Harwood must have completed the typescript by the end of December 1929 because a comparison of the *Apocalypse* notebook with the corrected typescript shows that the corrections to the latter and the revision of the last page are done with a fine, thin nib that differs from the pen used in the notebook. Lawrence had acquired a new pen on 28 December just as the old one had ceased to function.[106] *Apocalypse* was therefore almost certainly completed by 27 December 1929, and the corrections to the typescript made with the new pen thereafter. The precise date of the revised ending on Christianity and political power must remain conjectural, but it is reasonable to assume that it may be the writing Lawrence refers to in the letter to Koteliansky on 9 January 1930: 'I was just writing about the impossibility of fitting the Christian religion to the State – Send me the *Grand Inquisitor*, and I'll see if I can do an introduction. Tell me how *long* you'd like it. I did about 6,000 words for Carter's *Apocalypse* book.'[107]

[104] 'Introduction to *The Dragon of the Apocalypse*', p. 50.
[105] See Nehls, iii. 420 and Brewster, *D. H. Lawrence: Reminiscences and Correspondence*, p. 307. Harwood Brewster (1913–), the daughter of Earl and Achsah Brewster.
[106] Letter to Emil Krug, 28 December 1929. DHL thanks him for the new pen, saying that the old one is 'kaput'.
[107] Letter to Koteliansky, 9 January 1930.

It is unlikely that Lawrence did any more work on *Apocalypse* after 9 January. On 15 January, the day after Harwood left for England, he wrote to Carter: 'I shall lay my longer introduction by – not try to publish it now'[108] and although he completed the introduction to Koteliansky's translation of 'The Grand Inquisitor' from Dostoyevsky's *The Brothers Karamazov*[109] and was still writing some poetry and correcting the proofs of his *Nettles* poems as late as 5 February,[110] his vitality was diminishing with alarming rapidity and he was to read and write little more before his death. His letters reveal the encroaching ill-health and weakness: 'I'm not allowed now to read an MS. – but perhaps later'[111] and in two last references to *Apocalypse* on 30 January and [4? February] he simply wrote: 'I finished my little book on Offenbarung Johannis, but I shan't publish it. And of course I'm doing nothing at all, now'[112] and 'I am in bed – and probably going this week into a sanatorium. No luck. Have not finished my longer essay on Revelation – and am abandoning it.'[113] He entered the Ad Astra sanatorium at Vence on 6 February 1930. Only the very late review of Eric Gill's 'Art Nonsense and Other Essays' was still to come before he died on 2 March 1930.[114]

Apocalypse was Lawrence's last book. It is a searching examination of our civilisation and a radical criticism of the Christianity and scientific technology that shaped it; but it is also the revelation of Lawrence's belief in man's power to create 'a new heaven and a new earth'[115] if he can destroy the 'false, inorganic connections especially those related to money, and re-establish the living organic connections with the cosmos, the sun and earth, with mankind and nation and family'.[116] *Apocalypse* is a vigorously iconoclastic work, condemning nearly all our contemporary ways of life and searching for the causes of our malaise in the failure of Christian and democratic ideals as

---

[108] Letter to Carter, 15 January 1930.
[109] Letter to Koteliansky, [25? January 1930]. 'Pollinger took the Introd. back with him – about 4,000 words I suppose.' This book appeared as: *The Grand Inquisitor* by F. Dostoyevsky, translated by S. S. Koteliansky, with an Introduction by D. H. Lawrence (1930).
[110] Nehls, iii. 429. The Brewsters remember DHL 'correcting proofs of his *Nettles*' the morning before he left for the sanatorium.
[111] Letter to Lahr, 24 January 1930.
[112] Letter to Max Mohr, 30 January 1930.
[113] Letter to Carter [4? February 1930].
[114] See E. W. Tedlock, *The Frieda Lawrence Collection of D. H. Lawrence Manuscripts: A Descriptive Bibliography* (Albuquerque, 1948) p. 263: 'Frieda Lawrence has described this manuscript as the last thing Lawrence wrote, completed a few days before his death on March 2, 1930.'
[115] Revelation xxi. 1.
[116] *Apocalypse*, p. 149.

Lawrence saw them. Like Nietzsche before him, Lawrence criticised Christianity's emphasis on renunciation, love and equality, because he felt it denied individual potential and ignored the deep impulse to power in mankind: 'Man is a being of power, and then a being of love...And there must be a balance between the two. Man will achieve his highest nature and his highest achievements when he tries to get a living balance between his nature of power and his nature of love, without denying either.'[117] The power mode is collective, the love mode individual. In denying the power mode and concentrating on love, in rendering unto Caesar the things that are Caesar's, Christ inevitably relinquished power to the second-rate, the mediocre: 'mankind falls forever into the two divisions of aristocrat and democrat... We are speaking now not of political parties, but of the two sorts of human nature: those that feel themselves strong in their souls and those that feel themselves weak.'[118]

However, the mass of men have never been able to distinguish the difference between the 'earthly bread' or material things, and the 'heavenly bread'[119] which is the vivid life, the power of true living and of contact with God. Only the aristocrat – like Christ or the Buddha – can put humanity in touch, can interfuse the heavenly and the earthly so that 'the festivals of the earthly bread' once again 'go to the roots of the soul'.[120] Lawrence's distinction between 'aristocrat' and 'democrat' does not involve any of the undertones of authoritarianism or of what, since Mussolini coined the word for us, we have loosely termed 'fascism'. Lawrence's view of man is deeper; it is not political but spiritual, not a denial of men's individuality but a confirmation of it based on an acceptance of the innate and inexplicable differences between men. 'One man isn't any better than another, not because they are equal, but because they are intrinsically *other*, that there is no term of comparison. The minute you begin to compare, one man is seen to be far better than another, all the inequality you can imagine is there by nature'[121] says Birkin in *Women in Love*. And in *The Plumed Serpent*, perhaps the most controversial of Lawrence's expositions of the doctrine of power, he speaks of the aristocrats of the soul as masters and lords *among* men, not *of* men.[122]

Apocalypse recognises the need to give homage to the natural power and greatness of the aristocrat, that is the man 'who transmits the life of the

117 *Apocalypse*, Fragment 1, Appendix I, p. 163.
118 *Apocalypse*, p. 65.
119 'Introduction to *The Grand Inquisitor*', *Phoenix* 285.
120 Ibid., 288.
121 *Women in Love* (1920), chapter 8.
122 *The Plumed Serpent*, chapter 11.

universe'.[123] It is a belief strikingly similar to Blake's: '"The worship of God is: Honouring his gifts in other men, each according to his genius, and loving the greatest men best: those who envy or calumniate great men hate God; for there is no other God."'[124] And yet, Lawrence writes, 'It is not man's weakness that he needs someone to bow down to. It is his nature and his strength, for it puts him in touch with far, far greater life than if he stood alone.'[125] Ultimately 'individualism is really an illusion. I am part of the great whole, and I can never escape. But I *can* deny my connections, break them, become a fragment.'[126] In our scientific and materialistic age there exists more than ever before the need to regain the imaginative and spiritual values which alone can restore that sense of living connection and wholeness.

Lawrence did not live to revise *Apocalypse*, and although he re-wrote some passages and deleted others, the published version is essentially a first writing. It has some of the faults of a first draft; an occasional lack of coherence and some repetition, but the quality of spontaneity and freshness and the poetic beauty of the prose remain unimpaired. *Apocalypse* is an important document, not merely because it is Lawrence's last book, but because the ideas expressed in it – ranging over the entire system of his thought about Christianity, politics, man, God, religion, myth, art and symbol – are the summing up of issues that preoccupied him throughout his life and that he also explored in the writings of the final years. Indeed, *Apocalypse* stands in the same relation to these writings – to *Lady Chatterley's Lover*, the *Last Poems*, *Etruscan Places* and *The Escaped Cock* – as 'The Study of Thomas Hardy' and 'The Crown' do to *The Rainbow* and *Women in Love*. The *Apocalypse* essays embody Lawrence's final vision of man and the cosmos and are a last testament of his belief in the symbolic value of art as the way to creative integration: 'They wake the imagination and give us at moments a new universe to live in.'[127] These words written by Lawrence about Carter's book, are even more applicable to his own.

Publication

Lawrence had no control over the publication of either *Apocalypse* or the 'Introduction to *The Dragon of the Apocalypse*', both of which were first published after his death. His original foreword to Carter's *Dragon* became

[123] Letter to Burrow, 3 August 1927.
[124] 'The Marriage of Heaven and Hell', *Blake: The Complete Writings*, ed. Geoffrey Keynes, 158.
[125] 'Introduction to *The Grand Inquisitor*', *Phoenix* 290.
[126] *Apocalypse*, p. 149.
[127] 'Introduction to *The Dragon of the Apocalypse*', p. 54.

the longer *Apocalypse* – '25,000 words nearly' – and although the new 'Introduction' of 5,000 words had been sent to Carter by Curtis Brown, Lawrence's agent,[128] it was published separately in *The London Mercury* in July 1930. A note by the editor of the magazine reads: 'This introduction was the last MS. of Mr. Lawrence's to reach us before his death.'[129] Later a letter appeared in *The Times Literary Supplement* for 2 July 1931 from Carter's publishers[130] which wrongly attributed the genesis of Lawrence's ideas about Revelation, apocalyptic myth and symbol in his *Apocalypse* almost entirely to his association with Carter. It suggested that *Apocalypse* itself was an early draft which would have become part of Carter's book had Lawrence lived, and concluded with the statement that Carter's *Dragon* was 'the major document in an interesting and important collaboration'. Carter's subsequent letter to the editor of *The London Mercury* in September 1930 explained the discrepancy between the actual title of his book and the title Lawrence gave it in his 'Introduction' but Carter did not correct the misconception about the genesis of Lawrence's *Apocalypse*.

I believe that it will be of interest to your readers if you permit me to make clear certain points which otherwise may be found obscure in the late D. H. Lawrence's *Introduction* published by you in the July issue of *The London Mercury*. It will serve in some degree to simplify the position of my publishers, if it is announced that the title of the book for which it was written is not to be that of the *Dragon of the Apocalypse* as he had suggested and as he wrote it in his introduction.[131]

Lawrence's 'Introduction', however, was *not* included when the *Dragon* was published and Carter's letter continued to suggest misleadingly that Lawrence's final intention had been 'still to produce a joint work' with him in addition to the 5,000 word 'Introduction', whereas the correspondence in general and Lawrence's letter of 6 January 1930 to Carter in particular, make it perfectly clear that he considered the collaboration at an end, that the 'Introduction' was to be his only contribution to Carter's book, and that his own *Apocalypse* was an independent work.

The surviving materials of the 'Introduction' are at the Bancroft Library, University of California[132] and consist of: an autograph manuscript of twenty-one pages, a 'corrected' typescript of thirteen pages and two further

[128] See letter to Pearn [6? January 1930].

[129] *The London Mercury*, xxii (July 1930), 217. Presumably the article was placed by Nancy Pearn of the magazine department of Curtis Brown. DHL had written to her suggesting: 'This Introd. might possibly be serialised' (letter to Pearn, [6? January 1930]).

[130] The text of this letter was later reprinted as 'A Note by the Publisher' in *The Dragon of Revelation* (1931), p. 8.

[131] *The London Mercury*, xxii (September 1930), 451.

[132] See Roberts 330.

typescripts of twenty-four pages and twenty pages. However, none of the
three typescripts has any textual authority. The 'corrected' typescript has
been altered in a hand that is not Lawrence's, one of the other typescripts
bears a Curtis Brown stamp but no corrections, and the last typescript has
no distinguishing marks at all and is simply a copy. The base-text for the
present edition therefore is the manuscript which Lawrence sent to Curtis
Brown around 6 January 1930. This 'Introduction' has been reprinted in
Phoenix (1936) and in the Heinemann *Selected Literary Criticism* (1955). The
earlier 'A Review of *The Book of Revelation* by Dr. John Oman' which
Middleton Murry published in the *Adelphi* in April 1924 has been reprinted
only in *Phoenix II* (1968).

   Lawrence intended to publish *Apocalypse* – 'Probably I shall publish my
first Introduction' (6 January 1930) – although he later says 'I shall lay my
longer introduction by – not try to publish it now' (15 January 1930). At
the end of January he spoke of having 'finished my little book' (30 January
1930) but early in February to Carter: 'Have not finished my longer essay
on Revelation – and am abandoning it' [4? February 1930]. It is reasonable
to suppose that Lawrence would have revised *Apocalypse* further before
publication, but the manuscript (hereafter MS) and the corrected typed
carbon copy (hereafter TCC) are complete.

   The known materials of *Apocalypse* are at the University of Texas at Austin
and consist of: the autograph MS, torn from the notebook that Harwood
Brewster gave Lawrence in the autumn of 1929, which formed the basis for
the typescript made by her over the Christmas holidays of 1929–30. This
MS is numbered pages 1–105 but with added pages and many duplications
in the numbering it actually totals 160 pages of text. For example, page 51
of the MS has the pencilled instruction 'return to p. 33 for VI', at which
point the numbering begins again from page 33. Secondly, there is the TCC,
numbered 1–114, with Lawrence's extensive alterations and corrections.
Page 114 of this TCC has the original ending to *Apocalypse*, but a second,
fainter carbon copy of page 114 has the ending scored out and is completely
re-written on both sides of the page in black ink. Lawrence's new ending
was later typed to give four additional pages which are numbered 114–18.
These last four pages are an accurate transcription of his revised ending but
they are typed on different paper by another typist and although they are
corrected in ink and pencil the alterations are not in Lawrence's hand.[133]
They were presumably typed either when Lawrence was too ill to do any

[133] The paper on which these pages are typed also corresponds to that used for the title page
and for page 65 where the original typed page must have been lost and another copy typed
to replace it. Page 65 has no corrections in DHL's hand.

correcting himself or after his death. With these additional sheets the TCC
is numbered pages 1–118, and with the two duplicate copies of page 114,
it totals 120 pages.

In addition to the MS and the TCC described above there are several other
writings on *Apocalypse*. The most important of these is an autograph MS
totalling 102 pages which consists of five fragments in the original *Apocalypse*
notebook. These fragments are early versions of material that Lawrence
re-wrote and three of them are short, cancelled pieces that he clearly
discarded. However, the two uncancelled fragments are substantial writings
in themselves which often illuminate the argument of *Apocalypse* and they
are published for the first time in the Appendixes to this volume. These two
fragments are thirty-six and forty-three pages long and are numbered 23–58
and 11–53, respectively. Finally, there is a short uncancelled holograph MS
of only eleven pages, numbered by Lawrence 33–42, in a separate pink
notebook entitled *Apocalypsis II* and initialled, 'D.H.L.'. Presumably this
fragment is a continuation of some writing on Revelation in a first notebook
but no trace of one has been found.[134]

The only complete versions of *Apocalypse* therefore are the MS and TCC.
The TCC is extensively revised in Lawrence's hand-writing with many
interlinear alterations and re-written passages, for example:

And the Apocalypse, repellant though its chief spirit be, does also contain another
inspiration. It has also *another* voice. The very beginning surprises us: MS

And the Apocalypse, repellant though its chief spirit be, does also contain another
inspiration. It is repellant only because it resounds with the dangerous snarl of the
frustrated, suppressed collective self, the frustrated power-spirit in man, vengeful. But
it contains also some revelation of the true and positive Power-spirit. The very
beginning surprises us: TCC

---

[134] In addition to these writings there are several posthumous materials in private collections
which comprise: a set of uncorrected galley proofs (Whiteson); a set of 'corrected' page
proofs of 155 pages (Lazarus); a proof copy of the Orioli Florence edition of 1931 (House
of Books); another proof copy of the first edition (Blackwell). None of these is corrected
by DHL and none has any textual authority. The Whiteson galley proofs bear the printer's
stamp but are uncorrected apart from one revision on the first sheet. Although the Lazarus
page proofs are lightly corrected, these are corrections of printer's errors and some
accidental omissions. The corrections do not depart from the TCC. There is only one other
writing by DHL on Revelation. This is the set of notes entitled 'An Outline of Apocalypse'
(Roberts 324). Pages 1 and 3–7 of this autograph manuscript writen in pencil are in the
Bancroft Library, University of California. The missing page 2 is pasted on the inside back
cover of the *Apocalypse* notebook at the University of Texas, Austin. Tedlock's description
of this page in *The Frieda Lawrence Collection of D. H. Lawrence Manuscripts* (1948) is
accurate except that he has 'unseated' for 'unsealed' on p. 146. The 'Outline' is simply
a summary of the 'plot' of St John's Revelation, itemising what happens at the sounding
of each Trump, the breaking of each of the seven seals, etc. Since it is cancelled it has
not been included in the draft materials in the Appendixes of the present volume.

The final stage in the production of *Apocalypse* which has any textual authority is the TCC. The present edition uses the TCC as its base-text but also refers to the MS in a number of instances where the typist has been careless and Lawrence has not caught the error. At several points it seems that the typist's eye must have jumped between lines when Lawrence repeated a word, and the intervening line or lines were simply omitted, as in section 1 where the MS has: 'A man is more than a Christian, a rider on a white horse must be more than mere Faithfulness and Truth', which in the TCC becomes 'A man is more than mere Faithfulness and Truth'. On one occasion, however, Lawrence's habit of stylistic repetition resulted in the typist mistakenly repeating two lines, thus:

Come in silence, and say nothing. Come in touch, in soft new touch like a spring-time breeze, and shed   MS

Come in silence, and say nothing. Come in touch, in soft new touch like a spring-time, and say nothing. Come in touch, in soft new touch like a spring-time breeze, and shed   TCC

Moreover the typist occasionally substituted one substantive for another which makes grammatical sense but is a misreading of the MS, thus 'cycle' becomes 'circle' and 'One' becomes 'The'. The present edition accepts accidentals and substantives that Lawrence himself changed in the TCC, since this text is extensively corrected and forms the last stage in the writing of *Apocalypse*, but when the TCC varies from the MS the MS reading is adopted and the variant recorded in the textual apparatus. Except where he himself introduced changes into the TCC, Lawrence's use of accidentals and substantives in the MS must be assumed to have greater authority than that of the typist, especially since he was not aware that he was proof-reading a final copy for publication.

Lawrence had corresponded with Giuseppe Orioli about publishing Carter's *Dragon*,[135] and although he never approached him about *Apocalypse*, the Italian publisher was aware of the existence of the MS. After Lawrence's death Orioli secured a contract for the still unpublished poems and stories and for *Apocalypse*. Laurence Pollinger of Curtis Brown records having sent him a contract as early as 20 May 1930,[136] but it was not until December

[135] See letter to Orioli, 30 August 1929. Giuseppe Orioli (1884–1942), the Italian antiquarian bookseller and publisher, had known the Lawrences from 1916. He supervised the publication of *Lady Chatterley's Lover* (1928), published DHL's translation of *The Story of Doctor Manente* (1929), *The Virgin and the Gipsy* (1930), *Apocalypse* (1931) and with Richard Aldington co-edited the *Last Poems* (1932).

[136] Unpublished correspondence from Pollinger to Frieda Lawrence, 28 August 1930, in the Curtis Brown file at the University of Texas, Austin.

1930 that the Italian publisher wrote to Frieda, Lawrence and George Lawrence, and on 21 January 1931 they signed a contract with Orioli for limited editions of *Apocalypse* and the unpublished poems and short stories.[137]

It is not certain precisely when the text of *Apocalypse* reached the offices of Lawrence's agents and, later, Orioli. However on 29 December 1930 Pollinger wrote to Frieda: 'Do please let me have "The Apocalypse" and any other material that has not been published. It is most desirable that copies should be made of all of these MSS.'[138] And in an undated letter to Pollinger which refers to 'a good new year, for all of us' and was presumably a reply to the above, Frieda wrote: 'Aldous is bringing the Apocalypse in a day or two before going to London – Ada wants to read it –.'[139] It seems likely, therefore, that *Apocalypse* reached London some time in January 1931, and that Lawrence's agents sent a copy of the corrected TCC to Orioli to use as the base-text for the first edition. There are no printer's marks on the surviving TCC itself but the first edition follows the text of the TCC, not the MS, and incorporates all the additions and revisions made by Lawrence on the former.

Brigit Patmore, who had met the Lawrences on several occasions and was a particular friend of Richard Aldington, then engaged in editing the *Last Poems* with Orioli, recalls helping with the publication of *Apocalypse*:[140]

[137] Unpublished correspondence from Pollinger to DHL's brother, George Lawrence, and Frieda Lawrence, on 20 December 1930. A copy of the contract as well as subsequent correspondence are in the Curtis Brown files at the University of Texas, Austin. The contract signed on 21 January 1931 specifies a limited edition of 650 copies of each of the three volumes – *Apocalypse*, the last poems and the late stories – to be sold at not less than £1 1s 0d (one guinea) each, with the publishers paying the proprietors 50 per cent of the net profits. This general contract for all three posthumous volumes was later replaced by one drawn up in June 1931 for *Apocalypse* alone. It specified that the limited edition of *Apocalypse* would be 750 copies at 30s. A copy of this contract is also at the University of Texas, Austin.

[138] Unpublished letter from Pollinger to Frieda Lawrence in the Curtis Brown file at the University of Texas, Austin.

[139] Unpublished and undated letter headed 'Vence Sunday' from Frieda Lawrence to Pollinger in the Curtis Brown file at the University of Texas, Austin.
  Aldous Huxley (1894–1963), novelist, essayist, poet and biographer met DHL in December 1915 and from 1926 was often with him until his death. He edited *The Letters of D. H. Lawrence* (1932).
  Ada Clarke (née Lawrence), (1887–1948) was DHL's younger sister. With G. Stuart Gelder she wrote *Young Lorenzo: The Early Life of D. H. Lawrence* (Florence, 1931).

[140] Richard Aldington (1892–1962), poet, novelist, biographer, critic, editor, translator, was a friend of DHL's from July 1914 and the author of *D. H. Lawrence: An Indiscretion* (1927) and *D. H. Lawrence: Portrait of a Genius, But...* (1950). With Orioli he edited the *Last Poems* (1932) and compiled an anthology of DHL's prose, *The Spirit of Place* (1935). He is the author of introductions to DHL reprints by Penguin and Heinemann.

'After his death, when I was in Florence, Orioli asked me to correct the proofs of *The Apocalypse*. There were three versions in notebooks to be gone through but the alterations were slight, just the rejection of words which seemed superfluous.'[141] It is puzzling what Brigit Patmore could have meant by 'three versions in notebooks to be gone through' since in addition to the TCC and the complete MS there are only the five fragments listed above and the very short *Apocalypsis II* notebook: none of these can be described as 'versions'. Furthermore, examination of the 'corrected' Orioli page proofs[142] reveals that Brigit Patmore must have corrected from the TCC text since the page proofs follow the TCC, not the MS, and incorporate the additions and corrections of the former with considerable fidelity although there remain many printer's errors of omission, punctuation and spelling.

The errors of transmission between MS and TCC were perpetuated by Orioli and compounded since his compositor also omitted many lines and misread words. Lawrence's habit of stylistic repetition, which had caused similar difficulties for his typist, encouraged the compositor's eye to jump between lines, thus giving in section I 'mystification and of all' while both MS and TCC have 'mystification. On the whole, the modern mind dislikes mystification, and of all.' The first edition has many altered substantives, for example 'Sion' for 'Sin', 'sin' for 'six', 'reserved' for 'reversed'. Although Orioli followed the text of the TCC he was alarmed by the references to Mussolini in the last pages. The surviving set of lightly 'corrected' page proofs still contain Lawrence's original references but Orioli must have deleted them from the text before production. Thus both MS and TCC read: 'Mussolini is also a martyr' and 'like Mussolini', but in the first edition this becomes: 'others also are martyrs' and 'like those'. All subsequent editions have followed Orioli's altered text.

Orioli brought out *Apocalypse* on 3 June 1931 in a limited edition of 750 copies. Secker published the first English edition in May 1932, using the Orioli text but introducing emendations of capitalisation, punctuation and spelling, and an introduction by Richard Aldington about Lawrence's last writings (possibly to meet the objections of the first *Times Literary Supplement* reviewer who had complained that there was no indication when Lawrence had written the book).[143] Viking published the first American

---

Mrs Brigit Patmore (1882–1965), the writer, met DHL through Ford Madox (Hueffer) Ford before 1914 and was part of the Lawrence–Aldington circle in 1917. She saw DHL again in England in 1926 and as Aldington's guest at La Vigie, Ile de Port-Cros, Var, between October and November 1928.

[141] Nehls, iii. 256.
[142] These proofs are in the private collection of Mr George Lazarus.
[143] *The Times Literary Supplement*, 25 June 1931, p. 503.

edition on 27 November 1931, also from the Orioli text and also with its own editorial changes, and another edition which included the Aldington introduction on 13 February 1932. Albatross similarly used the Florence edition for its 'Modern Continental Library' paperback edition, also with the Aldington introduction, later in 1932.[144]

Apocalypse is a much neglected work which only appeared in three editions subsequent to the 1931 and 1932 publications. Viking renewed the American copyright in 1960 and reissued *Apocalypse* in 1966 with several subsequent impressions, but this was still derived from the Viking first edition. Heinemann published *Apocalypse* in the Phoenix edition in 1972, also using the Viking text; and the current Penguin paperback (1974 and 1975) is also derived from Heinemann's edition taken from Viking, not from the Florence first edition, with the result that it is the most inaccurate of them all, having reproduced not only the errors which Viking took over from Orioli and compounded, but a considerable number of its own mistakes and editorial changes.

No edition after Orioli's is based on Lawrence's TCC and none has any textual authority. The present edition is the first accurately to reproduce Lawrence's final corrected text, restoring the deletions made by Orioli in his first edition and correcting the compounded errors of his edition and of subsequent editions based on the Florence copy. These restorations and corrections are recorded in the textual apparatus.

Reviews

Lawrence's last book met with a disappointing reception. The first review in *The Times Literary Supplement* of 25 June 1931 criticised the publisher for omitting to say when the book was written, though it rightly placed *Apocalypse* among the last writings and recognised the affinity of its ideas with some of Lawrence's earlier work, in particular *Fantasia of the Unconscious*. The review pointed out that Lawrence was not simply condemning 'the religion of the self-glorification of the weak, the reign of the pseudo-humble'[145] but that he saw in Revelation the remnants of an older, universal religion which has an equal validity for our time. It praised the vitality of the writing, 'full of roving knowledge and poetry' but failed to grasp that *Apocalypse* is not a literal blueprint for regeneration but a poetic and symbolic one, using the imagery and myth of Revelation as its vehicle. The

144 The agreement between Frieda Lawrence and George Lawrence and the Albatross Verlag, dated 20 April 1932, is in the collection at the University of Texas, Austin.
145 *Apocalypse*, p. 65.

reviewer therefore found 'something...pathetic if not futile in Lawrence's final exhortation' and, quoting the last paragraph of the book, concluded the review with:

He is true when he says that, in more ways than one, we have lost the secret of connexion. But in this vivid and interesting book the clue looks rather like a dream. Lawrence, who says here that the individual cannot love and the Christian dare not, seems to have sundered the individual and collective selves so sharply that they cannot come together again. Once more he refuses to allow that another way is possible, and that 'he that loseth his life, the same shall save it'.

Joan Haslip, the reviewer for *The London Mercury* in November 1931 revealed a narrow bias, seeing the book as 'the product of a period of despair' with Lawrence 'so obsessed with the pagan cosmos' that he merely used 'Revelation as a medium in which to expound his own cult'. The reviewer ineptly conflated the author of Revelation with the writer of the fourth Gospel and also incorrectly assumed that Lawrence's *Apocalypse* was the product of several years' work.

It is astonishing that Lawrence's last book should have met with so little critical response. These two reviews were the only ones to appear in England following the publication of the Florence first edition, and only one periodical in America reviewed the book. This was the *Saturday Review* for 11 July 1931 which published a dismissive article by Osbert Burdett.

No one expecting further light upon the last book of the Bible would be thrilled to hear that D. H. Lawrence has now turned his attention thereto. No candid reader, I believe, was much interested in any of Lawrence's conclusions, in his judgments, his opinions, his verdicts, or his arguments. His readers were attracted or repelled by the man himself, and their interest lay in watching the struggles of this singularly awkward, partly gifted, but very undeveloped young man...I found nothing attractive in the spectacle of a nonconformist conscience in the grip of sex-obsession...His explosive obscenities were the nonconformist conscience turning on itself.

It is doubtful whether this reviewer can have read the book in its entirety. He was 'agreeably surprised' to find its style 'quiet and straightforward' and summarised the book as 'neither remarkable nor dull' – a curious description of some of Lawrence's most passionate and lyrical prose.

The publication of *Apocalypse* by Secker in 1932 with an introduction by Richard Aldington brought some further notice but only five comparatively short reviews appeared in Britain. *The Times Literary Supplement*, which had reviewed the Florence edition the previous year, included a paragraph on *Apocalypse* in its article 'D. H. Lawrence in Retrospect' on 5 May 1932, which revealed a baffled incomprehension, although it appreciated Richard

Aldington's assessment of Lawrence. The reviewer acknowledged Lawrence's 'passionately felt plea for the recovery of a lost union with the cosmos' but saw his symbolic writing as 'illusive if taken as a signpost', once again confusing literal truth with the psychological validity of what Lawrence was trying to say.

A short article by Dennis Campkins followed in the *Week-end Review* for 7 May 1932 which showed a sensitive response to Lawrence's style and praised its 'vivid imagery', concluding:

The thought of *Apocalypse* is often muddled, often incoherent, but the meaning behind, the force creative of the thought, this is clear and luminous, making for the sense-awareness which Lawrence preached to a world insensible. And the language, intense and starred with poetry, magnificently flowing, is pure Lawrence.

The Observer, reviewing both the Secker and Florence editions on 3 July 1932, recognised Lawrence's long quarrel with Christianity and, unlike the writer of the *Saturday Review* above, saw Lawrence as a religious man and the message of *Apocalypse* as the culmination of the doctrine he had been concerned to expound in his works.

Christianity was in essence his doctrine – the doctrine of being for the sake of life...*Apocalypse*...not only confutes those who regarded Lawrence as prurient: it convicts them quite simply of imbecility. It was because Lawrence believed in the resurrection of the body that he was able to understand the resurrection of the soul.

By contrast the *Adelphi* review of February 1933 written by Max Plowman,[146] displayed utter incomprehension of what it called the 'splenetic Lawrence' and confessed to an inability to finish reading the book.

Of all the English reviews only that by I. M. Parsons[147] in the *Spectator* for 14 May 1932 acclaimed the book as 'one of the most vital that Lawrence wrote: a magnificent last attempt to explain himself to the world' and recognised that its difficulties and occasional obscurities arose not because of its style but because Lawrence makes demands of his readers far greater than most of them are ready to meet.

In *Apocalypse* the mysteries are not so much different from what they are elsewhere in Lawrence's work, but they are described with the same intensity of feeling, the same urgent love of beauty and the same passionate pleading for a fuller life, which made each former revelation so fresh and so profoundly disturbing...To the end he is the preacher, the propagandist; but a propagandist once again for hope as against

---

[146] Max Plowman (1883–1941) had written to DHL in 1919 offering to write on behalf of *The Rainbow* which he admired. See letter to Plowman, 11 September 1919.

[147] I. M. Parsons (1906–   ) later became chairman of the publishing company Chatto and Windus, Ltd.

despair, for the strong freedom of the individual as against the weak tyranny of the many, for Life as against Death and a fire-insurance policy for the hereafter. It is all typical Lawrence, and like the rest of Lawrence it is not to be read or accepted at its face value. 'If people try to read *Apocalypse*', says Mr. Aldington, 'either as a work of scholarship or scientific analysis, they make a mistake, for it is nothing of the kind.'

The reception of *Apocalypse* in America, on publication of the Viking edition, was little better. The reviews were generally favourable, but most revealed fundamental misconceptions about the book and one or two were actively hostile. The *American Mercury* of June 1932 dismissed *Apocalypse* as 'altogether a slight book' although it acknowledged that Richard Aldington's introduction was 'one of the most brilliant and sympathetic studies of Lawrence in print'. W. R. Brooks, the reviewer in *Outlook* for March 1932 admitted that he had not read the book yet rejected it out of hand as an account of Lawrence's hatred of the Book of Revelation, his 'escape from the dreadful spell in which its savage imagery bound his childhood' and 'a further groping toward mysticism'.

Lorine Pruette wrote a full-page article for the 14 February 1932 *New York Herald Tribune*, 'Lawrence Makes Peace With His Childhood', in which she saw Lawrence's writing of *Apocalypse* as part of an attempt to exorcise the old childhood emotions associated with Revelation and Christianity. A. D. Emmart, writing for the *Baltimore Evening Sun*, 20 February 1932, paid tribute to Lawrence's originality and importance as a writer of the twentieth century in his review 'Lawrence On The Apocalypse'. The *New York Tribune Book Review* for 28 February 1932 contributed a short piece by Percy Hutchinson, 'Lawrence the Mystic in *Apocalypse*', which was favourably inclined but profoundly misguided in its attempt to interpret what it saw as the literal truth of Revelation. Nathan Haskell Dale, writing for the *Portland News*, 14 March 1932, discussed Lawrence's Congregationalist upbringing and compared his account of the nonconformist chapels of the English Midlands with some aspects of contemporary American religion, regretting, however: 'What a pity that he did not emerge into the serene philosophy of modern science...Instead he tried to find in the dim past, a happy barbarism, so immature as not even to recognize a god.' Both the unknown reviewer of the *Dayton Ohio Herald* for 26 March 1932 and Edwin H. Ford writing for the *Minneapolis Journal* for 17 April 1932, recognised that *Apocalypse* was not important as a commentary on Revelation but significant because it was the culmination of Lawrence's ideas on life and religion.

Three short, single paragraph reviews also announced the publication of the book in America. The anonymous reviewer of the *Plain Dealer* (Cleveland, Ohio) for 21 February 1932 recommended *Apocalypse*: 'Lawrence's commentary on the symbolism of this book will, I think, rank with the best he has written.' Hugh Cotterell of the *Southern California Trojan*, 1 March 1932, saw Lawrence's last testament as 'one of the finest wills that an author has left to his readers'. But the *Chicago News* for 2 March 1932 published a less discerning review which pointed out that Lawrence was 'not so thorough, competent, well informed or logical as many professional sociologists'.

Of the transatlantic reviews only three revealed any grasp of the significance of the book. E. S. Bates, writing for the *Saturday Review of Literature*, 13 February 1932, perceptively saw Lawrence as a writer whose essence lay 'in his ruling conflict' and as an exponent of four fundamental twentieth-century attitudes: the turning away from Christianity, the waning faith in democracy, a growing anti-intellectualism, and a rapidly spreading disillusionment with modern industry and technology. He paid tribute to the mastery and power of language in *Apocalypse* and in Lawrence's 'revelation of what Christianity actually is in practice – a hatred of excellence, an enthronement of mediocrity'.

It is equally a revelation of what democracy is in practice. The mistake has been to treat the individual as if he were, at least potentially, a whole man capable of self-fulfilment, whereas in fact men are 'by nature fragmentary', capable only of vicarious fulfilment in an ordered hierarchy in which they may identify themselves with beings above them, lords and kings, the nation, the race, the cosmos.
Here we have the tragic abandonment of our day, of the Jeffersonian, the Emersonian hope. This very Nietzschean Apocalypse is a new Anti-Christ.

The last sentence significantly echoes Lawrence's letter of June 1929 to his sister-in-law Else Jaffe, where he writes: 'The real principle of Evil is not anti-Christ or anti-Jehovah, but anti-life. I agree with you, in a sense, that I am with the anti-Christ. Only I am not anti-life.'[148]

The *New Republic* of 1 June 1932 published a discerning review by Kenneth White which predicted that *Apocalypse* would meet with the kind of resistance some of the earlier reviews had revealed.

Lawrence makes the unforgivable mistake of believing that writing made some intrusion, brought some emotional decision, into the life which it had attempted to enlarge and make more real. People naturally turn away from anything that confuses them and points to their deformities, whether these be social, political, or personal, after they have so carefully planned out ways of covering up the deformities, or

[148] Letter to Else Jaffe, 6 June 1929.

treating them lightly. . . Apocalypse will probably be dismissed as nonsense, because Lawrence talks of communing with the sun, of a 'blazing interchange', of responding to the cosmos, because Lawrence takes with intense seriousness the Revelation of John of Patmos.

The loss to us, if we were but aware, in Lawrence's death, is the loss of the revolution he wanted. He has left us only ill prepared. *Apocalypse* is remarkable; but it is grounded in 'Revelation', a work now in itself a curio. Consequently, it will appear to most people that a fine talent spent its last efforts on a document totally extraneous to the circumstances in which we live. Most people will not recognise that a powerful imagination was able to put itself at the very center of an important religious document, there to see radiating back into the life of all earlier people the hidden content, and to see the Christian content striking even into our own lives as inheritors, not of Christianity, but of Christianity's prejudices and hatreds.

The last review of *Apocalypse* to appear in America was by Geoffrey West in the *Yale Review* for December 1932, 'The Significance of D. H. Lawrence', a review which expressed a belief in Lawrence's greatness but revealed a deep misconception about his last book and its message.

Lawrence, one must protest, is more than negatively significant. If there is death in much of his work – and there is – there is life also. Though he could never open the way wide to us, indubitably he held the key to a mode of consciousness which, whether old or new, can revivify our perception of the world, enrich our whole scope of life, deepen intuition, reveal a warmer beauty, widen the total sphere of consciousness. In *Apocalypse*, a late study of the Book of Revelation, which, as Mr. Aldington says, must be read more for its exposition of Lawrence than as biblical exegesis, he sums up his positive creed. [The reviewer quotes from the last page beginning 'For man, the vast marvel. . .'] That is true, but it is not the whole truth, and in its half truth Lawrence found not liberty but a prison, a prison of the flesh.

Perhaps the finest critical assessment of *Apocalypse* to follow the book's publication was not in the form of a review at all. This was Richard Aldington's letter to Frieda Lawrence which has appeared as an introduction to every edition of *Apocalypse* since Orioli's Florence publication.

No other reviews[149] of the first editions are known on either side of the Atlantic, and from the available evidence Lawrence's last book seems to have made little impact on the reading public or in literary circles. Sadly this neglect has continued.

---

[149] Brief announcements of the book's publication in America also appeared in: *Nonpareil* (Council Bluff, Louisiana), 5 September 1931; *World* (Tulsa, Oklahoma), 13 September 1931; *News* (Charleston, South Carolina), 24 January 1932; *Times* (Portsmouth, Oregon) 24 January 1932; *Observer* (Raleigh, North Carolina), 31 January 1932; *Dispatch* (Columbus, Ohio), 26 February 1932; *Signal* (Zanesville, Ohio), 28 February 1932; *Cleveland Press*, 28 February 1932; *News* (Enid, Ohio) 28 February 1932; *Star* (Tucson, Arizona), 6 March 1932; *News* (Newark, New Jersey), 11 June 1932.

Appendixes

The draft material in these three Appendixes is probably from the early writing of *Apocalypse*, the 20,000 words that Frederick Carter recalled Lawrence had written by the end of November 1929. These fragments are included in this volume because they illuminate the argument of the main text and often contain fuller statements of issues that are only touched on in the final version and because they afford insight into the creative process of Lawrence's writing.

Fragment 1, numbered pages 11–53 in the MS, is an early version of sections II–VI. *Apocalypse* ends section I with the words 'It is popular religion, as distinct from thoughtful religion.' This is page 9 in the MS but page 10 is then cancelled and the original pages 11–53 discarded. The cancelled paragraphs on page 10 are included in the Appendix since they begin the argument of the material on pages 11–53. The MS of Fragment 1 is cancelled from 'After reading the Old Testament' to 'After all, how interesting the Bible is, when we can come to it fresh and find it human' and thereafter uncancelled. Fragment 1 contains a more complete discussion of Christianity and politics and of their love- and power-principles as Lawrence saw them. It postulates two modes of consciousness in man, traces the beginning of the Orphic mysteries and the dawn of religion in the Mediterranean, and discusses the nature of God. It suggests that art and the poetic imagination are essentially religious phenomena, a notion that is only briefly mentioned in *Apocalypse*, though the idea is present in many of Lawrence's late writings. And here the old division in Lawrence's doctrine between art and science, feeling and intellect, is finally resolved. The MS contains a fascinating glimpse of a new development in his thought: the belief that the scientific as well as the poetic modes of thought, the creativity of an Einstein and that of a poet, are essentially one and the same, each a manifestation of the vital act of imagination which Lawrence believed was the essence of creativity and of religion.

Fragment 2, numbered pages 23–58, was begun as a re-writing of part of Fragment 1, beginning at page 23 of that MS, and it contains much similar material re-worked, although it omits the detailed discussion of power and Christianity. But it also has what is possibly the fullest account in these last writings of Lawrence's ideas about the soul and the body. Lawrence believed that Revelation explored 'the opening and conquest of the great psychic centres of the body' (*Apocalypse*, p. 101) so that these passages complement the argument of the main text.

Apocalypsis II, numbered pages 33–42, is a continuation of a piece which

Lawrence must have begun in another, lost notebook. It is an earlier and fuller discussion of Pythagorean mathematics and the concept of mathematical symbols that comes in sections XVII and XX of the final text and is important for understanding Lawrence's notion of symbols and the way they work on the imagination. The argument develops into a discussion of the nature of human and divine consciousness.

The printed texts of these three fragments of apocalyptic writing follow Lawrence's manuscript.

A REVIEW OF
THE BOOK OF REVELATION
BY DR. JOHN OMAN

Note on the text

No manuscript or typescript of this review survives. The base-text is therefore the review as it was published in the *Adelphi* magazine for April 1924. There is no textual apparatus.

A REVIEW OF
THE BOOK OF REVELATION
BY DR. JOHN OMAN

The Apocalypse* is a strange and mysterious book. One therefore welcomes any serious work upon it. Now Dr. John Oman (*The Book of Revelation*, Cambridge University Press, 7s. 6d. net) has undertaken the arrangement of the sections into an intelligible order. The clue to the order lies in the idea that the theme is the conflict between true and false religion, false religion being established upon the Beast of world empire. Behind the great outward happenings of the world lie the greater, but more mysterious happenings of the divine ordination. The Apocalypse unfolds in symbols the dual event of the crashing-down of world-empire and world-civilization, and the triumph of men in the way of God.

Dr. Oman's rearrangement and his exposition give one a good deal of satisfaction. The main drift we can surely accept. John's passionate and mystic hatred of the civilization of his day, a hatred so intense only because he knew that the living realities of men's being were displaced by it, is something to which the soul answers now again. His fierce, new usage of the symbols of the four Prophets of the Old Testament* gives one a feeling of relief, of release into passionate actuality, after the tight pettiness of modern intellect.

Yet we cannot agree that Dr. Oman's explanation of the Apocalypse is exhaustive. No explanation of symbols is final. Symbols are not intellectual quantities, they are not to be exhausted by the intellect.

And an Apocalypse has, must have, is intended to have various levels or layers or strata of meaning. The fall of World Rule and World Empire before the Word of God is certainly one stratum. And perhaps it would be easier to leave it at that. Only it is not satisfying.

Why should Doctor Oman oppose the view that, besides the drama of the fall of World Rule and the triumph of the Word, there is another drama, or rather several other concurrent dramas? We gladly accept Dr. Oman's interpretation of the two Women and the Beasts. But why should he appear so unwilling to accept any astrological reference? Why should not the symbols have an astrological meaning, and the drama be also a drama of cosmic man, in terms of the stars?

As a matter of fact, old symbols have many meanings, and we only define one meaning in order to leave another undefined. So with the meaning of the Book of Revelation. Hence the inexhaustibility of its attraction.

— L. H. Davidson.*

INTRODUCTION TO
THE DRAGON OF THE APOCALYPSE
BY FREDERICK CARTER

Note on the text

The base-text for this 'Introduction' is the manuscript – 'about 5,000 words' – that DHL sent around 6 January 1930 to his agent Curtis Brown, by whom it was later typed and placed for publication with *The London Mercury*. It was published in the July 1930 issue. The typescripts, however, were never corrected by DHL, so that the final stage in the production of the 'Introduction' which had the author's sanction was the manuscript, now at the University of California.

The textual apparatus records the textual variants between the MS base-text and the 'Introduction' as it was printed in *The London Mercury*. Two editorial changes have been made: foreign words and book titles are italicised in accordance with DHL's usual practice in this MS, and the title of the Book of Revelation appears in roman type throughout.

INTRODUCTION TO
THE DRAGON OF THE APOCALYPSE
BY FREDERICK CARTER

It is some years now since Frederick Carter first sent me the manuscript of his *Dragon of the Apocalypse.** I remember it arrived   5
when I was staying in Mexico, in Chapala. The village post-master sent for me to the post-office: Will the honourable Señor please come to the post-office. I went, on a blazing April morning, there in the northern tropics. The post-master, a dark, fat Mexican with moustaches, was most polite: but also rather mysterious. There was   10
a packet—did I know there was a packet? No, I didn't. Well, after a great deal of suspicious courtesy, the packet was produced; the rather battered typescript of the *Dragon*, together with some of Carter's line-engravings, mainly astrological, which went with it. The post-master handled them cautiously. What was it? What was it? It was   15
a book, I said, the manuscript of a book, in English. Ah, but what sort of a book? What was the book about? I tried to explain, in my hesitating Spanish, what the *Dragon* was about, with its line-drawings. I didn't get far. The post-master looked darker and darker, more uneasy. At last he suggested, was it *magic*? I held my breath. It seemed   20
like the Inquisition again. Then I tried to accommodate him. No, I said, it was not magic, but the *history* of magic. It was the history of what magicians had thought, in the past, and these were the designs they had used.—Ah! The postman was relieved. The history of magic! A scholastic work! And these were the designs they had used!—He   25
fingered them gingerly, but fascinated.

And I walked home at last, under the blazing sun, with the bulky package under my arm. And then, in the cool of the patio, I read the beginning of the first *Dragon*.

The book was not then what it is now. Then, it was nearly all   30
astrology, and very little argument. It was confused: it was, in a sense, a chaos. And it hadn't very much to do with St. John's Revelation. But that didn't matter to me. I was very often smothered in words. And then would come a page, or a chapter, that would release my imagination and give me a whole great sky to move in. For the first   35
time I strode forth into the grand fields of the sky. And it was a real

45

experience, for which I have been always grateful. And always the sensation comes back to me, of the dark shade on the veranda in Mexico, and the sudden release into the great sky of the old world, the sky of the zodiac.

5   I have read books of astronomy which made me dizzy with the sense of illimitable space. But the heart melts and dies, it is the disembodied mind alone which follows on through this horrible hollow void of space, where lonely stars hang in awful isolation. And this is not a release. It is a strange thing, but when science extends space *ad infinitum*, and

10   we get the terrible sense of limitlessness, we have at the same time a secret sense of imprisonment. Three-dimensional space is homogeneous, and no matter *how* big it is, it is a kind of prison. No matter how vast the range of space, there is no release.

Why then, this sense of release, of marvellous release, in reading

15   the *Dragon?* I don't know. But anyhow, the *whole* imagination is released, not a part only. In astronomical space, one can only *move*, one cannot *be*. In the astrological heavens, that is to say, the ancient zodiacal heavens, the whole man is set free, once the imagination crosses the border. The whole man, bodily and spiritual, walks in the

20   magnificent fields of the stars, and the stars have names, and the feet tread splendidly upon—we know not what, but the heavens, instead of untreadable space.

It is an experience. To enter the astronomical sky of space is a great sensational experience. To enter the astrological sky of the zodiac and

25   the living, roving planets is another experience, another *kind* of experience; it is truly imaginative, and to me, more valuable. It is not a mere extension of what we know: an extension that becomes awful, then appalling. It is the entry into another world, another kind of world, measured by another dimension. And we find some prisoned

30   self in us coming forth to live in this world.

Now it is ridiculous for us to deny any experience. I well remember my first real experience of space, reading a book of modern astronomy. It was rather awful, and since then I rather hate the mere suggestion of illimitable space.

35   But I also remember very vividly my first experience of the astrological heavens, reading Frederick Carter's *Dragon:* the sense of being the macrocosm,* the great sky with its meaningful stars and its profoundly meaningful motions, its wonderful bodily vastness, not empty, but all alive and doing. And I value this experience more. For

40   the sense of astronomical space merely paralyses me. But the sense of

the living astrological heavens gives me an extension of my being, I
become big and glittering and vast with a sumptuous vastness. I am
the macrocosm, and it is wonderful. And since I am not afraid to feel
my own nothingness in front of the vast void of astronomical space,
neither am I afraid to feel my own splendidness in the zodiacal heavens.   5

The *Dragon* as it exists now is no longer the *Dragon* which I read
in Mexico. It has been made more—more argumentative, shall we say.
Give me the old manuscript and let me write an introduction to that!
I urge. But: No, says Carter. It isn't *sound*.

Sound what? He means his old astrological theory of the Apocalypse   10
was not sound, as it was exposed in the old manuscript. But who cares?
We do not care, vitally, about theories of the Apocalypse: what the
Apocalypse means. What we care about is the release of the imagination.
A real release of the imagination renews our strength and our vitality,
makes us feel stronger and happier. Scholastic works don't release the   15
imagination: at the best, they satisfy the intellect, and leave the body
an unleavened lump. But when I get the release into the zodiacal
cosmos my very feet feel lighter and stronger, my very knees are glad.

What does the Apocalypse matter, unless in so far as it gives us
imaginative release into another vital world? After all, what meaning   20
has the Apocalypse? For the ordinary reader, not much. For the
ordinary student and biblical student, it means a prophetic vision of
the martyrdom of the Christian Church, the Second Advent, the
destruction of worldly power, particularly the power of the great
Roman Empire, and then the institution of the Millennium,* the rule   25
of the risen Martyrs of Christendom for the space of one thousand
years: after which, the end of everything, the Last Judgment, and souls
in heaven; all earth, moon and sun being wiped out, all stars and all
space. The New Jerusalem,* and Finis!

This is all very fine, but we know it pretty well by now, so it offers   30
no imaginative release to most people. It is the orthodox interpretation
of the Apocalypse, and probably it is the true superficial meaning, or
the final intentional meaning of the work. But what of it? It is a bore.
Of all the stale buns, the New Jerusalem is one of the stalest. At the
best, it was only invented for the Aunties of this world.   35

Yet when we read Revelation, we feel at once there are meanings
behind meanings. The visions that we have known since childhood are
not so easily exhausted by the orthodox commentators. And the
phrases that have haunted us all our life, like: And I saw heaven
opened, and behold! A white horse!*—these are not explained quite   40

away by orthodox explanations. When all is explained and expounded
and commented upon, still there remains a curious fitful, half-spurious
and half-splendid wonder in the work. Sometimes the great figures
loom up marvellous. Sometimes there is a strange sense of incomprehensible drama. Sometimes the figures have a life of their own,
inexplicable, which cannot be explained away or exhausted.

And gradually we realize that we are in the world of symbol as well
as of allegory. Gradually we realize the book has no one meaning. It
has meanings. Not meaning *within* meaning: but rather, meaning
against meaning. No doubt the last writer left the Apocalypse as a sort
of complete Christian allegory, a Pilgrim's Progress to the Judgment
Day and the New Jerusalem: and the orthodox critics can explain the
allegory fairly satisfactorily. But the Apocalypse is a compound work.
It is no doubt the work of different men, of different generations and
even different centuries.

So that we don't have to look for *a meaning*, as we can look for a
meaning in an allegory like *Pilgrim's Progress,** or even like Dante.*
John of Patmos didn't *compose* the Apocalypse. The Apocalypse is the
work of no one man. The Apocalypse began probably two centuries
before Christ, as some small book, perhaps, of Pagan ritual, or some
small pagan-Jewish Apocalypse written in symbols. It was written over
by other Jewish apocalyptists, and finally came down to John of
Patmos. He turned it more or less, rather less than more, into a
Christian allegory. And later scribes trimmed up his work.

So the ultimate intentional, Christian meaning of the book is, in a
sense, only plastered over. The great images incorporated are like the
magnificent Greek pillars plastered into the Christian Church in Sicily:
they are not merely allegorical figures: they are symbols, they belong
to a bigger age than that of John of Patmos. And as symbols they defy
John's superficial allegorical meaning. You can't give a great symbol
a "meaning", any more than you can give a cat a "meaning". Symbols
are organic units of consciousness with a life of their own, and you
can never explain them away, because their value is dynamic,
emotional, belonging to the sense-consciousness of the body and soul,
and not simply mental. An allegorical image has a *meaning*. Mr.
Facing-both-ways has a meaning. But I defy you to lay your finger
on the full meaning of Janus,* who is a symbol.

It is necessary for us to realize very definitely the difference between
allegory and symbol. Allegory is narrative description using, as a rule,
images to express certain definite qualities. Each image means

something, and is a term in the argument and nearly always for a moral or didactic purpose, for under the narrative of an allegory lies a didactic argument, usually moral. Myth likewise is descriptive narrative using images. But myth is never an argument, it never has a didactic nor a moral purpose, you can draw no conclusion from it. Myth is an attempt to narrate a whole human experience, of which the purpose is too deep, going too deep in the blood and soul, for mental explanation or description. We *can* expound the myth of Kronos* very easily. We can explain it, we can even draw the moral conclusion. But we only look a little silly. The myth of Kronos lives on beyond explanation, for it describes a profound experience of the human body and soul, an experience which is never exhausted and never will be exhausted, for it is being felt and suffered now, and it will be felt and suffered while man remains man. You may explain the myths away: but it only means you go on suffering blindly, stupidly, "in the unconscious" instead of healthily and with the imaginative comprehension playing upon the suffering.

And the images of myth are symbols. They don't "mean something". They stand for units of human *feeling*, human experience. A complex of emotional experience is a symbol. And the power of the symbol is to arouse the deep emotional self, and the dynamic self, beyond comprehension. Many ages of accumulated experience still throb within a symbol. And we throb in response. It takes centuries to create a really significant symbol: even the symbol of the Cross, or of the horse-shoe, or the horns. No man can invent symbols. He can invent an emblem, made up of images: or metaphors: or images: but not symbols. Some images, in the course of many generations of men, become symbols, embedded in the soul and ready to start alive when touched, carried on in the human consciousness for centuries. And again, when men become unresponsive and half dead, symbols die.

Now the Apocalypse has many splendid old symbols, to make us throb. And symbols suggest schemes of symbols. So the Apocalypse, with its symbols, suggests schemes of symbols, deep underneath its Christian-allegorical surface meaning of the Church of Christ.

And one of the chief schemes of symbols which the Apocalypse will suggest to any man who has a feeling for symbols, as contrasted with the orthodox feeling for allegory, is the astrological scheme. Again and again the symbols of the Apocalypse are astrological, the movement is star-movement, and these suggest an astrological scheme. Whether

it is worth while to work out the astrological scheme from the impure
text of the Apocalypse depends on the man who finds it worth while.
Whether the scheme *can* be worked out remains for us to judge. In
all probability there was once an astrological scheme there.

5   But what is certain is that the astrological symbols and suggestions
are still there, they give us the lead. And the lead leads us sometimes
out into a great imaginative world where we feel free and delighted.
At least, that is my experience. So what does it matter whether the
astrological scheme can be restored intact or not? Who cares about
10   explaining the Apocalypse, either allegorically or astrologically or
historically or any other way. All one cares about is the lead, the lead
that the symbolic figures give us, and their dramatic movement: the
lead, and where it will lead us to. If it leads to a release of the
imagination into some new sort of world, then let us be thankful, for
15   that is what we want. It matters so little to us who care more about
life than about scholarship, what is correct or what is not correct. What
does "correct" mean, anyhow? *Sanahorias** is the Spanish for carrots:
I hope I am correct. But what are carrots correct for?

       What the ass wants is carrots; not the idea of carrots, nor
20   thought-forms of carrots, but carrots. The Spanish ass doesn't even
know that he is eating *sanahorias*. He just eats and feels blissfully full
of carrot. Now does *he* have more of the carrot, who eats it, or do I,
who know that in Spanish it is called a *sanahoria* (I hope I am correct)
and in botany it belongs to the *umbelliferæ*?

25   We are full of the wind of thought-forms, and starved for a good
carrot. I don't care *what* a man sets out to prove, so long as he will
interest me and carry me away. I don't in the least care whether he
proves his point or not, so long as he has given me a real imaginative
experience by the way, and not another set of bloated thought-forms.
30   We are starved to death, fed on the eternal sodom-apples* of
thought-forms. What we want is *complete* imaginative experience,
which goes through the whole soul and body. Even at the expense of
reason we want imaginative experience. For reason is certainly not the
final judge of life.

35   Though, if we pause to think about it, we shall realize that it is not
Reason herself whom we have to defy, it is her myrmidons, our
accepted ideas and thought-forms. Reason can adjust herself to almost
anything, if we will only free her from her crinoline and powdered
wig, with which she was invested in the eighteenth and nineteenth
40   centuries. Reason is a supple nymph, and slippery as a fish by nature.

She had as leave give her kiss to an absurdity any day, as to syllogistic truth. The absurdity may turn out truer.

So we need not feel ashamed of flirting with the zodiac. The zodiac is well worth flirting with. But not in the rather silly modern way of horoscopy and telling your fortune by the stars. Telling your fortune by the stars, or trying to get a tip from the stables, before a horse-race. You want to know what horse to put your money on. Horoscopy is just the same. They want their "fortune" told: never their misfortune.

Surely one of the greatest imaginative experiences the human race has ever had was the Chaldean* experience of the stars, including the sun and moon. Sometimes it seems it must have been greater experience than any god-experience. For God is only a great imaginative experience. And sometimes it seems as if the experience of the living heavens, with a living yet not human sun, and brilliant living stars in *live* space must have been the most magnificent of all experiences, greater than any Jehovah or Baal,* Buddha or Jesus. It may seem an absurdity to talk of *live* space. But is it? While we are warm and well and "unconscious" of our bodies, are we not all the time ultimately conscious of our bodies in the same way, as live or living space? And is not this the reason why void space so terrifies us?

I would like to know the stars again as the Chaldeans knew them, two thousand years before Christ. I would like to be able to put my ego into the sun, and my personality into the moon, and my character into the planets, and live the life of the heavens, as the early Chaldeans did. The human consciousness is really homogeneous. There is no complete forgetting, even in death. So that somewhere within us the old experience of the Euphrates, Mesopotamia* between the rivers, lives still. And in my Mesopotamian self I long for the sun again, and the moon and stars, for the Chaldean sun and the Chaldean stars. I long for them terribly. Because *our* sun and *our* moon are only thought-forms to us, balls of gas, dead globes of extinct volcanoes, things we *know* but never feel by experience. By *experience*, we should feel the sun as the savages feel him, we should "know" him as the Chaldeans knew him, in a terrific embrace. But our experience of the sun is dead, we are cut off. All we have now is the thought-form of the sun. He is a blazing ball of gas, he has spots occasionally, from some sort of indigestion, and he makes you brown and healthy if you let him. The first two "facts" we should never have known if men with telescopes, called astronomers, hadn't told us. It is obvious, they

are mere thought-forms. The third "fact", about being brown and healthy, we believe because the doctors have told us it is so. As a matter of fact, many neurotic people become more and more neurotic, the browner and "healthier" they become by sun-baking. The sun can
5   rot as well as ripen. So the third fact is also a thought-form.

And that is all we have, poor things, of the sun. Two or three cheap and inadequate thought-forms. Where, for us, is the great and royal sun of the Chaldeans? Where even, for us, is the sun of the Old Testament, coming forth like a strong man to run a race?* We have
10   lost the sun. We have lost the sun, and we have found a few miserable thought-forms. A ball of blazing gas! with spots! he browns you!

To be sure, we are not the first to lose the sun. The Babylonians themselves began the losing of him. The great and living heavens of the Chaldeans deteriorated already in Belshazzar's day* to the fortune-
15   telling disc of the night skies. But that was man's fault, not the heavens'. Man always deteriorates. And when he deteriorates he always becomes inordinately concerned about his "fortune" and his fate. While life itself is fascinating, fortune is completely uninteresting, and the idea of fate does not enter. When men become poor in life then
20   they become anxious about their fortune and frightened about their fate. By the time of Jesus, men had become so anxious about their fortunes and so frightened about their fates, that they put up the grand declaration that life was one long misery and you couldn't expect your fortune till you got to heaven; that is, till after you were dead. This
25   was accepted by all men, and has been the creed till our day, Buddha and Jesus alike. It has provided us with a vast amount of thought-forms, and landed us in a sort of living death.

So now we want the sun again. Not the spotted ball of gas that browns you like a joint of meat, but the living sun, and the living moon
30   of the old Chaldean days. Think of the moon, think of Artemis and Cybele,* think of the white wonder of the skies, so rounded, so velvety, moving so serene; and then think of the pock-marked horror of the scientific photographs of the moon!

But when we have seen the pock-marked face of the moon in
35   scientific photographs, need that be the end of the moon for us? Even rationally? I think not. It is a great blow: but the imagination can recover from it. Even if we have to believe the pock-marked photograph, even if we believe in the cold and snow and utter deadness of the moon—which we *don't* quite believe—the moon is not therefore a dead
40   nothing. The moon is a white strange world, great, white, soft-seeming

globe in the night sky, and what she actually communicates to me across space I shall never fully know. But the moon that pulls the tides, and the moon that controls the menstrual periods of women, and the moon that touches the lunatics, she is not the mere dead lump of the astronomist. The moon is the great moon still, she gives forth her soft 5 and feline influences, she sways us still, and asks for sympathy back again. In her so-called deadness there is enormous potency still, and power even over our lives. The Moon! Artemis! the great goddess of the splendid past of men! Are you going to tell me she is a dead lump?

She is not dead. But maybe we are dead, half-dead little modern 10 worms stuffing our damp carcasses with thought-forms that have no sensual reality. When we describe the moon as dead, we are describing the deadness in ourselves. When we find space so hideously void, we are describing our own unbearable emptiness. Do we imagine that we, poor worms with spectacles and telescopes and thought-forms, are 15 really more conscious, more vitally aware of the universe than the men in the past were, who called the moon Artemis, or Cybele, or Astarte?* Do we imagine that we really, livingly know the moon better than they knew her? That our knowledge of the moon is more real, more "sound"? Let us disabuse ourselves. We know the moon in terms of 20 our own telescopes and our own deadness. We know everything in terms of our own deadness.

But the moon is Artemis still, and a dangerous goddess she is, as she always was. She throws her cold contempt on you as she passes over the sky, poor, mean little worm of a man who thinks she is nothing 25 but a dead lump. She throws back the cold white vitriol of her angry contempt on to your mean, tense nerves, nervous man, and she is corroding you away. Don't think you can escape the moon, any more than you can escape breathing. She is on the air you breathe. She is active within the atom. Her sting is part of the activity of the electron. 30

Do you think you can put the universe apart, a dead lump here, a ball of gas there, a bit of fume somewhere else? How puerile it is, as if the universe were the back yard of some human chemical works! How gibbering man becomes, when he is really clever, and thinks he is giving the ultimate and final description of the universe! Can't he 35 see that he is merely describing himself, and that the self he is describing is merely one of the more dead and dreary states that man can exist in? When man changes his state of being, he needs an entirely different description of the universe, and so the universe changes its nature to him entirely. Just as the nature of our universe is entirely 40

different from the nature of the Chaldean cosmos. The Chaldeans
described the cosmos as they found it: magnificent. We describe the
universe as we find it: mostly void, littered with a certain number of
dead moons and unborn stars, like the back yard of a chemical works.

5   Is our description true? Not for a single moment, once you change
your state of mind: or your state of soul. It is true for our present
deadened state of mind. Our state of mind is becoming unbearable.
We shall have to change it. And when we have changed it, we shall
change our description of the universe entirely. We shall not call the
10   moon Artemis, but the new name will be nearer to Artemis than to
a dead lump or an extinct globe. We shall not get back the Chaldean
vision of the living heavens. But the heavens will come to life again
for us, and the vision will express also the new men that we are.

And so the value of these studies in the Apocalypse. They wake the
15   imagination and give us at moments a new universe to live in. We may
think it is the old cosmos of the Babylonians, but it isn't. We can never
recover an old vision, once it has been supplanted. But what we can
do is to discover a new vision in harmony with the memories of old,
far-off, far, far-off experience that lie within us. So long as we are not
20   deadened or drossy, memories of Chaldean experience still live within
us, at great depths, and can vivify our impulses in a new direction,
once we awaken them.

Therefore we ought to be grateful for a book like this of the *Dragon*.
What does it matter if it is confused? What does it matter if it repeats
25   itself? What does it matter if in parts it is not very interesting, when
in other parts it is intensely so, when it suddenly opens doors and lets
out the spirit into a new world, even if it is a very old world! I admit
that I cannot see eye to eye with Mr. Carter about the Apocalypse itself.
I cannot, myself, feel that old John of Patmos spent his time on his
30   island lying on his back and gazing at the resplendent heavens; then
afterwards writing a book in which all the magnificent cosmic and
starry drama is deliberately wrapped up in Jewish-Christian moral
threats and vengeances, sometimes rather vulgar.

But that, no doubt, is due to our different approach to the book.
35   I was brought up on the Bible, and seem to have it in my bones. From
early childhood I have been familiar with Apocalyptic language and
Apocalyptic image: not because I spent my time reading Revelation,
but because I was sent to Sunday School and to Chapel, to Band of
Hope and to Christian Endeavour,* and was always having the Bible
40   read at me or to me. I did not even listen attentively. But language

has a power of echoing and re-echoing in my unconscious mind. I can
wake up in the night and "hear" things being said—or hear a piece
of music—to which I had paid no attention during the day. The very
sound itself registers. And so the sound of Revelation had registered
in me very early, and I was as used to: "I was in the Spirit on the   5
Lord's day, and heard behind me a great voice, as of a trumpet, saying:
I am the Alpha and the Omega"*— as I was to a nursery rhyme like
Little Bo-Peep! I didn't know the meaning, but then children so
often prefer sound to sense. "Alleluia: for the Lord God omnipotent
reigneth".* The Apocalypse is full of sounding phrases, beloved by   10
the uneducated in the chapels for their true liturgical powers. "And
he treadeth the winepress of the fierceness and wrath of Almighty
God".*

No, for me the Apocalypse is altogether too full of fierce feeling,
fierce and moral, to be a grand disguised star-myth. And yet it has   15
intimate connexion with star-myths and the movement of the
astrological heavens: a sort of submerged star-meaning. And nothing
delights me more than to escape from the all-too-moral chapel meaning
of the book, to another wider, older, more magnificent meaning. In
fact, one of the real joys of middle age is in coming back to the Bible,   20
reading a new translation, such as Moffatt's,* reading the modern
research and modern criticism of some Old Testament books, and of
the Gospels, and getting a whole new conception of the Scriptures
altogether. Modern research has been able to put the Bible back into
its living connexions, and it is splendid: no longer the Jewish-moral   25
book and a stick to beat an immoral dog, but a fascinating account of
the adventure of the Jewish—or Hebrew or Israelite nation, among
the great old civilized nations of the past, Egypt, Assyria,* Babylon,
and Persia: then on into the Hellenic world, the Seleucids,* and the
Romans, Pompey and Anthony.* Reading the Bible in a new   30
translation, with modern notes and comments, is more fascinating than
reading Homer,* for the adventure goes even deeper into time and into
the soul, and continues through the centuries, and moves from Egypt
to Ur* and to Nineveh,* from Sheba to Tarshish* and Athens and
Rome. It is the very quick of ancient history.   35

And the Apocalypse, the last and presumably the latest of the books
of the Bible, also comes to life with a great new life, once we look at
its symbols and take the lead that they offer us. The text leads most
easily into the great chaotic Hellenic world of the first century:
Hellenic, not Roman. But the symbols lead much further back.   40

They lead Frederick Carter back to Chaldea and to Persia, chiefly, for his skies are the late Chaldean, and his mystery is chiefly Mithraic.* Hints, we have only hints from the outside. But the rest is within us, and if we can take a hint, it is extraordinary how far and into what fascinating worlds the hints can lead us. The orthodox critics will say: Fantasy! Nothing but fantasy! But then, thank God for fantasy, if it enhances our life.

And even so, the "reproach" is not quite just. The Apocalypse has an old, submerged astrological meaning, and probably even an old astrological scheme. The hints are too obvious and too splendid: like the ruins of an old temple incorporated in a Christian chapel. Is it any more fantastic to try to reconstruct the embedded temple, than to insist that the embedded images and columns are mere rubble in the Christian building, and have no meaning? It is as fantastic to deny meaning when meaning is there, as it is to invent meaning when there is none. And it is much duller. For the invented meaning may still have a life of its own.

APOCALYPSE

Note on the text

The base-text for this edition is the corrected typed carbon copy (TCC) of *Apocalypse* typed over the Christmas holidays of 1929–30; it has the last corrections and revisions DHL made before his death. It is owned by the University of Texas at Austin.

The apparatus records all textual variants including editorial interventions on the few occasions when the editor has found it necessary to emend the text. Both manuscript and TCC are inconsistent in using 'God' and 'god'. The present text adopts the most consistent usage and capitalises 'God' when referring either to the Old and New Testament deity or to the creative power which DHL saw informing the universe, and 'god' or 'gods' when referring to pagan deities and to an undifferentiated or more general force or potency. References to the Book of Revelation are in roman type throughout in accordance with DHL's usual, though not invariable, practice in both MS and TCC.

The following emendations have been made silently:

1 Clearly accidental spelling errors by DHL or his typist and obvious typesetters' mistakes have been corrected, e.g. 'arestocrat' becomes 'aristocrat'.

2 Accidental omissions have been supplied only in the case of incomplete quotation marks, final stops and apostrophes in colloquial contractions.

3 The section divisions have been numbered consecutively.

4 DHL's punctuation has been retained throughout. However, his typist was not always consistent in placing punctuation inside or outside quotation marks. Accordingly this has been regularised to the most consistent MS usage.

5 DHL's capitalisation has been retained. However neither MS nor TCC is consistent in the use of 'Apocalyptist' or 'apocalyptist' and both occur, often in a single paragraph. The lower case has been adopted throughout as DHL's most frequent practice.

APOCALYPSE

I

Apocalypse* means simply Revelation, though there is nothing simple about this one, since men have puzzled their brains for nearly two thousand years to find out what, exactly, is revealed in all its orgy of mystification. On the whole, the modern mind dislikes mystification, and of all the books in the Bible, it finds Revelation perhaps the least attractive.

That is my own first feeling about it. From earliest years right into manhood, like any other nonconformist* child I had the Bible poured every day into my helpless consciousness, till there came almost a saturation point. Long before one could think or even vaguely understand, this Bible language, these "portions" of the Bible were *douched* over the mind and consciousness, till they became soaked in, they became an influence which affected all the processes of emotion and thought. So that today, although I have "forgotten" my Bible, I need only begin to read a chapter to realise that I "know" it with an almost nauseating fixity. And I must confess, my first reaction is one of dislike, repulsion, and even resentment. My very instincts *resent* the Bible.

The reason is now fairly plain to me. Not only was the Bible, in portions, poured into the childish consciousness day in, day out, year in, year out, willy nilly, whether the consciousness could assimilate it or not, but also it was day in, day out, year in, year out expounded, dogmatically, and always morally expounded, whether it was in day-school or Sunday School, at home or in Band of Hope or Christian Endeavour.* The interpretation was always the same, whether it was a Doctor of Divinity in the pulpit, or the big blacksmith who was my Sunday School teacher.* Not only was the Bible verbally trodden into the consciousness, like innumerable foot-prints treading a surface hard, but the foot-prints were always mechanically alike, the interpretation was fixed, so that all real interest was lost.

The process defeats its own ends. While the Jewish poetry penetrates the emotions and the imagination, and the Jewish morality penetrates the instincts, the mind becomes stubborn, resistant, and at last

59

repudiates the whole Bible authority, and turns with a kind of
repugnance away from the Bible altogether. And this is the condition
of many men of my generation.

5   Now a book lives as long as it is unfathomed. Once it is fathomed,
it dies at once. It is an amazing thing, how utterly different a book
will be, if I read it again after five years. Some books gain immensely,
they are a new thing. They are so astonishingly different, they make
a man question his own identity. Again, other books lose immensely.
I read *War and Peace** once more, and was amazed to find how little
10   it moved me, I was almost aghast to think of the raptures I had once
felt, and now felt no more.

So it is. Once a book is fathomed, once it is *known*, and its meaning
is fixed or established, it is dead. A book only lives while it has power
to move us, and move us *differently*; so long as we find it *different* every
15   time we read it. Owing to the flood of shallow books which really are
exhausted in one reading, the modern mind tends to think every book
is the same, finished in one reading. But it is not so. And gradually
the modern mind will realise it again. The real joy of a book lies in
reading it over and over again, and always finding it different, coming
20   upon another meaning, another level of meaning. It is, as usual, a
question of values: we are so overwhelmed with *quantities* of books,
that we hardly realise any more that a book can be valuable, valuable
like a jewel, or a lovely picture, into which you can look deeper and
deeper and get a more profound experience every time. It is far, far
25   better to read one book six times, at intervals, than to read six several
books. Because if a certain book can call you to read it six times, it
will be a deeper and deeper experience each time, and will enrich the
whole soul, emotional and mental. Whereas six books read once only
are merely an accumulation of superficial interest, the burdensome
30   accumulation of modern days, quantity without real value.

We shall now see the reading public dividing again into two groups:
the vast mass, who read for amusement and for momentary interest,
and the small minority, who only want the books that have value to
themselves, books which yield experience, and still deeper experience.
35   The Bible is a book that has been temporarily killed for us, or for
some of us, by having its meaning arbitrarily fixed. We know it so
thoroughly, in its superficial or popular meaning, that it is dead, it gives
us nothing any more. Worse still, by old habit amounting almost to
instinct, it imposes on us a whole state of feeling which is now
40   repugnant to us. We detest the "chapel" and the Sunday School

feeling which the Bible must necessarily impose on us. We want to get rid of all that *vulgarity*—for vulgarity it is.

Perhaps the most detestable of all these books of the Bible, taken superficially, is Revelation. By the time I was ten, I am sure I had heard, and read, that book ten times over, even without knowing or taking real heed. And without ever knowing or thinking about it, I am sure it always roused in me a real dislike. Without realising it, I must, from earliest childhood have detested the pie-pie,* mouthing, solemn, portentous, loud way in which everybody read the Bible, whether it was parsons or teachers or ordinary persons. I dislike the "parson" voice through and through my bones. And this voice, I remember, was always at its worst when mouthing out some portion of Revelation. Even the phrases that still fascinate me I cannot recall without shuddering, because I can still hear the portentous declamation of a nonconformist clergyman: "And I saw heaven opened, and behold a white horse; and he that sat upon it was called "*—there my memory suddenly stops, deliberately blotting out the next words: "Faithful and True". I hated, even as a child, allegory: people having the names of mere qualities, like this somebody on a white horse, called "Faithful and True". In the same way I could never read *Pilgrim's Progress.** When as a small boy I learnt from Euclid that: "The whole is greater than the part",* I immediately knew that that solved the problem of allegory for me. A man is more than a Christian, a rider on a white horse must be more than mere Faithfulness and Truth, and when people are merely personifications of qualities they cease to be people for me. Though as a young man I almost loved Spenser and his *Faerie Queen,** I had to gulp at his allegory.

But the Apocalypse is, and always was from earliest childhood, to me antipathetic. In the first place its splendiferous imagery is distasteful because of its complete unnaturalness. "And before the throne there was a sea of glass like unto crystal: and in the midst of the throne and round about the throne were four beasts full of eyes before and behind.

"And the first beast was like a lion, and the second beast like a calf, and the third beast had a face as a man, and the fourth beast was like a flying eagle.

"And the four beasts had each of them six wings about him; and they were full of eyes within: and they rest not day and night, saying, Holy, holy, holy, Lord God Almighty, which was, and is, and is to come—".*

A passage like that irritated and annoyed my boyish mind because of its pompous unnaturalness. If it is imagery, it is imagery which cannot be imagined: for how can four beasts be "full of eyes before and behind", and how can they be "in the midst of the throne and round about the throne"? They can't be somewhere and somewhere else at the same time. But that is how the Apocalypse is.

Again, much of the imagery is utterly unpoetic and arbitrary, some of it really ugly, like all the wadings in blood, and the rider's shirt dipped in blood, and people washed in the blood of the Lamb.* Also such phrases as "the wrath of the Lamb"* are on the face of them ridiculous. But this is the grand phraseology and imagery of the nonconformist chapels, all the Bethels* of England and America, and all the Salvation armies.* And vital religion is said to be found, in all ages, down among the uneducated people.

Down among the uneducated people you will still find Revelation rampant. I think it has had, and perhaps still has more influence, actually, than the Gospels or the great Epistles. The huge denunciation of kings and Rulers, and of the whore that sitteth upon the waters, is entirely sympathetic to a Tuesday evening congregation of colliers and colliers' wives, on a black winter night, in the great barn-like Pentecost chapel.* And the capital letters of the name: MYSTERY, BABYLON THE GREAT, THE MOTHER OF HARLOTS AND ABOMINATIONS OF THE EARTH* thrill the old colliers today as they thrilled the Scotch Puritan peasants and the more ferocious of the early Christians. To the underground early Christians, Babylon the great meant Rome, the great city and the great empire which persecuted them. And great was the satisfaction of denouncing her and bringing her to utter, utter woe and destruction, with all her kings, her wealth and her lordliness. After the Reformation Babylon was once more identified with Rome, but this time it meant the Pope, and in Protestant and nonconformist England and Scotland out rolled the denunciations of John the Divine, with the grand cry: "Babylon the great is fallen, is fallen, and is become the habitation of devils, and the hold of every foul spirit, and a cage of every unclean and hateful bird—".* Nowadays the words are still mouthed out, and sometimes still they are hurled at the Pope and the Roman Catholics, who seem to be lifting their heads up again. But more often, today, Babylon means the rich and wicked people who live in luxury and harlotry somewhere in the vague distance, London, New York, or Paris worst of all, and who never once set foot in "chapel", all their lives.

It is very nice, if you are poor and *not* humble—and the poor may be obsequious, but they are almost *never* truly humble, in the Christian sense—to bring your grand enemies down to utter destruction and discomfiture, while you yourself rise up to grandeur. And nowhere does this happen so splendiferously as in Revelation. The great enemy in the eyes of Jesus was the Pharisee,* harping on the letter of the law. But the Pharisee is too remote and subtle for the collier and the factory-worker. The Salvation Army at the street corner rarely raves about Pharisees. It raves about the Blood of the Lamb, and Babylon, Sin, and Sinners, the great harlot, and angels that cry Woe, Woe, Woe! and Vials that pour out horrible plagues. And above all, about being Saved, and sitting on the Throne with the Lamb, and reigning in Glory, and having Everlasting Life, and living in a grand city made of jasper, with gates of pearl: a city that "had no need of the sun, neither of the moon, to shine in it".* If you listen to the Salvation Army you will hear that they are going to be very grand, very grand indeed, once they get to heaven. *Then* they'll show you what's what. *Then* you'll be put in your place, you superior person, you Babylon: down in hell and in brimstone.*

This is entirely the tone of Revelation. What we realise when we have read the precious book a few times is that John the Divine had, on the face of it, a grandiose scheme for wiping out and annihilating everybody who wasn't of the elect, the chosen people, in short, and of climbing up himself right on to the throne of God. With nonconformity, the chapel people took over to themselves the Jewish idea of the chosen people. They were "it", the elect, or the "saved". And they took over the Jewish idea of ultimate triumph and reign of the chosen people. From being bottom dogs they were going to be top dogs: in Heaven. If not sitting actually on the throne, they were going to sit in the lap of the enthroned Lamb. It is doctrine you can hear any night from the Salvation Army or in any Bethel or Pentecost Chapel. If it is not Jesus, it is John. If it is not Gospel, it is Revelation. It is popular religion, as distinct from thoughtful religion.

II

Or at least, it was popular religion when I was a boy. And I remember, as a child, I used to wonder over the curious sense of self-glory which one felt in the uneducated leaders, the men especially of the Primitive Methodist Chapels.* They were not on the whole pious or mealy-mouthed or objectionable, these colliers who spoke heavy dialect and ran the "Pentecost". They certainly were not humble or apologetic. No, they came in from the pit and sat down to their dinners with a bang, and their wives and daughters ran to wait on them quite cheerfully, and their sons obeyed them without overmuch resentment. The home was rough yet not unpleasant, and there was an odd sense of wild mystery or power about, as if the chapel men really had some dispensation of rude power from above. Not love, but a rough and rather wild, somewhat "special" sense of power. They were so *sure*, and as a rule their wives were quite humble to them. They ran a chapel, so they could run their household. I used to wonder over it, and rather enjoy it. But even I thought it rather "common". My mother, who was Congregationalist,* never set foot in a Primitive Methodist chapel in her life, I don't suppose. And she was certainly not prepared to be humble to her husband. If he'd been a real cheeky chapel man, she would no doubt have been much meeker with him. Cheek, that was the outstanding quality of chapel men. But a special kind of cheek, authorised from above, as it were. And I know now, a good deal of this special kind of religious cheek was backed up by the Apocalypse.

It was not till many years had gone by, and I had read something of comparative religion and the history of religion, that I realised what a strange book it was that had inspired the colliers on the black Tuesday nights in Pentecost or Beauvale Chapel* to such a queer sense of special authority and of religious cheek. Strange marvellous black nights of the north Midlands, with the gas-light hissing in the chapel, and the roaring of the strong-voiced colliers. Popular religion: a religion of self-glorification and power, forever! and of darkness. No wailing "Lead kindly Light"!* about it.

The longer one lives, the more one realises that there are two kinds of Christianity, the one focussed on Jesus and the Command: Love one another!*—and the other focussed, not on Paul or Peter or John the Beloved, but on the Apocalypse. There is the Christianity of tenderness. But as far as I can see, it is utterly pushed aside by the Christianity of self-glorification: the self-glorification of the humble.

There's no getting away from it, mankind falls forever into the two divisions of aristocrat and democrat. The purest aristocrats during the Christian era have taught democracy. And the purest democrats try to turn themselves into the most absolute aristocracy. Jesus was an aristocrat, so was John the Apostle, and Paul. It takes a great aristocrat to be capable of great tenderness and gentleness and unselfishness: the tenderness and gentleness of *strength*. From the democrat you may often get the tenderness and gentleness of weakness: that's another thing. But you usually get a sense of toughness.

We are speaking now not of political parties, but of the two sorts of human nature: those that feel themselves strong in their souls, and those that feel themselves weak. Jesus and Paul and the greater John felt themselves strong. John of Patmos felt himself weak, in his very soul.

In Jesus' day, the inwardly strong men everywhere had lost their desire to rule on earth. They wished to withdraw their strength from earthly rule and earthly power, and to apply it to another form of life. Then the weak began to rouse up and to feel *inordinately* conceited, they began to express their rampant hate of the "obvious" strong ones, the men in worldly power.

So that religion, the Christian religion especially, became dual. The religion of the strong taught renunciation and love. And the religion of the weak taught *down with the strong and the powerful, and let the poor be glorified*. Since there are always more weak people than strong, in the world, the second sort of Christianity has triumphed and will triumph. If the weak are not ruled, they will rule, and there's the end of it. And the rule of the weak is *Down with the strong!*

The grand biblical authority for this cry is the Apocalypse. The weak and pseudo-humble are going to wipe all worldly power, glory and riches off the face of the earth, and then they, the truly weak, are going to reign. It will be a millennium of pseudo-humble saints, and gruesome to contemplate. But it is what religion stands for today: down with all strong, free life, let the weak triumph, let the pseudo-humble reign. The religion of the self-glorification of the weak, the reign of the pseudo-humble. This is the spirit of society today, religious and political.

III

And this was pretty well the religion of John of Patmos. They say he was an old man already when he finished the Apocalypse in the year 96 A.D.: which is the date fixed by modern scholars, from "internal evidence".*

Now there were three Johns in early Christian history: John the Baptist, who baptised Jesus, and who apparently founded a religion, or at least a sect of his own, with strange doctrines that continued for many years after Jesus' death; then there was the Apostle John, who was supposed to have written the Fourth Gospel and some Epistles; then there was this John of Patmos who lived in Ephesus* and was sent to prison on Patmos for some religious offence against the Roman State. He was, however, released from his island after a term of years, returned to Ephesus and lived, according to legend, to a great old age.

For a long time it was thought that the Apostle John, to whom we ascribe the Fourth Gospel, had written the Apocalypse also. But it cannot be that the same man wrote the two works, they are so alien to one another. The author of the Fourth Gospel* was surely a cultured "Greek" Jew, and one of the great inspirers of mystic, "loving" Christianity. John of Patmos must have had a very different nature. He certainly has inspired very different feelings.

When we come to read it critically and seriously, we realise that the Apocalypse reveals a profoundly important Christian doctrine which has in it none of the real Christ, none of the real Gospel, none of the *creative* breath of Christianity, and is nevertheless perhaps the most effectual doctrine in the Bible. That is, it has had a greater effect on second-rate people throughout the Christian ages, than any other book in the Bible. The Apocalypse of John is, as it stands, the work of a second-rate mind. It appeals intensely to second-rate minds in every country and every century. Strangely enough, unintelligible as it is, it has no doubt been the greatest source of inspiration to the vast mass of Christian minds—the vast mass being always second-rate—since the first century. And we realise, to our horror, that this is what we are up against today: not Jesus nor Paul, but John of Patmos.

The Christian doctrine of love even at its best was an evasion. Even Jesus was going to reign "hereafter", when his "love" would be turned into confirmed power. This business of reigning in glory hereafter went to the root of Christianity: and is, of course, only an expression of frustrated desire to reign here and now. The Jews would not be put off: they were determined to reign on earth, so after the Temple of Jerusalem* was smashed for the second time, about 200 B.C., they started in to imagine the coming of a Messiah militant and triumphant, who would conquer the world. The Christians took this up as the Second Advent of Christ, when Jesus was coming to give the gentile world its final whipping, and establish a rule of saints. John of Patmos extended this previously modest rule of saints (about forty years) to the grand round number of a thousand years, and so the Millennium* took hold of the imagination of man.

And so there crept into the New Testament the grand Christian enemy, the Power-spirit. At the very last moment, when the devil had been so beautifully shut out, in he slipped, dressed in Apocalyptic disguise, and enthroned himself at the end of the book as Revelation.

For Revelation, be it said once and for all, is the revelation of the undying will-to-power in man, and its sanctification, its final triumph. If you have to suffer martyrdom, and if all the universe has to be destroyed in the process, still, still, still, O Christian, you shall reign as a king and set your foot on the necks of the old bosses!

This is the message of Revelation.

And just as inevitably as Jesus had to have a Judas Iscariot among his disciples, so did there have to be a Revelation in the New Testament.

Why? Because the nature of man demands it, and will always demand it.

The Christianity of Jesus applies to a part of our nature only. There is a big part to which it does not apply. And to this part, as the Salvation Army will show you, Revelation does apply.

The religions of renunciation, meditation, and self-knowledge are for individuals alone. But man is individual only in part of his nature. In another great part of him, he is collective.

The religions of renunciation, meditation, self-knowledge, pure morality are for individuals, and even then, not for complete individuals. But they express the individual side of man's nature. They isolate this side of his nature. And they cut off the other side of his nature, the collective side. The lowest stratum of society is always non-individual, so look there for the other manifestation of religion.

The religions of renunciation, like Buddhism or Christianity or Plato's philosophy, are for aristocrats, aristocrats of the spirit. The aristocrats of the spirit are to find their fulfilment in self-realisation and in service. Serve the poor. Well and good. But whom are the poor going to serve? It is the grand question. And John of Patmos answers it. The poor are going to serve themselves, and attend to their own self-glorification. And by the poor we don't mean the indigent merely: we mean the merely collective souls, terribly "middling", who have no aristocratic singleness and aloneness.

The vast mass are these middling souls. They *have* no aristocratic individuality, such as is demanded by Christ or Buddha* or Plato.* So they skulk in a mass and secretly are bent on their own ultimate self-glorification. The Patmossers.

Only when he is alone, can man be a Christian, a Buddhist, or a Platonist. The Christ statues and Buddha statues witness to this. When he is with other men, instantly distinctions occur, and levels are formed. As soon as he is with other men, Jesus is an aristocrat, a master. Buddha is always the lord Buddha, Francis of Assisi,* trying to be so humble, as a matter of fact finds a subtle means to absolute power over his followers. Shelley could not *bear* not be the aristocrat of his company. Lenin* was a Tyrannus in shabby clothes.

So it is! Power is there, and always will be. As soon as two or three men come together,* especially to *do* something, then power comes into being, and one man is a leader, a master. It is inevitable.

Accept it, recognise the natural power in the man, as men did in the past, and give it homage, then there is a great joy, an uplifting, and a potency passes from the powerful to the less powerful. There is a stream of power. And in this, men have their best collective being, now and forever. Recognise the flame of power, or glory, and a corresponding flame springs up in yourself. Give homage and allegiance to a hero, and you become yourself heroic. It is the law of men. Perhaps the law of women is different.

But act on the reverse, and what happens? Deny power, and power wanes. Deny power in a greater man, and you have no power yourself. But society, now and forever, must be ruled and governed. So that the mass must grant *authority* where they deny power. Authority now takes the place of power, and we have "ministers" and public officials and policemen. Then comes the grand scramble of ambition, competition, and the mass treading one another in the face, so afraid they are of power.

A man like Lenin is a great evil saint who believes in the utter destruction of power. It leaves men unutterably bare, stripped, mean, miserable, and humiliated. Abraham Lincoln* is a half-evil saint who almost believes in the utter destruction of power. President Wilson* is a quite evil saint who quite believes in the destruction of power—but who runs himself to megalomania and neurasthenic tryanny. Every saint becomes evil—and Lenin, Lincoln, Wilson are true saints so long as they remain purely individual;—every saint becomes evil the moment he touches the collective self of men. Then he is a perverter: Plato the same. The great saints are for the *individual* only, and that means, for one side of our nature only, for in the deep layers of ourselves we are collective, we can't help it. And the collective self either lives and moves and has its being in a full relationship of power: or it is reversed, and lives a frictional misery of trying to destroy power, and destroy itself.

But nowadays, the will to destroy power is paramount. Great kings like the late Tsar*—we mean great in position—are rendered almost imbecile by the vast anti-will of the masses, the will to negate power. Modern kings are negated till they become almost idiots. And the same of any man in power, unless he be a power-destroyer and a white-feathered evil bird: then the mass will back him up. How can the anti-power masses, above all the great middling masses, ever have a king who is more than a thing of ridicule or pathos?

The Apocalypse has been running for nearly two thousand years: the hidden side of Christianity: and its work is nearly done. For the Apocalypse does not worship power. It wants to murder the powerful, to seize power itself, the weakling.

Judas had to betray Jesus to the powers that be, because of the denial and subterfuge inherent in Jesus' teaching. Jesus took up the position of the pure individual, even with his disciples. He did not *really* mix with them, or even really work or act with them. *He was alone all the time.* He puzzled them utterly, and in some part of them, he let them down. He refused to be their physical power-lord. The power-homage in a man like Judas felt itself betrayed! So it betrayed back again: with a kiss.* And in the same way, Revelation had to be included in the New Testament, to give the death-kiss to the Gospels.

IV

It is a curious thing, but the collective will of a community really
reveals the *basis* of the individual will. The early Christian Churches,
or communities, revealed quite early a strange will to a strange kind
5   of power. They had a will to destroy all power, and so usurp themselves
the final, the ultimate power. This was not quite the teaching of Jesus,
but it was the inevitable implication of Jesus' teaching, in the minds
of the vast mass of the weak, the inferior. Jesus taught the escape and
liberation into unselfish, brotherly love: a feeling that only the strong
10   can know. And this, sure enough, at once brought the community of
the weak into triumphant being; and the will of the community of
Christians was anti-social, almost anti-human, revealing from the start
a frenzied desire for the end of the world, the destruction of humanity
altogether; and then, when this did not come, a grim determination
15   to destroy all mastery, all lordship, and all human splendour out of
the world, leaving only the community of saints as the final negation
of power, and the final power.
      After the crash of the Dark Ages, the Catholic Church emerged again
a *human* thing, a complete, not a half-thing, adjusted to seed-time and
20   harvest and the solstice of Christmas and of midsummer, and having
a good balance, in early days, between brotherly love and natural
lordship and splendour. Every man was given his little kingdom in
marriage, and every woman her own little inviolate realm. This
Christian marriage guided by the church was a great institution for
25   true freedom, true possibility of fulfilment. Freedom was no more, and
can be no more than the possibility of living fully and satisfactorily.
In marriage, in the great natural cycle of church ritual and festival,
the early Catholic Church tried to give this to men. But alas, the
Church soon fell out of balance, into worldly greed.
30   Then came the Reformation, and the thing started over again: the
old will of the Christian community to destroy human worldly power,
and to substitute the *negative* power of the mass. The battle rages today,
in all its horror. In Russia, the triumph over worldly power was accomplished, and the reign of saints set in, with Lenin for the chief saint.

And Lenin was a saint. He had every quality of a saint. He is worshipped today, quite rightly, as a saint. But saints who try to kill all brave power in mankind are fiends, like the Puritans who wanted to pull all the bright feathers out of the chaffinch. Fiends!

Lenin's rule of saints turned out quite horrible. It has more thou-shalt-nots than any rule of "Beasts",* or emperors. And this is bound to be so. Any rule of saints must be horrible. Why? Because the nature of man is not saintly. The *primal* need, the old-Adamic need in a man's soul is to be, in his own sphere and as far as he can attain it, master, lord, and splendid one. Every cock can crow on his own muck-heap, and ruffle gleaming feathers, every peasant could be a glorious little Tsar in his own hut, and when he got a bit drunk. And every peasant was consummated in the old dash and gorgeousness of the nobles, and in the supreme splendour of the Tsar. The supreme master, and lord and splendid one: their own, their own splendid one: they might see him with their own eyes, the Tsar! And this fulfilled one of the deepest, greatest and most powerful needs of the human heart. The human heart needs, needs, needs splendour, gorgeousness, pride, assumption, glory, and lordship. Perhaps it needs these even more than it needs love: at last, even more than bread. And every great king makes every man a little lord in his own tiny sphere, fills the imagination with lordship and splendour, satisfies the soul. The most dangerous thing in the world is to show man his own paltriness as a hedged-in male. It depresses him, and *makes* him paltry. We become, alas, what we think we are. Men have been depressed now for many years in their male and splendid selves, depressed into dejection and almost into abjection. Is not that evil? Then let men themselves do something about it.

And a great saint like Lenin—or Shelley or St. Francis—can only cry *anathema! anathema!*, to the natural proud self of power, and try deliberately to destroy all might and all lordship, and leave the people poor, oh, so poor! Poor, poor, poor, as the people are in all our modern democracies, though nowhere so absolutely impoverished in life as in the most absolute democracy, no matter how they be in money.

The community is inhuman, and less than human. It becomes at last the most dangerous because *bloodless* and insentient tyrant. For a long time, even a democracy like the American or the Swiss will answer to the call of a hero, who is somewhat of a true aristocrat: like Lincoln: so strong is the aristocratic instinct in man. But the willingness to give the response to the heroic, the true aristocratic call, gets weaker and weaker in every democracy, as time goes on. All history proves it. Then men turn against the heroic appeal, with a sort of venom. They will only listen to the call of mediocrity wielding the insentient bullying power of mediocrity: which is evil. Hence the success of painfully inferior and even base politicians.

Brave people add up to an aristocracy. The democracy of thou-shalt-not is bound to be a collection of weak men. And then the sacred "will of the people" becomes blinder, baser, colder and more dangerous than the will of any tyrant. When the will of the people becomes the sum of the weakness of a multitude of weak men, it is time to make a break.

So today. Society consists of a mass of weak individuals trying to protect themselves, out of fear, from every possible imaginary evil, and, of course, *by their very fear*, bringing the evil into being.

This is the Christian Community today, in its perpetual mean thou-shalt-not. This is how Christian doctrine has worked out in practice.

V

And Revelation was a foreshadowing of all this. It is above all what some psychologists would call the revelation of a thwarted "superiority" goal,* and a consequent inferiority complex. Of the positive side of Christianity, the peace of meditation and the joy of unselfish service, the rest from ambition and the pleasure of knowledge, we find nothing in the Apocalypse. Because the Apocalypse is for the non-individual side of a man's nature, written from the thwarted collective self, whereas meditation and unselfish service are for pure individuals, isolate. Pure Christianity anyhow *cannot* fit a nation, or society at large. The Great War made it obvious. It can only fit individuals. The collective whole must have some other inspiration.

And the Apocalypse, repellant though its chief spirit be, does also contain another inspiration. It is repellant only because it resounds with the dangerous snarl of the *frustrated, suppressed* collective self, the frustrated power-spirit in man, vengeful. But it contains also some revelation of the true and positive Power-spirit. The very beginning surprises us: "John to the seven churches in Asia: grace be to you and peace from HE WHO IS AND WAS AND IS COMING, and from the seven Spirits before his throne, and from Jesus Christ the faithful witness, the first-born from the dead, and the prince over the kings of the earth; to him who loves us and has loosed us from our sins by shedding his blood—he has made us a realm of priests for his God and Father,—to him be glory and dominion for ever and ever, Amen. Lo, he is coming on the clouds, to be seen by every eye, even by those who impaled him, and all the tribes of earth will wail because of him: even so, Amen ",*—I have used Moffatt's translation,* as the meaning is a little more explicit than in the authorised version.*

But here we have a curious Jesus, very different from the one in Galilee, wandering by the lake.* And the book goes on: "On the Lord's day I found myself rapt in the Spirit, and I heard a loud voice behind me like a trumpet calling, 'Write your vision in a book'.—So I turned to see whose voice it was that spoke to me; and on turning round I saw seven golden lampstands and in the middle of the lampstands One

who resembled a human being, with a long robe, and a belt of gold
round his breast; his head and hair were white as wool, white as snow;
his eyes flashed like fire, his feet glowed like burnished bronze, his voice
sounded like many waves, in his right hand he held seven stars, a sharp
5   sword with a double edge issued from his mouth, and his face shone
like the sun in full strength. When I saw him, I fell at his feet like
a dead man; but he laid his hand on me, saying: 'Do not be afraid;
I am the First and Last, I was dead and here I am alive for evermore,
holding the keys that unlock death and Hades. Write down your vision
10   of what is and what is to be hereafter. As for the secret symbol of the
seven stars which you have seen in my right hand, and of the seven
golden lampstands: the seven stars are the angels of the seven
churches, and the seven lampstands are the seven churches. To the
angel of the church at Ephesus write thus:—"These are the words
15   of him who holds the seven stars in his right hand, who moves among
the seven golden lampstands—"''".*

Now this being with the sword of the Logos* issuing from his mouth
and the seven stars in his hand is the Son of God, therefore, the
Messiah, therefore Jesus. It is very far from the Jesus who said in
20   Gethsemane: "My heart is sad, sad even unto death; stay here and
watch".*—But it is the Jesus that the early Church, especially in Asia,
prominently believed in.

And what is this Jesus? It is the great Splendid One, almost identical
with the Almighty in the visions of Ezekiel and Daniel.* It is a vast
25   Cosmic lord, standing among the seven eternal lamps of the archaic
planets, sun and moon and five great stars around his feet. In the sky
his gleaming head is in the north, the sacred region of the Pole, and
he holds in his right hand the seven stars of the Bear, that we call
the Plough, and he wheels them round the Pole star, as even now we
30   see them wheel, causing the universal revolution of the heavens, the
roundwise moving of the cosmos. This is the lord of all motion, who
swings the cosmos into its course. Again, from his mouth issues the
two-edged sword of the Word, the mighty weapon of the Logos which
will smite the world (and in the end destroy it). This is the sword indeed
35   that Jesus brought among men. And lastly, his face shines like the sun
in full strength, the source of life itself, the dazzler, before whom we
fall as if dead.

And this is Jesus: not only the Jesus of the early churches, but
the Jesus of popular religion today. There is nothing humble nor
40   suffering here. It is our "superiority goal", indeed. And it is a true

account of man's *other* conception of God; perhaps the greater and
more fundamental conception: the magnificent Mover of the Cosmos!
To John of Patmos, the Lord is *Kosmokrator*, and even *Kosmodynamos*:
the great Ruler of the Cosmos, and the Power of the Cosmos. But alas,
according to the Apocalypse man has no share in the ruling of the   5
Cosmos until after death. When a Christian has been put to death by
martyrdom, then he will be resurrected at the Second Advent and
become himself a little Kosmokrator, ruling for a thousand years. It
is the apotheosis of the weak man.

But the Son of God, the Jesus of John's vision, is more even than   10
this. He holds the keys that unlock death and Hades. He is Lord of
the Underworld. He is Hermes, the guide of souls through the
death-world, over the hellish stream. He is master of the mysteries of
the dead, he knows the meaning of the holocaust,* and has final power
over the powers below. The dead and the lords of death, who are always   15
hovering in the background of religion away down among the people,
these Chthonioi* of the primitive Greeks, these too must acknowledge
Jesus as a supreme lord.

And the lord of the dead is master of the future, and the god of the
present. He gives the vision of what was, and is, and shall be.   20

Here is a Jesus for you! What is modern Christianity going to make
of it? For it is the Jesus of the very first communities, and it is the
Jesus of the early Catholic Church, as it emerged from the Dark Ages
and adjusted itself once more to life and death and the cosmos, the
whole great adventure of the human soul, as contrasted with the little   25
petty personal adventure of modern Protestantism and Catholicism
alike, cut off from the cosmos, cut off from Hades, cut off from the
magnificence of the Star-mover. Petty little personal salvation, petty
morality instead of cosmic splendour, we have lost the sun and the
planets, and the Lord with the seven stars of the Bear in his right hand.   30
Poor, paltry, creeping little world we live in, even the keys of death
and Hades are lost. How shut in we are! All we can do, with our
brotherly love, is to shut one another in. We are so afraid somebody
else might be lordly and splendid, when we can't. Petty little
bolshevists, every one of us today, we are determined that *no* man shall   35
shine like the sun in full strength, for he would certainly outshine us.

Now again we realise a dual feeling in ourselves with regard to the
Apocalypse. Suddenly we see some of the old pagan splendour, that
delighted in the might and the magnificence of the Cosmos, and man
who was as a star in the cosmos. Suddenly we feel again the nostalgia   40

for the old pagan world, long before John's day, we feel an immense yearning to be freed from this petty personal entanglement of weak life, to be back in the far-off world before men became "afraid". We want to be freed from our tight little automatic "universe", to go
5   back to the great living cosmos of the "unenlightened" pagans!

Perhaps the greatest difference between us and the pagans lies in our different relation to the cosmos. With us, all is personal. Landscape and the sky, these are to us the delicious background of our personal life, and no more. Even the universe of the scientist is little more than
10 an extension of our personality, to us. To the pagan, landscape and personal background were on the whole indifferent. But the cosmos was a very real thing. A man *lived* with the cosmos, and knew it greater than himself.

Don't let us imagine we see the sun as the old civilisations saw it.
15 All we see is a scientific little luminary, dwindled to a ball of blazing gas. In the centuries before Ezekiel and John, the sun was still a magnificent reality, men drew forth from him strength and splendour, and gave him back homage and lustre and thanks. But in us, the connection is broken, the responsive centres are dead. Our sun is a
20 quite different thing from the cosmic sun of the ancients, so much more trivial. We may see what we call the sun, but we have lost Helios* forever, and the great orb of the Chaldeans* still more. We have lost the cosmos, by coming out of responsive connection with it, and this is our chief tragedy. What is our petty little love of nature—
25 Nature!!—compared to the ancient magnificent living with the cosmos, and being honoured by the cosmos!

And some of the great images of the Apocalypse move us to strange depths, and to a strange wild fluttering of freedom: of true freedom, really, an escape to *somewhere*, not an escape to nowhere. An escape
30 from the tight little cage of our universe; tight, in spite of all the astronomists' vast and unthinkable stretches of space; tight, because it is only a continuous extension, a dreary on and on, without any meaning: an escape from this into the vital Cosmos, to a sun who has a great wild life, and who looks back at us for strength or withering,
35 marvellous, as he goes his way. Who says the sun cannot speak to me! The sun has a great blazing consciousness, and I have a little blazing consciousness. When I can strip myself of the trash of personal feelings and ideas, and get down to my naked sun-self, then the sun and I can commune by the hour, the blazing interchange, and he gives me life,
40 sun-life, and I send him a little new brightness from the world of the

bright blood. The great sun, like an angry dragon, hates the nervous and personal consciousness in us. As all these modern sunbathers must realise, for they become disintegrated by the very sun that bronzes them. But the sun, like a lion, loves the bright red blood of life, and can give it an infinite enrichment if we know how to receive it. But we don't. We have lost the sun. And he only falls on us and destroys us, decomposing something in us: the dragon of destruction instead of the life bringer.

And we have lost the moon, the cool, bright, ever-varying moon. It is she who would caress our nerves, smooth them with the silky hand of her glowing, soothe them into serenity again with her cool presence. For the moon is the mistress and mother of our watery bodies, the pale body of our nervous consciousness and our moist flesh. Oh the moon could soothe us and heal us like a cool great Artemis between her arms. But we have lost her, in our stupidity we ignore her, and angry she stares down on us and whips us with nervous whips. Oh beware of the angry Artemis of the night heavens, beware of the spite of Cybele, beware of the vindictiveness of horned Astarte.*

For the lovers who shoot themselves in the night, in the horrible suicide of love, they are driven mad by the poisoned arrows of Artemis: the moon is against them: the moon is fiercely against them. And oh, if the moon is against you, oh beware of the bitter night, especially the night of intoxication.

Now this may sound nonsense, but that is merely because we are fools. There is an eternal vital correspondence between our blood and the sun: there is an eternal vital correspondence between our nerves and the moon. If we get out of contact and harmony with the sun and moon, then both turn into great dragons of destruction against us. The sun is a great source of blood-vitality, it streams strength to us. But once we resist the sun, and say: It is a mere ball of gas!—then the very streaming vitality of sunshine turns into subtle disintegrative force in us, and undoes us. The same with the moon, the planets, the great stars. They are either our makers or our unmakers. There is no escape.

We and the cosmos are one. The cosmos is a vast living body, of which we are still parts. The sun is a great heart whose tremors run through our smallest veins. The moon is a great gleaming nerve-centre from which we quiver forever. Who knows the power that Saturn has over us, or Venus?* But it is a vital power, rippling exquisitely through us *all the time*. And if we deny Aldebaran,* Aldebaran will pierce us with infinite dagger-thrusts. He who is not with me is against me!*—that is a cosmic law.

Now all this is *literally* true, as men knew in the great past, and as they will know again.

By the time of John of Patmos, men, especially educated men, had already almost lost the cosmos. The sun, the moon, the planets, instead of being the communers, the comminglers, the life-givers, the splendid ones, the awful ones, had already fallen into a sort of deadness, they were the arbitrary, almost mechanical engineers of fate and destiny. By the time of Jesus, men had turned the heavens into a mechanism of fate and destiny, a prison.* The Christians escaped this prison by denying the body altogether. But alas, these little escapes! especially the escapes by denial!—they are the most fatal of evasions. Christianity and our ideal civilisation has been one long evasion. It has caused endless lying and misery, misery such as people know today, not of physical want but of far more deadly *vital* want. Better lack bread than lack life. One long evasion, whose only fruit is the machine!

We have lost the cosmos. The sun strengthens us no more, neither does the moon. In mystic language, the moon is black to us, and the sun is as sackcloth.

Now we have to get back the cosmos, and it can't be done by a trick. The great range of responses that have fallen dead in us have to come to life again. It has taken two thousand years to kill them. Who knows how long it will take to bring them to life.

When I hear modern people complain of being lonely then I know what has happened. They have lost the cosmos.—It is nothing human and personal that we are short of. What we lack is cosmic life, the sun in us and the moon in us. We can't get the sun in us by lying naked like pigs on a beach. The very sun that is bronzing us is inwardly disintegrating us—as we know later. Process of katabolism.* We can only get the sun by a sort of worship: and the same the moon. By *going forth* to worship the sun, worship that is felt in the blood. Tricks and postures only make matters worse.

VI

And now we must admit that we are also grateful to St. John's Revelation for giving us hints of the magnificent cosmos and putting us into momentary contact. The contacts, it is true, are only for moments, then they are broken by this other spirit of hope-despair. But even for the moments we are grateful.

There are flashes throughout the first part of the Apocalypse of true cosmic worship. The cosmos became anathema to the Christians, though the early Catholic Church restored it somewhat after the crash of the Dark Ages. Then again the cosmos became anathema to the Protestants after the Reformation. They substituted the non-vital universe of forces and mechanistic order, everything else became abstraction, and the long slow death of the human being set in. This slow death produced science and machinery, but both are death products.

No doubt the death was necessary. It is the long, slow death of society which parallels the quick death of Jesus and the other dying gods. It is death none the less, and will end in the annihilation of the human race—as John of Patmos so fervently hoped—unless there is a change, a resurrection, and a return to the cosmos.

But these flashes of the cosmos in Revelation can hardly be attributed to John of Patmos. As an apocalyptist he uses other people's flashes to light up his way of woe and hope. The grand hope of the Christians is a measure of their utter despair.

It began, however, before the Christians. Apocalypse is a curious form of literature, Jewish and Jewish Christian. This new form arose somewhere about 200 B.C., when the Prophets had finished. An early Apocalypse is the Book of Daniel,* the latter part at least: another is the Apocalypse of Enoch,* the oldest parts of which are attributed to the second century B.C.

The Jews, the Chosen People, had always had an idea of themselves as a grand imperial people. They had their try, and failed disastrously. Then they gave it up. After the destruction of the temple by Antiochus Epiphanes,* the national imagination ceased to imagine a great natural

Jewish Empire. The prophets became silent forever. The Jews became a people of *postponed destiny*. And then the seers began to write Apocalypses.

The seers had to tackle this business of postponed destiny. It was no longer a matter of prophecy: it was a matter of vision. God would no longer *tell* his servant what would happen, for what would happen was almost untellable. He would show him a vision.

Every profound new movement makes a great swing also backwards to some older, half-forgotten way of consciousness. So the apocalyptists swung back to the old cosmic vision. After the second destruction of the Temple the Jews despaired, consciously or unconsciously, of the *earthly* triumph of the Chosen People. Therefore, doggedly, they prepared for an unearthly triumph. That was what the apocalyptists set out to do: to vision forth the unearthly triumph of the Chosen.

To do this, they needed an all-round view: they needed to know the end as well as the beginning. Never before had men wanted to know the end of creation: sufficient that it was created, and would go on for ever and ever. But now, the apocalyptists had to have a vision of the end.

They became then cosmic. Enoch's visions of the cosmos are very interesting, and not very Jewish. But they are curiously geographical.

When we come to John's Apocalypse, and come to know it, several things strike us. First, the obvious scheme, the division of the book into two halves, with two rather discordant intentions. The first half, before the birth of the baby Messiah, seems to have the intention of salvation and renewal, leaving the world to go on renewed. But the second half, when the Beasts rouse up, develops a weird and mystic hate of the world, of worldly power, and of everything and everybody who does not submit to the Messiah out and out. The second half of the Apocalypse is flamboyant hate and a simple lust, lust is the only word, for the end of the world. The apocalyptist *must* see the universe, or the known cosmos, wiped out utterly, and merely a heavenly city and a hellish lake of brimstone left.

The discrepancy of the two intentions is the first thing that strikes us. The first part, briefer, more condensed or abbreviated, is much more difficult and complicated than the second part, and the feeling in it is much more dramatic, yet more universal and significant. We feel in the first part, we know not why, the space and pageantry of the pagan world. In the second part is the individual frenzy of those early Christians, rather like the frenzies of chapel people and revivalists today.

Then again, we feel that in the first part we are in touch with great old symbols, that take us far back into time, into the pagan vistas. In the second part, the imagery is Jewish allegorical, rather modern, and has a fairly easy local and temporal explanation. When there is a touch of true symbolism, it is not of the nature of a ruin or a remains embedded in the present structure, it is rather an archaic reminiscence.

A third thing that strikes us is the persistent use of the great pagan, as well as Jewish power-titles, both for God and for the Son of Man. *King of Kings and Lord of Lords** is typical throughout, and Kosmokrator, and Kosmodynamos. Always the titles of power, and never the titles of love. Always Christ the omnipotent conqueror flashing his great sword and destroying, destroying vast masses of men, till blood mounts up to the horses' bridles. Never Christ the Saviour: never. The Son of Man of the Apocalypse comes to bring a new and terrible *power* on to the earth, power greater than that of any Pompey or Alexander or Cyrus.* Power, terrific, smiting power. And when praise is uttered, or the hymn to the Son of Man, it is to ascribe to him power, and riches, and wisdom, and strength, and honour, and glory, and blessing—all the attributes given to the great kings and Pharaohs of the earth, but hardly suited to a crucified Jesus.

So that we are left puzzled. If John of Patmos finished this Apocalypse in 96 A.D., he knew strangely little of the Jesus legend, and had just none of the spirit of the Gospels, all of which preceded his book. A curious being, this old John of Patmos, whoever he was. But anyhow he focussed the emotions of certain types of men for centuries to come.

What we feel about the Apocalypse is that it is not one book, but several, perhaps many. But it is not made up of pieces of several books strung together, like Enoch. It is one book, in several layers: like layers of civilisation as you dig deeper and deeper to excavate an old city. Down at the bottom is a pagan substratum, probably one of the ancient books of the Aegean civilisation:* some sort of a book of a pagan Mystery.* This has been written over by Jewish apocalyptists, then extended, and then finally written over by the Jewish-Christian apocalyptist John: and then, after his day, expurgated and corrected and pruned down and added to by Christian editors who wanted to make of it a Christian work.*

But John of Patmos must have been a strange Jew: violent, full of the Hebrew books of the Old Testament, but also full of all kinds of pagan knowledge, anything that would contribute to his passion, his

unbearable passion, for the Second Advent, the utter smiting of the
Romans with the great sword of Christ, the trampling of mankind in
the winepress of God's anger till blood mounted to the bridles of the
horses,* the triumph of the rider on a white horse, greater than any
5   Persian king: then the rule of Martyrs for one thousand years: and
then oh then the destruction of the entire universe, and the last
Judgment. "Come, Lord Jesus, Come"!*

And John firmly believed He was coming, and coming *immediately*.
Therein lay the trembling of the terrific and terrifying hope of the early
10   Christians: that made them, naturally, in pagan eyes, the enemies of
mankind altogether.

But He did not come, so we are not very much interested. What
does interest us is the strange pagan recoil of the book, and the pagan
vestiges. And we realise how the Jew, when he *does* look into the
15   outside world, has to look with pagan or gentile eyes. The Jews of the
post-David period* have no eyes of their own to see with. They peered
inward at their Jehovah till they were blind: then they looked at the
world with the eyes of their neighbours. When the prophets had to
see visions, they had to see Assyrian* or Chaldean visions. They
20   borrowed other gods to see their own invisible God by.

Ezekiel's great vision,* which is so largely repeated in the Apocalypse,
what is it but pagan, disfigured probably by jealous Jewish scribes:
a great pagan concept of the Time Spirit* and the Kosmokrator and
the Kosmodynamos! Add to this that the Kosmokrator stands among
25   the wheels of the heavens, known as the wheels of Anaximander,* and
we see where we are. We are in the great world of the pagan cosmos.

But the text of Ezekiel is hopelessly corrupt—no doubt deliberately
corrupted by fanatical scribes who wanted to smear over the pagan
vision. It is an old story.

30   It is none the less amazing to find Anaximander's wheels in Ezekiel.*
These wheels are an ancient attempt to explain the orderly yet complex
movement of the heavens. They are based on the first "scientific"
duality which the pagans found in the universe, namely, the moist and
the dry, the cold and the hot, air (or cloud) and fire. Strange and
35   fascinating are the great revolving wheels of the sky, made of dense
air or night-cloud and filled with the blazing cosmic fire, which fire
peeps through or blazes through at certain holes in the felloes of the
wheels, and forms the blazing sun or the pointed stars. All the orbs
are little holes in the black wheel which is full of fire: and there is wheel
40   within wheel, revolving differently.

Anaximander, almost the very first of the ancient Greek thinkers, is supposed to have invented this "wheel" theory of the heavens in Ionia in the sixth century B.C. Anyhow Ezekiel learnt it in Babylonia: and who knows whether the whole idea is not Chaldean. Surely it has behind it centuries of Chaldean sky-knowledge.

It is a great relief to find Anaximander's wheels in Ezekiel. The Bible at once becomes a book of the human race, instead of a corked-up bottle of "inspiration". And so it is a relief to find the four Creatures* of the four quarters of the heavens, winged and starry. Immediately we are out in the great Chaldean star-spaces, instead of being pinched up in a Jewish tabernacle. That the Jews managed, by pernicious anthropomorphising, to turn the four great Creatures into Archangels, even with names like Michael and Gabriel,* only shows the limit of the Jewish imagination, which can know nothing except in terms of the human ego. It is none the less a relief to know that these policemen of God, the great Archangels, were once the winged and starry creatures of the four quarters of the heavens, quivering their wings across space, in Chaldean lore.

In John of Patmos, the "wheels" are missing. They had been superseded long ago by the spheres of the heavens. But the Almighty is even more distinctly a cosmic wonder, amber-coloured like sky-fire, the great Maker and the great Ruler of the starry heavens, Demiurge* and Kosmokrator, the one who wheels the cosmos. He is a great *actual* figure, the great dynamic God, neither spiritual nor moral, but cosmic and vital.

Naturally or unnaturally, the orthodox critics deny this. Archdeacon Charles admits that the seven stars in the right hand of the "Son of Man" are the stars of the Bear, wheeling round the Pole, and that this is Babylonian: then he goes on to say "but our author can have had nothing of this in mind".*

Of course, excellent clergymen of today know exactly what "our author" had in mind. John of Patmos is a Christian saint, so he *couldn't* have had any heathenism in mind. This is what orthodox criticism amounts to. Whereas as a matter of fact we are amazed at the almost brutal paganism of "our author", John of Patmos. Whatever else he was, he was not afraid of a pagan symbol, nor even, apparently, of a whole pagan cult. The old religions were cults of vitality, potency, and power: we must never forget it. Only the Hebrews were moral: and they only in patches. Among the old pagans, morals were just social manners, decent behaviour. But by the time of Christ all religion and

all thought seemed to turn from the old worship and study of vitality, potency, power, to the study of death and death-rewards, death-penalties, and morals. All religion, instead of being religion of *life*, here and now, became religion of postponed destiny, death, and reward
5   *afterwards*, "if you are good".

John of Patmos accepted the postponement of destiny with a vengeance, but he cared little about "being good". What he wanted was the *ultimate* power. He was a shameless power-worshipping pagan Jew, gnashing his teeth over the postponement of his grand
10   destiny.

It seems to me he knew a good deal about the pagan value of symbols, as contrasted even with the Jewish or Christian value. And he used the pagan value just when it suited him, for he was no timid soul. To suggest that the figure of the Kosmodynamos wheeling the
15   heavens, the great figure of cosmic Fire with the seven stars of the Bear in his right hand, could be unknown to John of Patmos is beyond even an Archdeacon. The world of the first century was full of star-cults, the figure of the Mover of the Heavens must have been familiar to every boy in the east. Orthodox critics in one breath relate that "our author"
20   had no starry heathenism in mind, and in the next they expatiate on how thankful men must have been to escape, through Christianity, from the senseless and mechanical domination of the heavens, the changeless rule of the planets, the fixed astronomical and astrological fate. "Good heavens!" we still exclaim: and if we pause to consider,
25   we shall see how powerful was the idea of moving, fate-fixing heavens, half-cosmic, half-mechanical, but still not anthropomorphic.

I am sure not only John of Patmos, but St. Paul and St. Peter and St. John the Apostle knew a great deal about the stars, and about the pagan cults. They chose, perhaps wisely, to suppress it all. John of
30   Patmos did not. So his Christian critics and editors, from the second century down to Archdeacon Charles,* have tried to suppress it for him. Without success: because the kind of mind that worships the divine *power* always tends to think in symbols. Direct thinking in symbols, like a game of chess, with its king and queen and pawns,
35   is characteristic of those men who see power as the great desideratum— and they are the majority. The lowest substratum of the people still worships power, still thinks crudely in symbols, still sticks to the Apocalypse and is entirely callous to the Sermon on the Mount. But so, apparently, does the highest superstratum of church and state still
40   worship in terms of power: naturally, really.

But the orthodox critics like Archdeacon Charles want to have their cake and eat it. They *want* the old pagan power-sense in the Apocalypse, and they spend half their time denying it is there. If they *have* to admit a pagan element, they gather up the skirts of their clerical gowns and hurry past. And at the same time, the Apocalypse is a   5
veritable heathen feast for them. Only they must swallow it with pious appearances.

Of course the dishonesty, we can call it no less, of the Christian critic is based on fear. Once start admitting that *anything* in the Bible is pagan, of pagan origin and meaning, and you are lost, you won't know   10
where to stop. God escapes out of the bottle once and for all, to put it irreverently. The Bible is so splendidly full of paganisms and therein lies its greater interest. But once admit it, and Christianity must come out of her shell.

Once more then we look at the Apocalypse, and try to sense its   15
structure vertically, as well as horizontally. For the more we read it, the more we feel that it is a section through time, as well as a Messianic mystery. It is the work of no one man, and even of no one century. Of that we feel sure.

The oldest part, surely, was a pagan work, probably the description   20
of the "secret" ritual of initiation into one of the pagan Mysteries, Artemis, Cybele, even Orphic:* but most probably belonging there to   1
the east Mediterranean, probably actually to Ephesus: as would seem natural. If such a book existed, say two or perhaps three centuries before Christ, then it was known to all students of religion: and   25
perhaps it would be safe to say that every intelligent man in that day, especially in the east, was a student of religion. Men were religious-mad: not religious-sane. The Jews were just the same as the gentiles. The Jews of the dispersion* certainly read and discussed everything they could lay their hands on. We must put away forever the Sunday School   30
idea of a bottled-up Jewry with nothing but its own God to think about. It was very different. The Jews of the last centuries B.C. were as curious, as widely read, and as cosmopolitan as the Jews of today: saving, of course, a few fanatical sets and sects.

So that the old pagan book must quite early have been taken and   35
written over by a Jewish apocalyptist, with a view to substituting the Jewish idea of a Messiah and a Jewish salvation (or destruction) *of the whole world*, for the purely individual experience of pagan initiation. This Jewish Apocalypse, written over perhaps more than once, was surely known to all religious seekers of Jesus' day, including the writers   40

of the Gospels. And probably, even before John of Patmos tackled
it, a Jewish-Christian apocalyptist had re-written the work once more,
probably had already extended it in the prophetic manner of Daniel,
to foretell the utter downfall of Rome: for the Jews loved nothing in
5 the world so much as prophesying the utter downfall of the gentile
kingdoms. Then John of Patmos occupied his prison-years on the
island in writing the whole book over once more, in his own peculiar
style. We feel that he invented little, and had few ideas: but that he
did indeed have a fierce and burning passion against the Romans who
10 had condemned him. For all that, he shows no hatred of the pagan
Greek culture of the east. In fact, he accepts it almost as naturally as
his own Hebrew culture, and far more naturally than the new Christian
spirit, which is alien to him. He rewrites the older Apocalypse,
probably cuts the pagan passages still shorter, simply because they have
15 no Messianic anti-Rome purport, not for any objection to their
paganism; and then he lets himself go in the second half of the book,
where he can lash the Beast called Rome (or Babylon), the Beast called
Nero, or Nero redivivus,* and the Beast called Antichrist, or the
Roman priesthood of the Imperial cult. How he left the final chapters
20 about the New Jerusalem we don't know, but they are now in a state
of confusion.

We feel that John was a violent but not very profound person. If
he invented the letters to the seven churches, they are a rather dull
and weak contribution. And yet it is his curious fervid intensity which
25 gives to Revelation its lurid power. And we cannot help liking him
for leaving the great symbols on the whole intact.

But after John had done with it, the real Christians started in. And
them we really resent. The Christian fear of the pagan outlook has
damaged the whole consciousness of man. The one fixed attitude of
30 Christianity towards the pagan religious vision has been an attitude
of stupid denial, denial that there was anything in the pagans at all,
except bestiality. And all pagan evidence in the books of the Bible had
to be expurgated, or twisted into meaninglessness, or smeared over into
Christian or Jewish semblances.

35 This is what happened to the Apocalypse after John left it. How
many bits the little Christian scribes have snipped out, how many bits
they have stuck in, how many times they have forged "our author's"
style, we shall never know: but there are certainly many evidences of
their pettifogging work.* And all to cover up the pagan traces, and
40 make this plainly unchristian work passably Christian.

We cannot help hating the Christian *fear*, whose method, from the very beginning, has been to deny everything that didn't fit: or better still, suppress it. The system of suppression of all pagan evidence has been instinctive, a fear-instinct, and has been thorough, and has been, really, criminal, in the Christian world, from the first century until today. When a man thinks of the vast stores of priceless pagan documents that the Christians have wilfully destroyed, from the time of Nero to the obscure parish priests of today, who still burn any book found in their parish that is unintelligible, and therefore possibly heretical, the mind stands still!—and we reflect with irony on the hullabaloo over Rheims Cathedral.* How many of the books we would give our fingers to possess, and can't, are lost because the Christians burnt them on purpose! They left Plato and Aristotle, feeling these two kin. But the others—!

The instinctive policy of Christianity towards all true pagan evidence has been and is still: suppress it, destroy it, deny it. This dishonesty has vitiated Christian thought from the start. It has, even more curiously, vitiated ethnological scientific thought the same. Curiously enough, we do not look on the Greeks and the Romans after about 600 B.C., as *real* pagans: not like Hindus or Persians, Babylonians or Egyptians or even Cretans, for example. We accept the Greeks and Romans as the initiators of our intellectual and political civilisation, the Jews as the fathers of our moral-religious civilisation. So these are "our sort". All the rest are mere nothing, amost idiots. All that can be attributed to the "barbarians" beyond the Greek pale: that is, to Minoans,* Etruscans,* Egyptians, Chaldeans, Persians and Hindus, is, in the famous phrase of a famous German professor: *Urdummheit.** Urdummheit, or primal stupidity, is the state of all mankind before precious Homer, and of all races, all, except Greek, Jew, Roman and—ourselves!

The strange thing is that even true scholars, who write scholarly and impartial books about the early Greeks, as soon as they mention the autochthonous races of the Mediterranean, or the Egyptians, or the Chaldeans, insist on the childishness of these peoples, their perfectly trivial achievement, their necessary Urdummheit. These great civilised peoples knew nothing: all *true* knowledge started with Thales* and Anaximander and Pythagoras,* with the Greeks. The Chaldeans knew no true astronomy, the Egyptians knew no mathematics nor science, and the poor Hindus, who for centuries were supposed to have invented that highly important reality, the arithmetical zero, or nought,

are now not allowed even this merit. The Arabs, who are almost "us",
invented it.

It is most strange. We can understand the *Christian* fear of the pagan
way of knowledge. But why the scientific fear? Why should science
betray its fear in a phrase like Urdummheit? We look at the wonderful
remains of Egypt, Babylon, Assyria, Persia, and old India, and we
repeat to ourselves: *Urdummheit!* Urdummheit? We look at the
Etruscan tombs and ask ourselves again, *Urdummheit?* primal stupidity? Why, in the oldest of peoples, in the Egyptian friezes and the
Assyrian, in the Etruscan paintings and the Hindu carvings we see a
splendour, a beauty, and very often a joyous, sensitive intelligence
which is certainly lost in our world of *Neufrecheit.** If it is a question
of primal stupidity or new impudence, then give me primal stupidity.

The Archdeacon Charles is a true scholar and authority in Apocalypse, a far-reaching student of his subject. He tries, without success,
to be fair in the matter of pagan origins. His predisposition, his terrific
prejudice, is too strong for him. And once, he gives himself away, so
we understand the whole process. He is writing in time of war—at the
end of the late war—so we must allow for the fever. But he makes a
bad break, none the less. On page 86 of the second volume of his
commentary on Revelation, he writes of the Antichrist in the Apocalypse that it is "a marvellous portrait of the great god-opposing power
that should hereafter arise, who was to exalt might above right, and
attempt, successfully or unsuccessfully for the time, to seize the
sovereignty of the world, backed by hosts of intellectual workers, who
would uphold all his pretensions, justify all his actions, and enforce
his political aims by an economic warfare, which menaced with
destruction all that did not bow down to his arrogant and godless
claims. And though the justness of this forecast is clear to the student
who approaches the subject with some insight, and to all students who
approach it with the experience of the present world war, we find that
as late as 1908, Bousset in his article on the "Antichrist" in Hastings'
Encyclopedia of Religion and Ethics, writes as follows: 'The interest in
the (Antichrist) legend...is now to be found only among the lower
classes of the Christian community, among sects, eccentric individuals,
and fanatics.'*

"No great prophecy receives its full and final fulfilment in any single
event, or single series of events. In fact, it may not be fulfilled at all
in regard to the object against which it was primarily delivered by the
prophet or Seer. But, if it is the expression of a great moral and spiritual

truth, it will of a surety be fulfilled at sundry times and in divers manners and in varying degrees of completeness. The present attitude of the Central Powers of Europe on this question of might against right, of Caesarism* against religion, of the state against God, is the greatest fulfilment that the Johannine prophecy in XIII has as yet received. Even the very indefiniteness regarding the chief Antichrist in XIII is reproduced in the present upheaval of evil powers. In XIII the Antichrist is conceived as a single individual, i.e. the demonic Nero; but even so, behind him stands the Roman Empire, which is one with him in character and purpose, and in itself the Fourth Kingdom or the Kingdom of the Antichrist—in fact, the Antichrist itself. So in regard to the present war, it is difficult to determine whether the Kaiser or his people can advance the best claims to the title of a modern Antichrist. If he is a present-day representative of the Antichrist, so just as surely is the empire behind him, for it is one in spirit and purpose with its leader—whether regarded from its military side, its intellectual, or its industrial. They are in a degree far transcending that of ancient Rome 'those who are destroying the earth'".*

So there we have Antichrist talking German to Archdeacon Charles, who, at the same moment, is using the books of German scholars for his work on the Apocalypse. It is as if Christianity and ethnological science alike could not exist unless they had an opposite, an Antichrist or an Urdummheit, for an offset. The Antichrist and the Urdummheit are just the fellow who is different from me. Today Antichrist speaks Russian, a hundred years ago he spoke French, tomorrow he may speak cockney or the Glasgow brogue. As for Urdummheit, he speaks any language that isn't Oxford or Harvard or an obsequious imitation of one of these.

VII

It is childish. What we have now to admit is that the beginning of the new era (our own) coincided with the dying of the old era of the true pagans or, in the Greek sense, barbarians. As our present civilisation was showing the first sparks of life, say in 1000 B.C., the great and ancient civilisation of the older world was waning: the great river civilisations of the Euphrates,* the Nile and the Indus,* with the lesser sea-civilisation of the Aegean. It is puerile to deny the age and the greatness of the three river civilisations, with their intermediary cultures in Persia or Iran, and in the Aegean, Crete or Mycene.* That any of these civilisations could do a sum in long division we do not pretend. They may not even have invented the wheel-barrow. A modern child of ten could lick them hollow in arithmetic, geometry, or even, maybe, astronomy. And what of it?

What of it? Because they lacked our modern mental and mechanical attainments, were they any less "civilised" or "cultures", the Egyptians and the Chaldeans, the Cretans and the Persians and the Hindus of the Indus, than we are? Let us look at a great seated statue of Rameses,* or at Etruscan tombs, let us read of Assiburnipal* or Darius,* and then say. How do our modern factory workers show beside the delicate Egyptian friezes of the common people of Egypt? or our khaki soldiers, beside the Assyrian friezes? or our Trafalgar Square lions beside these of Mycene? Civilisation? it is revealed rather in sensitive life than in inventions; and have we anything as good as the Egyptians of two or three thousand years before Christ, as a people? Culture and civilisation are tested by vital consciousness. Are we more vitally conscious than an Egyptian 3000 years B.C. was? Are we? Probably we are less. Our conscious range is wide, but shallow as a sheet of paper. We have no depth to our consciousness.

A rising thing is a passing thing, says Buddha. A rising civilisation is a passing civilisation. Greece rose upon the passing of the Aegean: and the Aegean was the link between Egypt and Babylon. Greece rose as the passing of the Aegean civilisation, and Rome rose as the same, for the Etruscan civilisation was a last strong wave from the Aegean, and Rome rose, truly, from the Etruscans. Persia arose from between the great cultures of the Euphrates and the Indus, and no doubt, in the passing of these.

Perhaps every rising civilisation must fiercely repudiate the passing civilisation. It is a fight within the self. The Greeks fiercely repudiated the barbarians. But we know now, the barbarians of the east Mediterranean were as much Greeks as most of the Greeks themselves. They were only Greeks, or autochthonous Hellenes who adhered to the old way of culture instead of taking on the new. The Aegean must always have been, in the primitive sense, Hellenic. But the old Aegean culture is different from what we call Greek, especially in its religious basis. Every old civilisation, we may be certain of it, had a definitely religious basis. The nation was, in a very old sense, a church, or a vast cult-unit. From cult to culture is only a step, but it took a lot of making. Cult-lore was the wisdom of the old races. We now have culture.

It is fairly difficult for one culture to understand another. But for culture to understand cult-lore is extremely difficult, and, for rather stupid people, impossible. Because culture is chiefly an activity of the mind, and cult-lore is an activity of the senses. The pre-Greek ancient world had not the faintest inkling of the lengths to which mental activity could be carried. Even Pythagoras, whoever he was, had no inkling: nor Herakleitos* nor even Empedokles* or Anaxagoras.* Socrates and Aristotle* were the first to *perceive* the dawn.

But on the other hand, we have not the faintest conception of the vast range that was covered by the ancient sense-consciousness. We have lost almost entirely the great and intricately developed sensual awareness, or sense-awareness, and sense-knowledge, of the ancients. It was a great depth of knowledge arrived at direct, by instinct and intuition, as we say, not by reason. It was a knowledge based not on words but on images. The abstraction was not into generalisations or into qualities, but into symbols. And the connection was not logical but emotional. The word "therefore" did not exist. Images or symbols succeeded one another in a procession of instinctive and arbitrary physical connection—some of the Psalms give us examples—and they "get nowhere" because there was nowhere to get to, the desire was to achieve a consummation of a certain state of consciousness, to fulfill a certain state of feeling-awareness. Perhaps all that remains to us today of the ancient way of "thought-process" are games like chess and cards. Chess-men and card-figures are symbols: their "values" are fixed in each case: their "movements" are non-logical, arbitrary, and based on the power-instinct.

Not until we can grasp a little of the working of the ancient mind can we appreciate the "magic" of the world they lived in. Take even the sphinx conundrum:* *What is it that goes first on four legs, then on two and then on three?*—The answer is: Man.—To us it is rather silly, the great question of the sphinx. But in the uncritical ancient who *felt* his images, there would spring up a great complex of emotions and fears. The thing that goes on four legs is the animal, in all its animal difference and potency, its hinterland consciousness which circles round the isolated consciousness of man. And when, in the answer, it is shown that the baby goes on four legs, instantly there springs up another emotional complex, half fear, half amusement, as man realises himself as an animal, especially in the infantile state, going on all fours with face to the ground and belly or navel polarised to the earth's centre, like a true animal, instead of navel polarised to the sun, as in the true man, according to primitive conception. The second clause, of the two-legged creature, would bring up complex images of men, monkeys, birds and frogs, and the weird falling into relationship of these four would be an instant imaginative act, such as is very hard for us to achieve, but which children still make. The last clause, of the three-legged creature, would bring wonder, faint terror, and a searching of the great hinterlands beyond the deserts and the sea for some still-unrevealed beast.

So we see that the emotional reaction to such a conundrum was enormous. And even kings and heroes like Hector* or Menelaus* would make the same reaction, as a child now does, but a thousandfold stronger and wider. Men were not fools for so doing. Men are far more fools today, for stripping themselves of their emotional and imaginative reactions, and feeling nothing. The price we pay is boredom and deadness. Our bald processes of thought no longer are life to us. For the sphinx-riddle of man is as terrifying today as it was before Oedipus, and more so. For now it is the riddle of the dead-alive man, which it never was before.

VIII

Man thought and still thinks in images. But now our images have hardly any emotional value. We always want a "conclusion", an *end*, we always want to come, in our mental processes, to a decision, a finality, a full-stop. This gives us a sense of satisfaction. All our mental consciousness is a movement onwards, a movement in stages, like our sentences, and every full-stop is a mile-stone that marks our "progress" and our arrival somewhere. On and on we go, for the mental consciousness labours under the illusion that there is somewhere to go to, a goal to consciousness. Whereas of course there is no goal. Consciousness is an end in itself. We torture ourselves getting somewhere, and when we get there it is nowhere, for there is nowhere to get to.

While men still thought of the heart or the liver as the seat of consciousness, they had no idea of this on-and-on process of thought. To them a thought was a completed state of feeling-awareness, a cumulative thing, a deepening thing, in which feeling deepened into feeling in consciousness till there was a sense of fulness. A completed thought was the plumbing of a depth, like a whirlpool, of emotional awareness, and at the depth of this whirlpool of emotion the resolve formed. But it was no stage in a journey. There was no logical chain to be dragged further.

This should help us to appreciate the prophetic method of the past, and also the oracular method. The old oracles were not supposed to say something that fitted plainly in the whole chain of circumstance. They were supposed to deliver a set of images or symbols of the real dynamic value, which should set the emotional consciousness of the enquirer, as he pondered them, revolving more and more rapidly, till out of a state of intense emotional absorption the resolve at last formed; or, as we say, the decision was arrived at. As a matter of fact, we do very much the same, in a crisis. When anything very important is to be decided we withdraw and ponder and ponder until the deep emotions are set working and revolving together, revolving, revolving, till a centre is formed and we "know what to do". And the fact that no politician today has the courage to follow this intensive method of "thought" is the reason of the absolute paucity of the political mind today.

IX

Well then, let us return to the Apocalypse with this in mind: that the
Apocalypse is still, in its movement, one of the works of the old pagan
civilisation, and in it we have, not the modern process of progressive
thought, but the old pagan process of rotary image-thought. Every
image fulfills its own little cycle of action and meaning, then is
superseded by another image. This is specially so in the first part,
before the birth of the Child.* Every image is a picture-graph, and
the connection between the images will be made more or less
differently by every reader. Nay, every image will be understood
differently by every reader, according to his emotion-reaction. And yet
there is a certain precise plan or scheme.

We must remember that the old human conscious-process has to
see something happen, every time. Everything is concrete, there are no
abstractions. And everything *does* something.

To the ancient consciousness, Matter, Materia, or Substantial things
are God. A great rock is God. A pool of water is God. And why not?
The longer we live the more we return to the oldest of all visions. A
great rock *is* God. I can touch it. It is undeniable. It is God.

Then those things that move are doubly God. That is, we are doubly
aware of their godhead: that which is, and that which moves: twice
godly. Everything is a "thing": and every "thing" acts and has effect:
the universe is a great complex activity of things existing and moving
and having effect. And all this is God.*

Today, it is almost impossible for us to realise what the old Greeks
meant by god, or *theos*.* Everything was *theos*; but even so, not at the
same moment. At the moment, whatever *struck* you was god. If it was
a pool of water, the very watery pool might strike you: then that was
god; or the blue gleam might suddenly occupy your consciousness:
then that was god; or a faint vapour at evening rising might catch the
imagination: then that was *theos*; or thirst might overcome you at the
sight of the water: then the thirst itself was god; or you drank, and
the delicious and indescribable slaking of thirst was the god; or you
felt the sudden chill of the water as you touched it: and then another

god came into being, "the cold": and this was not a *quality*, it was
an existing entity, almost a creature, certainly a *theos*: the cold; or
again, on the dry lips something suddenly alighted: it was "the moist",
and again a god. Even to the early scientists or philosophers, "the
5 cold", "the moist", "the hot", "the dry" were things in themselves,
realities, gods, *theoi*. And they *did things*.

With the coming of Socrates and "the spirit", the cosmos died. For
two thousand years man has been living in a dead or dying cosmos,
hoping for a heaven hereafter. And all the religions have been religions
10 of the dead body and the postponed reward: eschatological, to use a
pet word of the scientists.*

It is very difficult for us to understand the pagan mind. When we
are given translations of stories from the ancient Egyptian, the stories
are almost entirely unintelligible. It may be the translations' fault: who
15 can pretend really to *read* hieroglyph script? But when we are given
translations from Bushman folk-lore, we find ourselves in almost the
same puzzled state. The words may be intelligible, but the connection
between them is impossible to follow. Even when we read translations
of Hesiod,* or even of Plato, we feel that a meaning has been arbitrarily
20 *given* to the work, which is not its own meaning. It is the movement
that is wrong, the inner connection. Flatter ourselves as we may, the
gulf between Professor Jowett's mentality and Plato's mentality is
almost impassable; and Professor Jowett's Plato* is, in the end, just
Professor Jowett, with hardly a breath of the living Plato. Plato
25 divorced from his great pagan background is really only another
Victorian statue in a toga—or a chlamys.*

To get at the Apocalypse we have to appreciate the mental working
of the pagan thinker or poet—pagan thinkers were necessarily poets—
who starts with an image, sets the image in motion, allows it to achieve
30 a certain course or circuit of its own, and then takes up another image.
The old Greeks were very fine image-thinkers, as the myths prove.
Their images were wonderfully natural and harmonious. They followed
the logic of action rather than of reason, and they had no moral axe to
grind. But still they are nearer to us than the orientals, whose
35 image-thinking often followed no plan whatsoever, not even the
sequence of action. We can see it in some of the Psalms, the flitting
from image to image with no essential connection at all, but just the
curious image-association. The oriental loved that.

To appreciate the pagan manner of thought we have to drop our
40 own manner of on-and-on-and-on, from a start to a finish, and allow

the mind to move in cycles, or to flit here and there over a cluster of images. Our idea of time as a continuity in an eternal straight line has crippled our consciousness cruelly. The pagan conception of time as moving in cycles is much freer, it allows movement upwards and downwards, and allows for a complete change of the state of mind, at any moment. One cycle finished, we can drop or rise to another level, and be in a new world at once. But by our time-continuum method, we have to trail wearily on over another ridge.

The old method of the Apocalypse is to set forth the image, make a world, and then suddenly depart from this world in a cycle of time and movement and event, an *epos;** and then return again to a world not quite like the original one, but on another level. The "world" is established on twelve: the number twelve is basic for an established cosmos. And the cycles move in sevens.*

This old plan still remains, but very much broken up. The Jews always spoilt the beauty of a plan by forcing some ethical or tribal meaning in. The Jews have a moral instinct against design. Design, lovely plan, is pagan and immoral. So that we are not surprised, after the experience of Ezekiel and Daniel, to find the *mise en scène* of the vision muddled up, Jewish temple furniture shoved in, and twenty-four elders or presbyters who no longer quite know what they are, but are trying to be as Jewish as possible, and so on. The sea as of glass has come in from the Babylonian cosmos, the bright waters of heaven, as contrasted with the bitter or dead waters of the earthly sea: but of course it has to be put in a dish, a temple laver. Everything Jewish is *interior*. Even the stars of heaven and the waters of the fresh firmament have to be put inside the curtains of that stuffy tabernacle or temple.*

But whether John of Patmos actually left the opening vision of the throne and the four starry Creatures and the twenty-four elders or witnesses, in the muddle we find them in, or whether later editors deliberately, in true Christian spirit, broke up the design, we don't know. John of Patmos was a Jew, so he didn't much mind whether his vision was imaginable or not. But even then, we feel the Christian scribes smashed up the pattern, to "make it safe". Christians have always been "making things safe".

The book had difficulty in getting into the Bible at all: the eastern Fathers* objected to it so strongly. So if, in Cromwellian fashion, the heathen figures had their noses and hands knocked off, to "make them safe", we can't wonder. All we can do is to remember that there is

probably a pagan kernel to the book: that this was written over,
perhaps more than once, by Jewish apocalyptists, before the time of
Christ: that John of Patmos probably wrote over the whole book once
more, to make it Christian: and after that Christian scribes and editors
5   tinkered with it to make it safe. They could go on tinkering for more
than a hundred years.

Once we allow for pagan symbols more or less distorted by the
Jewish mind and the Christian iconoclast,* and for Jewish temple and
ritual symbols arbitrarily introduced to make the heavens fit inside that
10   precious Israelitish tabernacle, we can get a fairly good idea of the *mise
en scène*, the vision of the throne with the cosmic beasts giving praise,
and the rainbow-shrouded Kosmokrator about whose presence the
prismatic glory glows like a rainbow and a cloud: "Iris too is a cloud".*
This Kosmokrator gleams with the colour of jasper and the sardine
15   stone:* the commentators* say greenish yellow, whereas in Ezekiel it
was amber yellow, as the effulgence of the cosmic fire. Jasper equates
with the sign *Pisces*, which is the astrological sign of our era. Only now
are we passing over the border of Pisces, into a new sign and a new
era.* And Jesus was called The Fish,* for the same reason, during the
20   first centuries. Such a powerful hold had star-lore, originally Chaldean,
over the mind of man!

From the throne proceed thunders and lightnings and voices.
Thunder indeed was the first grand cosmic utterance. It was a being
in itself: another aspect of the Almighty or the Demiurge: and its voice
25   was the first great cosmic noise, betokening creation.* The grand
Logos of the beginning* was a thunderclap laughing throughout chaos,
and causing the cosmos. But the Thunder, which is also the Almighty,
and the Lightning, which is the Fiery Almighty putting forth the first
jet of life-flame—the fiery Logos—have both also their angry or
30   sundering aspect. Thunder claps creative through space, Lightning
darts in fecund fire: or the reverse, destructive.

Then before the throne are the seven Lamps, which are explained
as the seven Spirits of God.* Explanations are fishy, in a work like
this. But the seven lamps are the seven planets (including sun and
35   moon) who are the seven Rulers from the heavens over the earth and
over us. The great sun that makes day and makes all life on earth, the
moon that sways the tides and sways our physical being, unknown
sways the menstrual period in women and the sexual rhythm in a man,
then the five big wandering stars, Mars, Venus, Saturn, Jupiter,
40   Mercury, these, which are also our days of the week are as much our

Rulers now as ever they were: and as little. We know we live by the sun: how much we live by the others, we don't know. We reduce it all to simple gravitation-pull. Even at that, strange fine threads hold us to the moon and stars. That these threads have a psychic pull on us, we know from the moon. But what of the stars? How can we say? We have lost that sort of awareness.

However, we have the *mise en scène* of the drama of the Apocalypse: call it heaven, if you like. It really means the complete cosmos as we now have it: the "unregenerate" cosmos.

The Almighty has a book in his hand.* The book is no doubt a Jewish symbol. They were a bookish people: and always great keepers of accounts: reckoning up sins throughout the ages. But the Jewish symbol of a book will do fairly well, with its seven seals, to represent a cycle of seven: though how the book is to be *opened* piece by piece, after the breaking of each seal, I myself cannot see: since the book is a rolled up scroll, and therefore could not *actually* be opened till all seven seals were broken.* However, it is a detail: to the apocalyptist and to me. Perhaps there is no intention of opening it, till the end.

The Lion of Judah is supposed to open the book. But Lo! when the kingly beast comes on to the stage, it turns out to be a Lamb with seven horns* (of power, the seven powers or potencies) and seven eyes (the same old planets). We are always hearing a terrific roaring as of lions, and we are always seeing a Lamb exhibiting this wrath. John of Patmos' Lamb is, we suspect, the good old lion in sheep's clothing. It behaves like the most terrific lion. Only John insists that it is a Lamb.

He has to insist on the Lamb, in spite of his predilection for lions, because Leo must now give way to Aries; for, throughout the whole world, the God who, like a lion, was given blood sacrifice must be shoved into the background, and the sacrificed god must occupy the foreground. The pagan mysteries of the sacrifice of the god for the sake of a greater resurrection are older than Christianity, and on one of these mysteries the Apocalypse is based.* A Lamb it has to be: or with Mithras,* a bull: and the blood drenches over the initiate from the cut throat of the bull (they lifted his head up as they cut his throat) and makes him a new man.

> "Wash me in the blood of the Lamb
> And I shall be whiter than snow—"*

shrieks the Salvation Army in the market place. How surprised they would be if you told them it might just as well have been a bull. But perhaps they wouldn't. They might twig at once. In the lowest stratum of society religion remains pretty much the same, throughout the ages.

(But when it was for a hecatomb,* they held the head of the bull downwards, to earth, and cut his throat over a pit. We feel that John's Lamb was for a hecatomb).

God became the animal that was slain, instead of the animal that does the slaying. With the Jews, then, it had to be a lamb, partly because of their ancient paschal sacrifice. The Lion of Judah put on a fleece: but by their bite ye shall know them.* John insists on a Lamb "as it were slain":* but we never see it slain, we only see it slaying mankind by the million. Even when it comes on in a victorious bloody shirt at the end, the blood is not its *own* blood: it is the blood of inimical kings.

> "Wash me in the blood of my enemies
> And I shall be that I am—"

says John of Patmos in effect.

There follows a paean. What it is is a real pagan paean of praise to the god who is about to demonstrate. The elders, those twice twelve of the established cosmos, who are really the twelve signs of the zodiac on their "seats", keep getting up and bowing to the throne, like the sheaves to Joseph. Vials of sweet odour are labelled: Prayers of the saints; probably an after-touch of some little Christian later on. Flocks of Jewish angels flock in. And then the drama begins.*

X

With the famous four horsemen,* the real drama begins. These four horsemen are obviously pagan. They are not even Jewish. In they ride, one after the other—though why they should come from the opening of the seals of a *book*, we don't know. In they ride, short and sharp, and it is over. They have been cut down to a minimum.

But there they are: obviously astrological, zodiacal, prancing in to a purpose. To what purpose? This time, really individual and human, rather than cosmic. The famous book of seven seals in this place is the body of man: of a man: of Adam: of any man: and the seven seals are the seven centres or gates of his dynamic consciousness. We are witnessing the opening, and conquest of the great psychic centres of the human body. The old Adam is going to be conquered, die, and be re-born as the new Adam: but in stages: in seven-fold stages: or in six stages, and then a climax, seven. For man has seven levels of awareness, deeper and higher: or seven spheres of consciousness. And one by one these must be conquered, transformed, transfigured.*

And what are these seven spheres of consciousness in a man? Answer as you please, any man can give his own answer. But taking a common "popular" view, they are, shall we say, the four dynamic natures of man and the three "higher" natures.* Symbols mean something: yet they mean something different to every man. Fix the meaning of a symbol, and you have fallen into the commonplace of allegory.

Horses, always horses! How the horse dominated the mind of the early races, especially of the Mediterranean! You were a lord if you had a horse. Far back, far back in our dark soul the horse prances. He is a dominant symbol: he gives us lordship: he links us, the first palpable and throbbing link with the ruddy-glowing Almighty of potency: he is the beginning even of our godhead in the flesh. And as a symbol he roams the dark underworld meadows of the soul. He stamps and threshes in the dark fields of your soul and of mine. The sons of God who came down and knew the daughters of men and begot the great Titans, they had "the members of horses", says Enoch.*

Within the last fifty years man has lost the horse. Now man is lost.

Man is lost to life and power—an underling and a wastrel. While horses thrashed the streets of London, London lived.

The horse, the horse! the symbol of surging potency and power of movement, of action, in man. The horse, that heroes strode. Even Jesus
5   rode an ass, a mount of humble power. But the horse for true heroes. And different horses for the different powers, for the different heroic flames and impulses.

The rider on the white horse! Who is he then? The man who needs an explanation will never know. Yet explanations are our doom.
10   Take the old four natures of man: the sanguine, the choleric, the melancholic, the phlegmatic! There you have the four colours of the horses, white, red, black, and *pale*, or yellowish. But how should sanguine be white?—Ah, because the blood was the life itself, the very life: and the very power of life itself was white, dazzling. In our old
15   days, *the blood was the life*, and visioned as power it was like white light. The scarlet and the purple were only the clothing of the blood. Ah the vivid blood clothed in bright red!—itself it was like pure light.

The red horse is choler: not mere anger, but natural fieryness, what we call passion.
20   The black horse was the black bile, refractory.

And the phlegm, or lymph of the body was the pale horse: in excess it causes death, and is followed by Hades.

Or take the four planetary natures of man: jovial, martial, saturnine and mercurial. This will do for another correspondence, if we go a little
25   behind the *Latin* meaning, to the older Greek. Then Great Jove is the sun, and the living blood: the white horse: and angry Mars rides the red horse: Saturn is black, stubborn, refractory and gloomy: and Mercury is really Hermes, Hermes of the Underworld, the guide of souls, the watcher over two ways, the opener of two doors, he who
30   seeks through hell, or Hades.

There are two sets of correspondence, both physical. We leave the cosmic meanings, for the intention here is more physical than cosmic.

You will meet the white horse over and over again, as a symbol. Does not even Napoleon have a white horse? The old meanings control our
35   actions, even when our minds have gone inert.

But the rider on the white horse is crowned. He is the royal me, he is my very self, and his horse is the whole *mana** of a man. He is my very me, my sacred ego, called into a new cycle of action by the Lamb and riding forth to conquest, the conquest of the old self for
40   the birth of a new self. It is he, truly, who shall conquer all the other

"powers" of the self. And he rides forth, like the sun, with arrows, to conquest, but not with the sword, for the sword implies also judgment, and this is my dynamic or potent self. And his bow is the bended bow of the body, like the crescent moon.*

The true action of the myth, or ritual-imagery, has been all cut away. The rider on the white horse appears, then vanishes. But we know why he has appeared. And we know why he is paralleled at the end of the Apocalypse by the last rider on the white horse, who is the heavenly Son of Man riding forth after the last and final conquest over the "kings". The son of man, even you or I, rides forth to the small conquest: but the Great Son of Man mounts his white horse after the last universal conquest, and leads on his hosts. His shirt is red with the blood of monarchs, and on his thigh is his title: King of Kings and Lord of Lords. (Why on his thigh? Answer for yourself. Did not Pythagoras show his golden thigh* in the temple? Don't you know the old and powerful Mediterranean symbol of the thigh?) But out of the mouth of the final rider on the white horse comes that fatal sword of the logos of judgment. Let us go back to the bow and arrows of him to whom judgment is not given.

The myth has been cut down to the bare symbols. The first rider only rides forth. After the second rider, peace is lost, strife and war enter the world—really the inner world of the self. After the rider on the black horse, who carries the balances of measure, that weigh out the measures or true proportions of the "elements" in the body, bread becomes scarce, though wine and oil are not hurt. Bread, barley is here the body or flesh which is symbolically sacrificed—as in the barley scattered over the victim in a Greek sacrifice: "Take this bread of my body with thee".* The body of flesh is now at famine stage, wasted down. Finally, with the rider on the pale horse, the last, the physical or dynamic self is dead in the "little death" of the initiate, and we enter the Hades or underworld of our being.

We enter the Hades or underworld of our being, for our body is now "dead". But the powers or demons of this underworld can only hurt a fourth part of the earth: that is, a fourth part of the body of flesh: Which means, the death is only mystical, and that which is hurt is only the body that belongs to already-established creation. Hunger and physical woes befall the physical body in this little death, but there is as yet no greater hurt.—There are no plagues: these are divine wrath, and here we have no anger of the Almighty.

There is a crude and superficial explanation of the four horsemen:

but probably it hints at the true meaning. The orthodox commentators*
who talk about famines in the time of Titus or Vespasian* may be
reading the bit about barley and wheat correctly, according to a late
apocalyptist. The *original* meaning, which was pagan, is smeared over
5   intentionally with a meaning that can fit this "Church of Christ versus
the wicked Gentile Powers" business. But none of that touches the
horsemen themselves. And perhaps here better than anywhere else in
the book can we see the peculiar way in which the old meaning has
been cut away and confused and changed, deliberately, while the bones
10   of the structure have been left.

But there are three more seals. What happens when these are
opened?

After the fourth seal and the rider on the pale horse, the initiate,
in pagan ritual, is bodily dead. There remains, however, the journey
15   through the underworld, where the living "I" must divest itself of soul
and spirit, before it can at last emerge naked from the far gate of hell
into the new day. For the soul, the spirit, and the living "I" are the
three divine natures of man. The four bodily natures are put off on
earth. The *two* divine natures can only be divested in Hades. And the
20   last is a stark flame which, on the new day, is clothed anew and
successively by the spiritual body, the soul-body, and then the
"garment" of flesh, with its fourfold terrestrial natures.

Now no doubt the pagan script recorded this passage through
Hades, this divesting of the soul, then of the spirit, till the mystic death
25   is fulfilled six-fold, and the seventh seal is at once the last thunder of
death and the first thundrous paean of new birth and tremendous joy.

But the Jewish mind hates the mortal and terrestrial divinity of
man: the Christian mind the same. Man is only postponedly divine:
when he is dead and gone to glory. He *must not* achieve divinity in
30   the flesh. So the Jewish and Christian apocalyptists abolish the mystery
of the individual adventure into Hades and substitute a lot of martyred
souls crying under the altar for vengeance—vengeance was a sacred
duty with the Jews. These souls are told to wait awhile—always the
postponed destiny—until more martyrs are killed; and they are given
35   white robes: which is premature, for the white robes are the new
resurrected bodies, and how could these crying "souls" put them on
in Hades: in the grave? However—such is the muddle that Jewish and
Christian apocalyptists have made of the fifth seal.

The sixth seal, the divesting of the spirit from the last living quick
40   of the "I", this has been turned by the apocalyptist into a muddled

cosmic calamity. The sun goes black as sack-cloth of hair: which means that he is a great black orb streaming forth visible darkness; the moon turns to blood, which is one of the horror-reversals of the pagan mind, for the moon is mother of the watery body of men, the blood belongs to the sun, and the moon, like a harlot or demon woman, can only be drunk with red blood in her utterly maleficent aspect of meretrix,* blood-drinker, she who should give the cool water of the body's fountain of flesh; the stars fall from the sky, and the heavens depart like a scroll rolled together, and "every mountain and island were moved out of their places".* It means the return of chaos, and the end of our cosmic order, or creation. Yet it is not *annihilation:* for the kings of the earth and all the rest of men keep on hiding in the shifted mountains, from the ever-recurrent wrath of the Lamb.

This cosmic calamity no doubt corresponds to the original final death of the initiate, when his very spirit is stripped off him and he knows death indeed, yet still keeps the final flame-point of life, down in Hades.—But it is a pity the apocalyptists were so interfering: the Apocalypse is a string of cosmic calamities, monotonous. We would give the New Jerusalem cheerfully, to have back the pagan record of initiation; and this perpetual "wrath of the Lamb" business exasperates one like endless threats of toothless old men.

However, the six stages of mystic death are over. The seventh stage is a death and birth at once. Then the final flame-point of the eternal self of a man emerges from hell, and at the very instant of extinction becomes a new whole cloven flame of a new-bodied man with golden thighs and a face of glory. But first there is a pause: a natural pause. The action is suspended, and transferred to another world, to the outer cosmos. There is a lesser cycle of ritual to fulfill, before the seventh seal, the crash and the glory.

XI

Creation, we know, is four-square, and the number of creation, or of the created universe, is four.* From the four corners of the world four winds can blow, three bad winds, one good one. When all the winds
5　are loosed, it means chaos in the air, and destruction on earth.
　　So the four angels of the winds* are told to hold back their winds and hurt neither earth nor sea nor trees: that is, the actual world.
　　But there is a mystic wind from the east* which lifts the sun and the moon like full-sailed ships, and bears them across the sky like
10　vessels slowly scudding.—This was one of the beliefs, in the second century B.C.—Out of this east rises the angel crying for a pause in the blowing of the winds of destruction, while he shall seal the servants of God in their foreheads. Then the twelve tribes of Jews are tediously enumerated and sealed: a tedious Jewish performance.
15　　　The vision changes, and we see a great multitude, clothed in white robes and with palms in their hands, standing before the throne and before the Lamb, and crying with a loud voice: "Salvation to our God which sitteth upon the throne, and to the Lamb".* Thereupon angels and elders and the four winged beasts fall on their faces and worship
20　God saying: "Blessing, and glory, and wisdom, and thanksgiving, and honour, and power, and might be unto our God for ever and ever. Amen".—*
　　This suggests that the seventh seal is opened. The angel cries to the four winds to be still, while the blessed, or the new-born appear. And
25　then those who "went through the great tribulation",* or initiation into death and re-birth, appear in glory, clothed in the white dazzling robes of their new bodies, carrying branches of the tree of life in their hands, and appearing in a grand blaze of light before the Almighty. They hymn their praise, and the angels take it up.
30　　　Here we can see, in spite of the apocalyptist, the pagan initiate, perhaps in a temple of Cybele, suddenly brought forth from the under-dark of the temple into the grand blaze of light in front of the pillars. Dazzled, re-born, he wears white robes and carries the palm-branch, and the flutes sound out their rapture round him, and

the dancing women lift the garlands over him. The lights flash, the
incense rolls up, the brilliant priests and priestesses throw up their
arms and sing the hymn to the new glory of the re-born, as they form
around him and exalt him in a kind of ecstasy. The crowd beyond is
breathless.   5

This vivid scene in front of the temple, of the glorification of a new
initiate and his identification or assimilation to the god, amid grand
brilliance and wonder, and the sound of flutes and the swaying of
garlands, in front of the awed crowd of on-lookers was, we know, the
end of the ritual of the Mysteries of Isis.* Such a scene has been turned   10
by the apocalyptists into a Christian vision. But it really takes place
after the opening of the seventh seal. The cycle of individual initiation
is fulfilled. The great conflict and conquest is over. The initiate is dead,
and alive again in a new body. He is sealed in the forehead, like a
Buddhist monk,* as a sign that he has died the death, and that his   15
seventh self is fulfilled, he is twice-born, his mystic eye or "third eye"*
is now open. He sees in two worlds. Or, like the Pharaohs with the
serpent Uraeus* rearing between their brows, he has charge of the last
proud power of the sun.

But all this is pagan and impious. No Christian is allowed to rise   20
up new and in a divine body, here on earth and in the midst of life.
So we are given a crowd of martyrs in heaven, instead.

The seal in the forehead may be ashes: the seal of the death of the
body: or it may be scarlet or glory, the new light or vision. It is, really,
in itself the seventh seal.   25

Now it is finished, and there is silence in heaven for the space of
about half an hour.*

XII

And here, perhaps, the oldest pagan manuscript ended. At any rate
the first cycle of the drama is over. With various hesitations, some old
apocalyptist starts the second cycle, this time the cycle of the death
and regeneration of earth or world, instead of the individual. And this
part, too, we feel is much older than John of Patmos. Nevertheless,
it is very Jewish, the curious distortion of paganism through the Jewish
moral and cataclysmic vision: the monomaniacal insistence on
punishment and woes, which goes right through the Apocalypse. We
are now in a real Jewish atmosphere.

But still there are old pagan ideas. Incense rises up to the nostrils
of the Almighty in great clouds of smoke. But these clouds of
incense-smoke are allegorised, and made to carry up the prayers of the
saints. Then the divine fire is cast down to earth, to start the little death
and final regeneration of the world, the earth and the multitude. Seven
angels, the seven angels of the seven dynamic natures of God,* are
given seven trumpets to make seven annunciations.

And then the now-Jewish Apocalypse starts to unroll its second
cycle of the Seven Trumps.

There is again a division into four and three. We are witnessing the
death (the little death) of the cosmos at divine command, and therefore
each time there is a trumpet blast, a third part, not a fourth, of the
world is destroyed. The divine number is three: the number of the
world, four-square, is four.

At the first Trump, a third part of vegetable life is destroyed.

At the second Trump, a third part of all marine life, even ships.

At the third Trump, a third part of the fresh waters of earth are
embittered and become poison.

At the fourth Trump, a third part of the heavens, sun, moon and
stars, are destroyed.

This corresponds to the four horsemen of the first cycle, in a clumsy
Jewish-apocalyptic parallel. The *material* cosmos has now suffered the
little death.

What follows are the "three woes", which affect the spirit and soul of the world (symbolised now as men), instead of the material part. A star falls to earth: Jewish figure for an angel descending. He has the key of the abyss—Jewish counterpart of Hades. And the action now moves to the underworld of the cosmos instead of the underworld of the self, as in the first cycle.

It is now all Jewish and allegorical, not symbolical any more. The sun and the moon are darkened because we are in the underworld.

The abyss, like the underworld, is full of malefic powers, injurious to man.

For the abyss, like the underworld, represents the superseded powers of creation.

The old nature of man must yield and give way to a new nature. In yielding, it passes away down into Hades, and there lives on, undying and malefic, superseded, yet malevolent-potent in the underworld.

This very profound truth was embodied in all old religions, and lies at the root of the worship of the underworld powers. The worship of the underworld powers, the chthonioi, was perhaps the very basis of the most ancient Greek religion. When man has neither the strength to subdue his underworld powers—which are really the ancient powers of his old, superseded self; nor the wit to placate them with sacrifice and the burnt holocaust; then they come back at him, and destroy him again. Hence every new conquest of life means a "harrowing of Hell".*

In the same way, after every great cosmic change, the power of the *old* cosmos, superseded, becomes demonic and harmful to the new creation. It is a great truth which lies behind the Gea-Ouranos-Kronos-Zeus series of myths.*

Therefore the whole cosmos has its malefic aspect. The sun, the great sun, in so far as he is the *old* sun of a superseded cosmic day, is hateful and malevolent to the new-born, tender thing I am. He does me harm, in my struggling self, for he still has power over my old self, and he is hostile.

Likewise the waters of the cosmos, in their *oldness* and their superseded or abysmal nature, are malevolent to life, especially to the life of man. The great Moon and mother of my inner water-streams, in so far as she is the old, dead moon is hostile, hurtful and hateful to my flesh, for she still has a power over my old flesh.

This is the meaning away back of the "two woes":* a very deep meaning, too deep for John of Patmos. The famous locusts of the first woe, which emerge from the abyss at the fifth Trump, are complex

but not unintelligible symbols. They do not hurt vegetable earth, only the men who have not the new seal on their foreheads. These men they torture, but cannot kill: for it is the little death. And they can torture only for five months, which is a season, the sun's season, and more
5   or less a third part of the year.

Now these locusts are like horses prepared unto battle, which means, horses, horses,* that they are hostile potencies or *powers*.

They have hair as the hair of women—the steaming crest of the sun-powers, or sun-rays.
10   They have the teeth of the lion—the red lion of the sun in his malefic aspect.

They have faces like men: since they are directed only against the *inward* life of men.

They have crowns like gold: they are royal, of the royal orb of the
15   sun.

They have stings in their tails: which means, they are in the reversed or hellish aspect, creatures which once were good, but being superseded, of a past order, are now reversed and hellish, stinging, as it were, backwards.
20   And their king is Apollyon*—which is Apollo, great Lord of the (pagan and therefore hellish) sun.

Having made his weird, muddled composite symbol at last intelligible, the old Jewish apocalyptist declares the first woe is past, and that there are two more still to come.*

XIII

The sixth Trump sounds. The voice from the golden altar says:
"Loose the four angels which are bound in the great river
Euphrates".—*

These are evidently four angels of four corners,* like those of the   5
four winds. So Euphrates, the evil river of Babylon, will no doubt stand
for the waters under the earth, or the abysmal under-ocean, in its
hellish aspect.

And the angels are loosed, whereupon, apparently the great army
of demon-horsemen, two hundred million, all told, issue from the   10
abyss.

The horses of the two hundred million horsemen have heads as the
heads of lions, and out of their mouth issue fire and brimstone. And
these kill a third part of men, by the fire, smoke and brimstone which
come out of their mouths. Then unexpectedly we are told that their   15
power is in their mouth and in their tails; for their tails are like
serpents, and have heads, and with them they do hurt.*

These weird creatures are Apocalyptic images, surely: not symbols,
but personal images of some old apocalyptist long before John of
Patmos. The horses are powers, and divine instruments of woe: for   20
they kill a third part of men, and later we are told they are plagues.
Plagues are the whips of God.

Now they ought to be the reversed or malevolent powers of the
abysmal or underworld waters. Instead of which they are sulphureous,
evidently volcanic beasts of the abysmal or underworld fires, which   25
are the hellish fires of the sun. And they have lions' heads, like powers
of the hellish sun.

Then suddenly they are given serpent tails, and they have evil power
in their tails. Here we are back at the right thing—the horse-bodied
serpent-monster of the salty deeps of hell: the powers of the underworld   30
waters seen in their reversed aspect, malevolent, striking a third of men,
probably with some watery and deadly disease; as the locusts of the
fifth Trump smote men with some hot and agonising, yet not deadly
disease, which ran for a certain number of months.

So that here probably two apocalyptists have been at work. The later one did not understand the scheme. He put in his brimstone horses with their riders having breastplates of fire and jacinth and brimstone (red, dark blue, and yellow), following his own gay fancy, and perhaps influenced by some volcanic disturbance and some sight of splendid red, blue and yellow cavalry of the east.* That is a true Jewish method.

But then he had to come back to the old manuscript, with serpent-tailed watery monsters. So he tacked on the serpent tails to his own horses, and let them gallop.

This apocalyptist of the brimstone horses is probably responsible for the "lake of fire burning with brimstone"* into which the souls of fallen angels and wicked men are cast to burn for ever and ever more. This pleasant place is the prototype of the Christian hell, specially invented by the Apocalypse. The old Jewish hells of Sheol and Gehenna* were fairly mild, uncomfortable abysmal places like Hades, and when a New Jerusalem was created from heaven, they disappeared. They were part of the old cosmos, and did not outlast the old cosmos. They were not eternal.

This was not good enough for the brimstone apocalyptist and John of Patmos. They must have a marvellous, terrific lake of sulphureous fire that could burn for ever and ever, so that the souls of the enemy could be kept writhing. When, after the last Judgment, earth and sky and all creation were swept away, and only glorious heaven remained, still, away down, there remained this burning lake of fire in which the souls were suffering. Brilliant glorious eternal heaven above: and brilliant sulphureous torture-lake away below. This is the vision of eternity of all Patmossers. They could not be happy in heaven unless they *knew* their enemies were unhappy in hell.

And this vision was specially brought into the world with the Apocalypse. It did not exist before.

Before, the waters of the hellish underworld were bitter like the sea. They were the evil aspect of the waters under the earth, which were conceived as some wondrous lake of sweet, lovely water, source of all the springs and streams of earth, lying away down below the rocks.

The waters of the abyss were salt like the sea. Salt had a great hold on the old imagination. It was supposed to be the product of "elemental" injustice. Fire and water, the two great living elements and opposites, gave rise to all substance in their slippery unstable "marriage". But when one triumphed over the other, there was "injustice".—So, when the sun-fire got too strong for the sweet waters, it *burnt* them, and when water was burnt by fire, it produced salt, child of injustice. This child of injustice corrupted the waters and made them bitter.* So the sea came into being. And thence the dragon of the sea, leviathan.*

And so the bitter waters of hell were the place where souls were drowned: the bitter, anti-life ocean of the end.

There was for ages a resentment against the sea: the bitter, corrupt sea, as Plato calls it.* But this seems to have died down in Roman times: so our apocalyptist substitutes a brimstone burning lake, as being more horrific, and able to make the souls suffer more.

A third of men are killed by these brimstone horsemen. But the remaining two-thirds do not refrain from worshipping idols which can "neither see nor hear nor walk".*

That sounds as if the Apocalypse here was still quite Jewish and pre-Christian. There is no Lamb about.

Later, this second woe winds up with the usual earthquakes. But since the shiver of the earth must immediately give rise to a new movement, it is postponed awhile.

XIV

Six Trumps are blown, so now there is a pause: just as there was a
pause after the Six Seals were opened, to let the angels of the four winds
arrange themselves, and the action transfer itself to heaven.

5   Now, however, come various interruptions. First there comes down
a mighty angel, a cosmic lord, something like the Son of Man in the
first vision. But the Son of Man, indeed all Messianic reference seems
missing in this part of the Apocalypse. This mighty angel sets one
burning foot upon the sea and one on earth, and roars like a lion
10   throughout space. Whereupon the seven creative thunders* roll out
their creative utterances. These seven thunders, we know, are the
seven tonal natures of the Almighty, Maker of heaven and earth: and
now they are giving voice to seven vast new commands, for a new
cosmic day, a new phase in creation. The seer is in a hurry to write
15   down these seven new words, but he is commanded not to do so. He is
not allowed to divulge the nature of the new commands, which will
bring the new cosmos into being. We must wait for the actuality. Then
this great "angel" or cosmic lord raises his hand and swears, by heaven
and earth and water under the earth, which is the great Greek oath
20   of the gods,* that the old Time is over, the mystery of God is about
to be fulfilled.

Then the seer is given the little book to eat. It is the lesser general
or universal message of the destruction of the old world and creation
of the new: a lesser message than that of the destruction of the old
25   Adam and the creation of new man, which the seven-sealed book told.
And it is sweet in the mouth—as revenge is sweet—but bitter in
experience.

Then another interruption: the measuring of the temple, a pure
Jewish interruption; the measuring or counting of the "chosen of
30   God", before the end of the old world; and the exclusion of the
unchosen.

Then comes the most curious interruption of the two witnesses.
Orthodox commentators* identify these two witnesses with Moses and
Elija who were with Jesus in the transfiguration on the mount.* They

are something much older too. These two witnesses are prophets clothed in sack-cloth: that is, they are in their woeful aspect, hostile or reversed. They are the two candlesticks and the two olive trees which stand before "Adonai", the God of the earth.* They have power over the waters of the sky (rain), power to turn water into blood, and to smite the earth with all the plagues. They make their testimony, then the beast out of the Abyss rises and slays them. Their dead bodies lie out in the street of the great city, and the people of the earth rejoice because these two who tormented them are dead. But after three and a half days, the spirit of life from God enters the dead two, they rise to their feet, and a great voice says from heaven "Come up hither".* So they rise to heaven on a cloud, and their enemies in fear behold them.

It looks as if we had here a layer of very old myth referring to the mysterious twins, "the little ones", who had such power over the nature of men. But both the Jewish and Christian apocalyptists have balked this bit of Revelation: they have not given it any plain meaning of any sort.

The twins belong to a very old cult which apparently was common to all ancient European peoples; but it seems they were heavenly twins, belonging to the sky. Yet when they were identified by the Greeks with the Tyndarids, Kastor and Polydeukes,* already in the Odyssey, they lived alternately in Heaven and in Hades, witnessing to both places. And as such, they may be the candlesticks, or stars of heaven, on the one hand, and the olive trees of the underworld, on the other.

But the older a myth, the deeper it goes in the human consciousness, the more varied will be the forms it takes in the upper consciousness. We have to remember that some symbols, and this of the twins is one of them, can carry even our modern consciousness back for a thousand years, for two thousand years, for three thousand years, for four thousand years, and even beyond that. The power of suggestion is most mysterious. It may not work at all: or it may carry the unconscious mind back in great cyclic swoops through eras of time: or it may go only part way.

If we think of the heroic Dioskouroi,* the Greek Twins, the Tyndarids, we go back only half way. The Greek heroic age did a strange thing, it made every cosmic conception anthropomorphic, yet kept a great deal of the cosmic wonder. So that the Dioskouroi are and are not the ancient twins.

But the Greeks themselves were always reverting to the pre-heroic, pre-Olympian gods and potencies. The Olympic-heroic period was only an interlude. The Olympic-heroic vision was always felt to be too shallow, the old Greek soul would drop continually to deeper, older, darker levels of religious consciousness, all through the centuries. So

5 that the mysterious Tritopatores* at Athens, who were also called The Twins, and Dioskouroi, were the lords of the winds, and mysterious watchers at the procreation of children. So here again we are back in the old levels.

When the Samothracian cult spread in Hellas, in the third and

10 second centuries B.C., then the twins became the *Kabeiroi*, or the Kabiri,* and then again they had an enormous suggestive influence over the minds of men. The Kabiri were a swing back to the old idea of the dark or mysterious twins, connected with the movement of the cloudy skies and the air, and with the movement of fertility, and the

15 perpetual and mysterious balance between these two. The apocalyptist sees them in their woeful aspect, masters of sky-water and the waters of earth, which they can turn into blood, and masters of plagues from Hades: the heavenly and hellish aspects of the twins, malevolent.

But the Kabiri were connected with many things: and it is said their

20 cult is still alive in Mohammedan countries. They were the two secret little ones, the homunculi,* and the "rivals". They were also connected with thunder, and with two round black thunder-stones. So they were called the "sons of thunder", and had power over rain: also power to curdle milk, and, malefic, power to turn water into blood.

25 As thunderers they were sunderers, sundering cloud, air and water. And always they have this aspect of rivals, dividers, separaters, for good as well as for ill: balancers.*

By another symbolic leap, they were also the ancient gods of gateposts, and then they were the guardians of the gate, and then the

30 twin beasts that guard the altar, or the tree, or the urn, in so many Babylonian and Aegean and Etruscan paintings and sculpture. They were often panthers, leopards, gryphons, earth and night creatures, jealous ones.

It is they who hold things asunder to make a space, a gateway. In

35 this way, they are rain-makers: they open the gates in the sky: perhaps as thunder-stones. In the same way they are the secret lords of sex, for it was early recognised that sex is a holding of two things asunder, that birth may come through between them. In the sexual sense, they can change water into blood: for the phallos itself was the homunculus,

40 and, in one aspect, it was itself the twins of earth, the small one who

made water and the small one who was filled with blood: the rivals
within a man's own very nature and earthly self: symbolised again in
the twin stones of the testes. They are thus the roots of the twin olive
trees, producing the olives, and the oil of the procreative sperm. They
are also the two candlesticks which stand before the lord of earth,   5
Adonai. For they give the two alternate forms of elemental consciousness, our day-consciousness and our night-consciousness, that which
we are in the depths of night, and that other, very different being which
we are in bright day. A creature of dual and jealous consciousness is
man, and the twins witness jealously to the duality.* Physiologically,   10
in the same meaning, it is they who hold apart the two streams of the
water and of the blood in our bodies. If the water and blood ever
mingled in our bodies, we should be dead. The two streams are kept
apart by the little ones, the rivals. And on the two streams depends
the dual consciousness.   15

Now these little ones, these rivals, they are "witnesses" to life, for
it is between their opposition that the Tree of Life itself grows, from
the earthly root. They testify before the god of earth or fecundity all
the time. And all the time, they put a limit on man. They say to him,
in every earthly or physical activity: Thus far and no further.—They   20
limit every action, every "earth" action, to its own scope, and
counterbalance it with an opposite action. They are gods of gates, but
they are also gods of limits: each forever jealous of the other, keeping
the other in bounds. They make life possible; but they make life
limited. As the testes, they hold the phallic balance forever, they are   25
the two phallic witnesses. They are the enemies of intoxication, of
ecstasy, and of licence, of licentious freedom. Always they testify to
Adonai. Hence the men in the cities of licence rejoice when the beast
from the abyss, which is the hellish dragon or demon of the earth's
destruction, or man's bodily destruction, at last kills these two   30
"guardians", regarded as a sort of policemen in "Sodom" and
"Egypt".* The bodies of the slain two lie unburied for three and a
half days: that is, half a week, or half a period of time, when all decency
and restraint has departed from among men.

The language of the text, "rejoice and make merry and send gifts   35
to one another"* suggests a pagan Saturnalia, like the Hermaia of Crete
or the Sakaia at Babylon,* the feast of unreason. If this is what the
apocalyptist meant, it shows how intimately he follows pagan practice,
for the ancient saturnalian feasts all represented the breaking, or at least
the interruption of an old order of rule and law: and this time it is   40

the "natural rule" of the two witnesses which is broken. Men escape from the laws even of their own nature for a spell: for three days and a half, which is half the sacred week, or a "little" period of time. Then, as heralding the new earth and the new body of man, the two witnesses
5   stand up again: men are struck with terror: the voice from heaven calls the two witnesses, and they go up in a cloud.

"Two, two for the lily-white boys, clothed all in green-O!—"*

Thus the earth, and the body, cannot die its death till these two sacred twins, the rivals, have been killed.
10   An earthquake comes, the seventh angel blows his trumpet and makes the great announcement: "The kingdoms of this world are become the kingdoms of our Lord and of his Christ, and he shall reign for ever and ever".*—So there is again worship and thanksgiving in heaven, that God takes the reign again. And the temple of God is
15   opened in heaven, the holy of holies is revealed, and the ark of the testament. Then there are the lightnings, voices, thunderings, earthquakes and hail which end a period and herald another. The third woe is ended.

And here ends the first part of the Apocalypse: the old half. The
20   little myth that follows stands quite alone in the book, dramatically, and is really out of keeping with the rest. One of the apocalyptists put it in as part of a theoretic scheme: the birth of the Messiah after the little death of earth and man. And the other apocalyptists left it there.

XV

What follows is the myth of the birth of a new sun-god from a great
sun-goddess, and her pursuit by the great red dragon. This myth is
left as the centre-piece of the Apocalypse, and figures as the birth of
the Messiah. Even orthodox commentators admit that it is entirely   5
unchristian, and almost entirely unjewish.* We are down pretty well
to a pagan bed-rock, and we can see at once how many Jewish and
Jewish-Christian overlays there are in the other parts.

But this pagan birth-myth is very brief—as was the other bit of pure
myth, that of the four horsemen.   10

"And there appeared a great wonder in heaven; a woman clothed
with the sun, and the moon under her feet, and upon her head a crown
of twelve stars: and she being with child cried, travailing in birth, and
pained to be delivered.

And there appeared another wonder in heaven: and behold, a great   15
red dragon having seven heads and ten horns, and seven crowns upon
his heads. And his tail drew a third part of the stars of heaven, and
did cast them to the earth; and the dragon stood before the woman
which was ready to be delivered, for to devour her child as soon as
it was born.   20

And she brought forth a man child, who was to rule all nations with
a rod of iron; and her child was caught up unto God, and to his throne.
And the woman fled into the wilderness, where she hath a place
prepared of God, that they should feed her there twelve hundred and
sixty days.   25

And there was war in heaven; Michael and his angels fought against
the dragon; and the dragon fought and his angels, and prevailed not;
neither was their place found any more in heaven.

And the great dragon was cast out, that old serpent called the Devil,
and Satan, which deceiveth the whole world: he was cast forth into   30
the earth, and his angels were cast out with him"—*

This fragment is really the pivot of the Apocalypse. It looks like late
pagan myth suggested from various Greek, Egyptian and Babylonian
myths. Probably the first apocalyptist added it to the original pagan

manuscript, many years before the birth of Christ, to give his vision of a Messiah's birth, born of the sun. But connecting with the Four Horsemen, and with the two witnesses, the goddess clothed in the sun and standing upon the moon's crescent is difficult to reconcile with a Jewish vision. The Jews hated pagan gods, but they more than hated the great pagan goddesses: they would not even speak of them, if possible. And this wonder-woman clothed in the sun and standing upon the crescent of the moon was too splendidly suggestive of the great goddess of the east, the great Mother, the Magna Mater as she became to the Romans. This great woman goddess with a child stands looming far, far back in history in the eastern Mediterranean, in the days when matriarchy was still the natural order of the obscure nations. How then does she come to tower as the central figure in a Jewish Apocalypse? We shall never know: unless we accept the old law that when you drive the devil out of the front door he comes in at the back. This great goddess has suggested many pictures of the Virgin Mary. She has brought into the Bible what it lacked before: the great cosmic Mother robed and splendid, but persecuted. And she is, of course, essential to the scheme of power and splendour, which must have a queen: unlike the religions of renunciation, which are womanless. The religions of power must have a great queen and queen mother. So here she stands in the Apocalypse, the book of thwarted power-worship.

After the flight of the great Mother from the dragon, the whole Apocalypse changes tone. Suddenly Michael the archangel is introduced: which is a great jump from the four starry beasts of the Presence, who have been the Cherubim till now. The dragon is identified with Lucifer and Satan, and even then has to give his power to the beast from the sea: alias Nero.

There is a great change. We leave the old cosmic and elemental world, and come to the late Jewish world of angels like policemen and postmen. It is a world essentially uninteresting, save for the great vision of the Scarlet Woman,* which has been borrowed from the pagans, and is, of course, the reversal of the great woman clothed in the sun. The late apocalyptists are much more at their ease cursing her and calling her a harlot and other vile names, than in seeing her clothed in the sun and giving her due reverence.

Altogether the latter half of the Apocalypse is a come-down. We see it in the chapter of the seven vials. The seven vials of the wrath of the Lamb are a clumsy imitation of the seven seals and the seven Trumps. The apocalyptist no longer knows what he is about. There is no division into four and three, no re-birth or glory after the seventh vial—just a clumsy succession of plagues. And then the whole thing falls to earth in the prophesying and cursing business which we have met already in the old prophets and in Daniel. The visions are amorphous and have fairly obvious allegorical meanings: treading the winepress of the wrath of the Lord, and so on. It is stolen poetry, stolen from the old prophets. And for the rest, the destruction of Rome is the blatant and rather boring theme. Rome was anyhow more than Jerusalem.

Only the great whore of Babylon rises rather splendid, sitting in her purple and scarlet upon her scarlet beast. She is the Magna Mater in malefic aspect, clothed in the colours of the angry sun, and throned upon the great red dragon of the angry cosmic power. Splendid she sits, and spendid is her Babylon. How the late apocalyptists love mouthing out all about the gold and silver and cinnamon of evil Babylon. How they *want* them all! How they *envy* Babylon her splendour, envy, envy! How they love destroying it all. The harlot sits magnificent with her golden cup of the wine of sensual pleasure in her hand. How the apocalyptists would have loved to drink out of her cup! And since they couldn't, how they loved smashing it!

Gone is the grand pagan calm which can see the woman of the cosmos wrapped in her warm gleam like the sun, and having her feet upon the moon, the moon who gives us our white flesh. Gone is the great Mother of the cosmos, crowned with a diadem of the twelve great stars of the zodiac. She is driven to the desert, and the dragon of the watery chaos spues floods upon her. But kind earth swallows the floods, and the great woman, winged for flight like an eagle, must remain lost in the desert for a time, and times, and half a time. Which is like the three-and-a-half days, or years of other parts of the Apocalypse, and means half of a time-period.

That is the last we have seen of her. She has been in the desert ever since, the great cosmic Mother crowned with all the signs of the zodiac. Since she fled, we have had nothing but virgins and harlots, half-women: the half-women of the Christian era. For the great Woman of the pagan cosmos was driven into the wilderness at the end of the old epoch, and she has never been called back. That Diana of Ephesus,* John of Patmos' Ephesus, was already a travesty of the great woman crowned with the stars.

Yet perhaps it was a book of her "mystery" and initiation ritual which gave rise to the existing Apocalypse. But if so, it has been written

over and over, till only a last glimpse is left of her: and one other
corresponding glimpse, of the great woman of the cosmos "seen red".
Oh how weary we get, in the Apocalypse, of all these woes and plagues
and deaths! how infinitely weary we are of the mere thought of that
5   jeweller's paradise of a New Jerusalem at the end! All this maniacal
anti-life! They can't bear even to let the sun and the moon exist, these
horrible salvationists. But it is envy.

XVI

The woman is one of the "wonders". And the other wonder is the Dragon. The Dragon is one of the oldest symbols of the human consciousness. The dragon and serpent symbol goes so deep in every human consciousness, that a rustle in the grass can startle the toughest "modern" to depths he has no control over.

First and foremost, the dragon is the symbol of the fluid, rapid, startling movement of life within us. That startled life which runs through us like a serpent, or coils within us potent and waiting, like a serpent, this is the dragon. And the same with the cosmos.

From earliest times, man has been aware of a "power" or potency within him—and also outside him—which he has no ultimate control over. It is a fluid, rippling potency which can lie quite dormant, sleeping, and yet be ready to leap out unexpectedly. Such are the sudden angers that spring upon us from within ourselves, passionate and terrible in passionate people: and the sudden accesses of violent desire, wild sexual desire, or violent hunger, or a great desire of any sort, even for sleep. The hunger which made Esau* sell his birthright would have been called his dragon: later, the Greeks would even have called it a "god" in him. It is something beyond him, yet within him. It is swift and surprising as a serpent, and overmastering as a dragon. It leaps up from somewhere inside him, and has the better of him.

Primitive man, or shall we say early man was in a certain sense afraid of his own nature, it was so violent and unexpected inside him, always "doing things to him". He early recognised the half-divine, half-demonish nature of this "unexpected" potency inside him. Sometimes it came upon him like a glory, as when Samson* slew the lion with his hands, or David slew Goliath* with a pebble. The Greeks before Homer would have called both these two acts "the god", in recognition of the superhuman nature of the deed, *and of the doer of the deed*, who was *within* the man. This "doer of the dead", the fluid, rapid, invincible, even clairvoyant potency that can surge through the whole body and spirit of a man, this is the dragon, the grand divine dragon of his superhuman potency, or the great demonish dragon of his inward destruction. It is this which surges in us to make us move, to make us act, to make us bring forth something: to make us spring up and live. Modern philosophers may call it Libido or *Elan Vital*,* but the words are thin, they carry none of the wild suggestion of the dragon.

And men "worshipped" the dragon. A hero was a hero, in the great past, when he had conquered the hostile dragon, when he had the power of the dragon *with him* in his limbs and breast. When Moses set up the brazen serpent* in the wilderness, an act which dominated the imagination of the Jews for many centuries, he was substituting the potency of the good dragon for the sting of the bad dragon, or serpents. That is, man can have the serpent with him or against him. When his serpent is with him, he is almost divine. When his serpent is against him, he is stung and envenomed and defeated from within. The great problem, in the past, was the conquest of the *inimical* serpent, and the liberation within the self of the gleaming bright serpent of gold, golden fluid life within the body, the rousing of the splendid divine dragon within a man, or within a woman.

What ails men today is that thousands of little serpents sting and envenom them all the time, and the great divine dragon is inert. We cannot wake him to life, in modern days. He wakes on the lower planes of life: for a while in an air-man like Lindberg* or in a boxer like Dempsey.* It is the little serpent of gold that lifts these two men for a brief time into a certain level of heroism. But on the higher planes, there is no glimpse or gleam of the great dragon.

The usual vision of the dragon is, however, not personal but cosmic. It is in the vast cosmos of the stars that the dragon writhes and lashes. We see him in his maleficent aspect, red. But don't let us forget that when he stirs green and flashing on a pure dark night of stars it is he who makes the wonder of the night, it is the full rich coiling of his folds which makes the heavens sumptuously serene, as he glides around and guards the immunity, the precious strength of the planets, and gives lustre and new strength to the fixed stars, and still more serene beauty to the moon. His coils within the sun make the sun glad, till the sun dances in radiance. For in his good aspect, the dragon is the great vivifier, the great enhancer of the whole universe.

So he persists still to the Chinese. The long green dragon with which we are so familiar on Chinese things is the dragon in his good aspect of life-bringer, life-giver, life-maker, vivifier. There he coils, on the breasts of the mandarins' coats, looking very horrific, coiling round the centre of the breast and lashing behind with his tail. But as a matter of fact, proud and strong and grand is the mandarin who is within the folds of the green dragon, lord of the dragon.—It is the same dragon which, according to the Hindus, coils quiescent at the base of the spine of a man, and unfolds sometimes lashing along the spinal way: and the yogi is only trying to set this dragon in controlled motion.* Dragon-cult is still active and still potent all over the world, particularly in the east.

But alas, the great green dragon of the stars at their brightest is coiled up tight and silent today, in a long winter sleep. Only the red dragon sometimes shows his head, and the millions of little vipers. The millions of little vipers sting us as they stung the murmuring Israelites, and we want some Moses to set the brazen serpent aloft: the serpent which was "lifted up" even as Jesus later was "lifted up" for the redemption of men.*

The red dragon is the kakodaimon, the dragon in his evil or inimical aspect. In the old lore, red is the colour of *man's* splendour, but the colour of evil in the cosmic creatures or the gods. The red lion is the sun in his evil or destructive aspect. The red dragon is the great "potency" of the cosmos in its hostile and destructive activity.

The agathodaimon becomes at last the kakodaimon.* The green dragon becomes with time the red dragon. What was our joy and our salvation becomes with time, at the end of the time-era, our bane and our damnation. What was a creative god, Ouranos, Kronos, becomes at the end of the time-period a destroyer and a devourer. The god of the beginning of an era is the evil principle at the end of that era. For time still moves in cycles. What was the green dragon, the good potency, at the beginning of the cycle has by the end gradually changed into the red dragon, the evil potency. The good potency of the beginning of the Christian era is now the evil potency of the end.

This is a piece of very old wisdom, and it will always be true. Time still moves in cycles, not in a straight line. And we are at the end of the Christian cycle. And the Logos, the good dragon of the beginning of the cycle is now the evil dragon of today. It will give its potency to no new thing, only to old and deadly things. It is the red dragon, and it must once more be slain by the heroes, since we can expect no more from the angels.

And, according to old myth, it is woman who falls most absolutely into the power of the dragon, and has no power of escape till man frees her. The new dragon is green or golden, green with the vivid ancient

meaning of green which Mohammed took up again, green with that
greenish dawn-light which is the quintessence of all new and life-giving
light. The dawn of all creation took place in greenish pellucid gleam
that was the shine of the very presence of the Creator. John of Patmos
harks back to this when he makes the iris or rainbow which screens
the face of the Almighty green like smaragd or emerald. And this lovely
jewel-green gleam is the very dragon itself, as it moves out wreathing
and writhing into the cosmos. It is the power of the Kosmodynamos
coiling throughout space, coiling along the spine of a man, leaning forth
between his brows like the Uraeus between the brows of a Pharaoh.
It makes a man splendid, a king, a hero, a brave man gleaming with
the gleam of the dragon, which is golden when it wreathes round a
man.

So the Logos came, at the beginning of our era, to give men another
sort of splendour. And that same Logos today is the evil snake, the
Laocoön* which is the death of all of us. The Logos which was like
the great green breath of spring-time is now the grey stinging of
myriads of deadening little serpents. Now we have to *conquer* the
Logos, that the new dragon gleaming green may lean down from among
the stars and vivify us and make us great.

And no-one is coiled more bitterly in the folds of the old Logos than
woman. It is always so. What was a breath of inspiration becomes in
the end a fixed and evil *form*, which coils us round like mummy
clothes. And then woman is more tightly coiled even than man. Today,
the best part of womanhood is wrapped tight and tense in the folds
of the Logos, she is bodiless, abstract, and driven by a self-determination
terrible to behold. A strange "spiritual" creature is woman today,
driven on and on by the evil demon of the old Logos, never for a
moment allowed to escape and be herself. The evil Logos says she must
be "significant", she must "make something worth while" of her life.
So on and on she goes, making something worth while, piling up the
evil forms of our civilisation higher and higher, and never for a second
escaping to be wrapped in the brilliant fluid folds of the new green
dragon. *All* our present life-forms are evil. But with a persistence that
would be angelic if it were not devilish woman insists on the *best* in
life, by which she means the *best* of our evil life-forms, unable to realise
that the best of evil life-forms are the most evil.

So, tragic and tortured by all the grey little snakes of modern shame
and pain, she struggles on, fighting for "the best", which is, alas, the
evil best. All women today have a large streak of the police-woman

in them. Andromeda* was chained naked to a rock, and the dragon of the old form fumed at her. But poor modern Andromeda, she is forced to patrol the streets more or less in police-woman's uniform, with some sort of a banner and some sort of a bludgeon—or is it called a baton!—up her sleeve, and who is going to rescue her from this? Let her dress up fluffy as she likes, or white and virginal, still underneath it all you can see the stiff folds of the modern police-woman,* doing her best, her level best.

Ah God, Andromeda at least had her nakedness, and it was beautiful, and Perseus wanted to fight for her. But our modern police-women have no nakedness, they have their uniforms. And who could want to fight the dragon of the old form, the poisonous old Logos, for the sake of a police-woman's uniform?

Ah woman, you have known many bitter experiences. But never, never before have you been condemned by the old dragon to be a police-woman.

Oh lovely green dragon of the new day, the undawned day, come, come in touch, and release us from the horrid grip of the evil-smelling old Logos! Come in silence, and say nothing. Come in touch, in soft new touch like a spring-time breeze,* and shed these horrible police-woman sheaths from off our women, let the buds of life come nakedly!

In the days of the Apocalypse the old dragon was red. Today he is grey. He was red, because he represented the old way, the old form of power, kingship, riches, ostentation, and lust. By the days of Nero, this old form of ostentation and sensational lust had truly enough become evil, the foul dragon. And the foul dragon, the red one, had to give way to the white dragon of the Logos—Europe has never known the green dragon. When our era began, it began with the glorification of white: the white dragon. It ends with the same sanitary worship of white, but the white dragon is now a great white worm, dirty and greyish. Our colour is dirty-white, or grey.

But just as our Logos colour began dazzling white—John of Patmos insists on it, in the white robes of the saints—and ends in a soiled colourlessness, so the old red dragon started marvellously red. The oldest of old dragons was a marvellous red, glowing golden and blood-red. He was bright, bright, bright red, like the most dazzling vermilion. This, this vivid gold-red was the first colour of the first dragon, far, far back under the very dawn of history. The farthest-off men looked at the sky and saw in terms of gold and red, not in terms of green and dazzling white. In terms of gold and red, and the reflection of the dragon in a man's face, in the far-off, far-off past, showed glowing brilliant vermilion. Ah then the heroes and the hero-kings glowed in the face red as poppies that the sun shines through.

5   It was the colour of glory:* it was the colour of the wild bright blood, which was life itself. The red, racing bright blood, that was the supreme mystery: the slow, purplish, oozing dark blood, the royal mystery.

The ancient kings of Rome, of the ancient Rome, who were really
10 a thousand years behind the civilisation of the eastern Mediterranean, they painted their faces vermilion, to be divinely royal. And the Red Indians of North America do the same. They are not red save by virtue of this very vermilion paint, which they call "medicine". But the Red Indians belong almost to the Neolithic stage of culture, and of religion.
15 Ah the dark vistas of time in the pueblos of New Mexico, when the men come out with faces glistening scarlet! Gods! they look like gods! It is the red dragon, the beautiful red dragon.

But he became old, and his life-forms became fixed. Even in the pueblos of New Mexico, where the old life-forms are the life-forms
20 of the great red dragon, the greatest dragon, even there the life-forms are really evil, and the men have a passion for the colour blue, the blue of the turquoise, to escape the red. Turquoise and silver, these are the colours they yearn for. For gold is of the red dragon. Far-off down the ages gold was the very stuff of the dragon, its soft, gleaming body,
25 prized for the glory of the dragon, and men wore soft gold for glory,* like the Aegean and Etruscan warriors in their tombs. And it was not till the red dragon became the kakodaimon, and men began to yearn for the green dragon and the silver arm-bands, that gold fell from glory and became money. What makes gold into money? the Americans ask
30 you. And there you have it. The death of the great gold dragon, the coming of the green and silver dragon—how the Persians and Babylonians loved turquoise blue, the Chaldeans loved lapis lazuli; so far back they had turned from the red dragon! The dragon of Nebuchadnezzar* is blue, and is a blue-scaled unicorn stepping
35 proudly. He is very highly developed. The dragon of the Apocalypse is a much more ancient beast: but then, he is kakodaimon.

But the royal colour still was red: the vermilion and the purple, which is not violet but crimson, the true colour of living blood, these were kept for kings and emperors. They became the very colours of
40 the evil dragon. They are the colours in which the apocalyptist clothes

the great harlot-woman whom he calls Babylon. The colour of life itself becomes the colour of abomination.

And today, in the day of the dirty-white dragon of the Logos and the steel-age, the socialists have taken up the oldest of life-colours, and the whole world trembles at a suggestion of vermilion. For the majority today, red is the colour of destruction. "Red for danger", as the children say. So the cycle goes round: the red and gold dragons of the Gold Age and the Silver Age, the green dragon of the Bronze Age, the white dragon of the Iron Age, the dirty-white dragon, or grey dragon of the Steel Age:* and then a return once more to the first billiant red dragon.

But every heroic epoch turns instinctively to the red dragon, or the gold: every non-heroic epoch instinctively turns away. Like the Apocalypse, where the red and the purple are anathema.

The great red dragon* of the Apocalypse has seven heads, each of them crowned: which means his power is royal or supreme in its own manifestation. The seven heads mean he has seven lives, as many lives as a man has natures, or as there are "potencies" to the cosmos. All his seven heads have to be smitten off: that is, man has another great series of seven conquests to make, this time over the dragon. The fight goes on.

The dragon, being cosmic, destroys a third part of the cosmos before he is cast down out of heaven into earth: he draws down a third part of the stars with his tail. Then the woman brings forth the child who is "to shepherd mankind with an iron flail".* Alas, if that is a prophecy of the reign of the Messiah, or Jesus, how true it is! For all men today are ruled with a flail of iron. This child is caught up to God: we almost wish the dragon had got him. And the woman fled into the wilderness. That is, the great cosmic mother has no place in the cosmos of men any more. She must hide in the desert since she cannot die.—And there she hides, still, during the weary three and a half mystic years which are still going on, apparently.

Now begins the second half of the Apocalypse. We enter the rather boring process of Danielesque prophecy, concerning the Church of Christ and the fall of the various kingdoms of the earth. We cannot be very much interested in the prophesied collapse of Rome and the Roman Empire.

XVII

But before we look at this second half, let us glance at the dominant
symbols, especially at the symbols of number. The whole scheme is
so entirely based on the numbers seven, four and three, that we may
as well try to find out what these numbers meant to the ancient mind.*
Three was the sacred number: it is still, for it is the number of the
Trinity: it is the number of the nature of God. It is perhaps from the
scientists, or the very early philosophers, that we get the most revealing
suggestions of the ancient beliefs. The early scientists took the extant
religious symbol-ideas and transmuted them into true "ideas". We
know that the ancients saw number concrete—in dots or in rows of
pebbles. The number three was three pebbles. And the number three
was held by the Pythagoreans to be the perfect number, in their
primitive arithmetic, because you could not divide it and leave a gap
in the middle. This is obviously true of three pebbles. You cannot
destroy the integrity of the three. If you remove one pebble on each
side, it still leaves the central stone poised and in perfect balance
between the two, like the body of a bird between the two wings. And
even as late as the third century, this was felt as the perfect or divine
condition of being.*
Again, we know that Anaximander, in the fifth century, conceived
of the Boundless, the infinite substance, as having its two "elements",
the hot and the cold, the dry and the moist, or fire and the dark, the
great "pair", on either side of it, in the first primordial creation.*
These three were the beginning of all things. This idea lies at the back
of the very ancient division of the *living* cosmos into three, before the
idea of God was separated out.
In parenthesis let us remark that the very ancient world was entirely
religious and godless. While men still lived in close physical unison,
like flocks of birds on the wing, in a close physical oneness, an ancient
tribal unison in which the individual was hardly separated out, then
the tribe lived breast to breast, as it were, with the cosmos, in naked
contact with the cosmos, the whole cosmos was alive and in contact
with the flesh of man, there was no room for the intrusion of the god

idea. It was not till the individual began to feel separated off, not till
he fell into awareness of himself, and hence into apartness; not,
mythologically, till he ate of the Tree of Knowledge instead of the Tree
of Life, and knew himself *apart* and separate, that the conception of
of a God arose, to intervene between man and the cosmos. The very
oldest ideas of man are *purely* religious, and there is no notion of any
sort of God or gods. God and gods enter when man has "fallen" into
a sense of separateness and loneliness. The oldest philosophers,
Anaximander with his divine Boundless and the divine two elements,
and Anaximenes with his divine "air",* are going back to the great
conception of the naked cosmos, before there was God. At the same
time, they know all about the gods of the sixth century: but they are
not strictly interested in them. Even the first Pythagoreans, who were
religious in the conventional way, were more profoundly religious in
their conceptions of the two primary forms, Fire and the Night, or
Fire and Dark, dark being conceived of as a kind of thick air or vapour.
These two were the Limit and the Unlimited, Night, the Unlimited,
finding its Limit in Fire.* These two primary forms, being in a tension
of opposition, prove their oneness by their very *opposedness.* Herakleitos
says that all things are an exchange for fire: and that the sun is new
every day.* "The limit of dawn and evening is the Bear: and opposite
the Bear is the boundary of bright Zeus".* Bright Zeus is here
supposed to be the bright blue sky, so his boundary is the Horizon,
and Herakleitos means probably that opposite the Bear, that is down,
down in the antipodes, it is always night, and Night lives the death
of Day, as Day lives the death of Night.*

This is the state of mind of great men in the fifth and fourth
centuries before Christ, strange and fascinating and a revelation of the
old symbolic mind. Religion was already turning moralistic or ecstatic,
with the Orphics the tedious idea of "escaping the wheel of birth"*
had begun to abstract men from life. But early science is a source of
the purest and oldest religion. The mind of man recoiled, there in
Ionia, to the oldest religious conception of the cosmos, from which to
start thinking out the scientific cosmos. And the thing the oldest
philosophers disliked was the new sort of religion, with its ecstasies
and its escape and its purely *personal* nature: its loss of the cosmos.

So the first philosophers took up the sacred three-part cosmos of
the ancients. It is paralleled in Genesis, where we have a God creation,
in the division into heaven, and earth, and water: the first three *created*
elements, presupposing a God who creates. The ancient three-fold

division of the living heavens, the Chaldean, is made when the heavens themselves are divine, and not merely God-inhabited. Before men felt any need of God or gods, while the vast heavens lived of themselves and lived breast to breast with man, the Chaldeans gazed up in the religious rapture. And then, by some strange intuition, they divided the heavens into three sections. And then they really *knew* the stars, as the stars have never been known since.

Later, when a God or Maker or Ruler of the skies was invented or discovered, then the heavens were divided into the four quarters, the old four quarters that lasted so long. And then, gradually with the invention of a God or a Demiurge, the old star-knowledge and true worship declined with the Babylonians into magic and astrology, the whole system was "worked". But still the old Chaldean cosmic knowledge persisted, and this the Ionians must have picked up again.

Even during the four-quarter centuries, the heavens still had three primary rulers, sun, moon, and morning-star. But the Bible says, sun, moon, and stars.

The morning-star was always a god, from the time when gods began. But when the cult of dying and re-born gods started all over the old world, about 600 B.C., he became symbolic of the new god, because he rules in the twilight, between day and night, and for the same reason he is supposed to be lord of both, and to stand gleaming with one foot on the flood of night and one foot on the world of day, one foot on sea and one on shore.* We know that night was a form of vapour or flood.*

XVIII

Three is the number of things divine, and four is the number of creation. The world is four, four-square, divided into four quarters which are ruled by four great creatures, the four winged creatures that surround the throne of the Almighty.* These four great creatures make up the sum of mighty space, both dark and light, and their wings are the quivering of this space, that trembles all the time with thunderous praise of the Creator: for these are Creation praising their Maker, as Creation shall praise its Maker forever. That their wings (strictly) are full of eyes before and behind, only means that they are the stars of the trembling heavens forever changing and travelling and pulsing. In Ezekiel, muddled and mutiliated as the text is, we see the four great creatures amid the wheels of the revolving heavens* a conception which belongs to the seventh, sixth, and fifth centuries—and supporting on their wing-tips the crystal vault of the final heaven of the Throne.

In their origin, the Creatures are probably older than God himself. They were a very grand conception, and some suggestion of them is at the back of most of the great winged Creatures of the East. They belong to the last age of the living cosmos, the cosmos that was not created, that had yet no god in it because it was in itself utterly divine and primal. Away behind all the creation myths lies the grand idea that the Cosmos *always was*, that it could not have had any beginning, because it always was there and always would be there. It could not have a god to start it, because it was itself all god and all divine, the origin of everything.

This living cosmos man first divided into three parts: and then, at some point of great change, we cannot know when, he divided it instead into four quarters, and the four quarters demanded a whole, a conception of the whole, and then a Maker, a Creator. So the four great elemental creatures became subordinate, they surround the supreme central unit, and their wings cover all space. Later still, they are turned from vast and living elements into beasts or Creatures or Cherubim*—it is a process of degradation—and given the four elemental or cosmic natures of man, lion, bull and eagle. In Ezekiel, each of the creatures is all four at once, with a different face looking in each direction. But in the Apocalypse each beast has its own face. And as the cosmic idea dwindled, we get the four cosmic natures of the four Creatures applied first to the great Cherubim, then to the personified Archangels, Michael, Gabriel etc., and finally they are applied to the four Evangelists, Matthew, Mark, Luke and John. "Four for the Gospel Natures".* It is all a process of degradation or personification of a great old concept.

Parallel to the division of the cosmos into four quarters, four parts, and four dynamic "natures" comes the other division, into four elements. At first, it seems as if there had been only three elements: heaven, earth, and sea, or water: heaven being primarily Light or Fire.* The recognition of air came later. But with the elements of Fire, earth and water the cosmos was complete, air being conceived of as a form of vapour, darkness the same.

And the earliest scientists (philosophers) seemed to want to make one element, or at most two, responsible for the cosmos. Anaximenes said all was water.* Xenophanes said all was earth and water.* Water gave off moist exhalations, and in these moist exhalations were latent sparks, these exhalations blew aloft as clouds, they blew far, far aloft, and condensed *upon their sparks* instead of into water, and thus they produced stars: thus they even produced the sun. The sun was a great "cloud" of assembled sparks from the moist exhalations of the watery earth.* This is how science began: far more fantastic than myth, but using processes of reason.

Then came Herakleitos with his: All is Fire, or rather: All is an exchange for Fire—, and his insistence on Strife, which holds things asunder and so holds them integral and makes their existence even possible, as the creative *principle:* Fire being an element.*

After which the Four Elements become almost inevitable. With Empedokles in the fifth century the Four Elements of Fire, Earth, Air and Water established themselves in the imagination of men for ever, the four *living* or cosmic elements, the radical elements: the Four Roots* Empedokles called them, the four cosmic roots of all existence. And they were controlled by two principles, Love and Strife.—"Fire and Water and Earth and the mighty height of Air; dread Strife, too, apart from these, of equal weight to each, and Love in their midst, equal in length and breadth".* And again Empedokles calls the Four: "shining Zeus, life-bringing Hera, Aidoneus and Nestis".* So we see the Four also as gods:* the Big Four of the ages. When we consider the Four elements, we shall see that they are, now and forever, the four elements of our experience. All that science has taught about fire does not make fire any different. The processes of combustion are not fire, they are thought-forms. H_2O is not water, it is a thought-form derived from experiments with water. Thought-forms are thought-forms, they do not make our life. Our life is made still of elemental fire and water, earth and air: by these we move and live and have our being.*

From the four elements we come to the four natures of man* himself, based on the conception of blood, bile, lymph and phlegm, and their properties. Man is still a creature that thinks with his blood: "the heart, dwelling in the sea of blood that runs in opposite directions, where chiefly is what men call thought; for the blood round the heart is the thought of men".*—And maybe this is true. Maybe all basic thought takes place in the blood around the heart, and is only transferred to the brain. Then there are the Four Ages,* based on the four metals gold, silver, bronze and iron. In the sixth century already the Iron Age had set in, and already man laments it. The Golden Age, before the eating of the Fruit of Knowledge, is left far behind.

The first scientists, then, are very near to the old symbolists. And so we see in the Apocalypse, that when St. John is referring to the old primal or divine cosmos, he speaks of a third part of this that or another: as when the dragon, who belongs to the old divine cosmos, draws down a third part of the stars with his tail: or where the divine trumps destroy a third part of things: or the horsemen from the abyss, which are divine demons, destroy a third part of men.* But when the destruction is by non-divine agency, it is usually a fourth part that is destroyed.*—Anyhow there is far too much destroying in the Apocalypse. It ceases to be fun.

XIX

The numbers four and three together make up the sacred number seven: the cosmos with its god. The Pythagoreans called it "the number of the right time".* Man and the cosmos alike have four created natures, and three divine natures. Man has his four earthly natures, then soul, spirit, and the eternal I. The universe has the four quarters and the four elements, then also the three divine quarters of heaven, Hades, and the Whole, and the three divine motions of Love, Strife and Wholeness. The oldest cosmos had no heaven nor Hades. But then it is probable that seven is not a sacred number in the oldest consciousness of man.

It is always, from the beginning, however, a semi-sacred number because it is the number of the seven ancient planets, which began with sun and moon, and included the five great "wandering" stars, Jupiter, Venus, Mercury, Mars and Saturn. The wandering planets were always a great mystery to men, especially in the days when he lived breast to breast with the cosmos, and watched the moving heavens with a profundity of passionate attention quite different from any form of attention today.

The Chaldeans always preserved some of the elemental immediacy of the cosmos, even to the end of Babylonian days. They had, later, their whole mythology of Marduk* and the rest, and the whole bag of tricks of their astrologers and magi,* but it seems never to have ousted, entirely, the serious* star-lore, nor to have broken altogether the breast to breast contact of the star-gazer and the skies of night. The magi continued, apparently, through the ages concerned only in the mysteries of the heavens, without any god or gods dragged in. That the heaven-lore degenerated into tedious forms of divination and magic later on is only part of human history: everything human degenerates, from religion downwards, and must be renewed and revived.

It was this preserving of star-lore naked and without gods that prepared the way for astronomy later, just as in the eastern Mediterranean a great deal of old cosmic lore about water and fire must have lingered and prepared the way for the Ionian philosophers and modern science.

The great control of the life of earth from the living and intertwining heavens was an idea which had far greater hold of the minds of men before the Christian era, than we realise. In spite of all the gods and goddesses, the Jehovah and the dying and redeeming Saviours of many nations, underneath, the old cosmic vision remained, and men believed, perhaps, more radically in the rule of the stars than in any of the gods. Man's consciousness has many layers, and the lowest layers continue to be crudely active, especially down among the common people, for centuries after the cultured consciousness of the nation has passed to higher planes. And the consciousness of man always tends to revert to the original levels; though there are two modes of reversion: by degeneration and decadence; and by deliberate return in order to get back to the roots again, for a new start.

In Roman times there was a great slipping back of the human consciousness to the oldest levels, though it was a form of decadence and a return to superstition. But in the first two centuries after Christ the rule of the heavens returned on man as never before, with a power of superstition stronger than any religious cult. Horoscopy was the rage. Fate, fortune, destiny, character, everything depended on the stars, which meant, on the seven planets. The seven planets were the seven Rulers of the heavens, and they fixed the fate of man irrevocably, inevitably. Their rule became at last a form of insanity, and both the Christians and the Neo-Platonists set their faces against it.

Now this element of superstition bordering on magic and occultism is very strong in the Apocalypse. The Revelation of John is, we must admit it, a book to conjure with. It is full of suggestions for occult use, and it has been used, throughout the ages, for occult purposes, for the purpose of divination and prophecy especially. It lends itself to this. Nay, the book is written, especially the second half, in a spirit of lurid prophecy very like the magical utterances of the occultists of the time. It reflects the spirit of the time: as *The Golden Ass** reflects that of less than a hundred years later, not very different.

So that the number seven ceases almost to be the "divine" number, and becomes the magical number of the Apocalypse. As the book proceeds, the ancient divine element fades out and the "modern", first-century taint of magic, prognostication, and occult practice takes its place. Seven is the number now of divination and conjuring, rather than of real vision.

So the famous "time, times and a half"*—which means three-and-a-half years. It comes from Daniel, who already starts the semi-occult business of prophesying the fall of empires. It is supposed to represent the half of a sacred week—all that is ever allowed to the princes of evil, who are never given the full run of the sacred week of seven "days". But with John of Patmos it is a magic number.

5   In the old days, when the moon was a great power in heaven, ruling men's bodies and swaying the flux of the flesh, then seven was one of the moon's quarters. The moon still sways the flux of the flesh, and still we have a seven-day week. The Greeks of the sea had a nine-day week.* That is gone.

10   But the number seven is no longer divine. Perhaps it is still to some extent magical.

XX

The number ten is the natural number of a series. "It is by nature that the Hellenes count up to ten and then start over again".* It is of course the number of the fingers of the two hands. This repetition of five observed throughout nature was one of the things that led the   5
Pythagoreans to assert that "all things are number".* In the Apocalypse, ten is the "natural" or complete number of a series. The Pythagoreans, experimenting with pebbles, found that ten pebbles could be laid out in a triangle of $4+3+2+1$: and this sent their minds off in imagination.*—But the ten heads or crowned horns of John's   10
two evil beasts probably represent merely a complete series of emperors or kings, horns being a stock symbol for empires or their rulers. The old symbol of horns, of course, is the symbol of power, originally the divine power that came to man from the vivid cosmos, from the starry green dragon of life, but especially from the vivid   15
dragon within the body, that lies coiled at the base of the spine, and flings himself sometimes along the spinal way till he flushes the brow with magnificence, the gold horns of power that bud on Moses' forehead,* or the gold serpent, Uraeus, which came down between the brows of the royal Pharaohs of Egypt, and is the dragon of the   20
individual. But for the commonalty, the horn of power was the ithyphallos,* the phallos, the cornucopia.*

XXI

The final number, twelve, is the number of the established or
unchanging cosmos, as contrasted with the seven of the wandering
planets, which are the physical (in the old Greek sense) cosmos, always
in motion apart from the rest of motion. Twelve is the number of the
signs of the zodiac, and of the months of the year. It is three times
four, or four times three: the complete correspondence. It is the whole
round of the heavens, and the whole round of man. For man had seven
natures in the old scheme: that is, $6+1$, the last being the nature of
his wholeness. But now he has another quite new nature, as well as
the old one: for we admit he still is made up of the old Adam *plus*
the new. So now his number is twelve, $6+6$ for his natures, and one
for his wholeness. But his wholeness is now in Christ: no longer
symbolised between his brows. And now that his number is twelve,
man is perfectly rounded and established, established and unchanging,
unchanging, for he is now perfect and there is no need for him to
change, his wholeness, which is his thirteenth number (unlucky in
superstition) being with Christ in heaven. Such was the opinion of the
"saved", concerning themselves. Such is still the orthodox opinion:
those that are saved in Christ are perfect and unchanging, no need for
them to change. They are perfectly individualised.

XXII

When we come to the second half of Revelation, after the newborn
child is snatched to heaven and the woman has fled into the wilderness,
there is a sudden change, and we feel we are reading purely Jewish
and Jewish Christian Apocalypse, with none of the old background.   5
    "And there was war in heaven: Michael and his angels fought
against the dragon".*—They cast down the dragon out of heaven into
the earth, and he becomes Satan, and ceases entirely to be interesting.
When the great figures of mythology are turned into rationalised or
merely moral forces, then they lose interest. We are acutely bored by   10
moral angels and moral devils. We are acutely bored by a "rationalised"
Aphrodite.* Soon after 1000 B.C. the world went a little insane about
morals and "sin". The Jews had always been tainted.
    What we have been looking for in the Apocalypse is something older,
grander than the ethical business. The old, flaming love of life and   15
the strange shudder of the presence of the invisible dead made the
rhythm of really ancient religion. Moral religion is comparatively
modern, even with the Jews.
    But the second half of the Apocalypse is all moral: that is to say,
it is all sin and salvation. For a moment there is a hint of the old cosmic   20
wonder, when the dragon turns again upon the woman, and she is
given wings of an eagle and flies off into the wilderness: but the dragon
pursues her and spues out a flood upon her, to overwhelm her: "and
the earth helped the woman, and the earth opened her mouth and
swallowed up the flood. And the dragon was wroth with the woman,   25
and went to make war on the remnant of her seed, *which keep the
commandments of God, and have the testimony of Jesus Christ*".*
    The last words are, of course, the moral ending tacked on by some
Jew-Christian scribe to the fragment of myth. The dragon is here the
watery dragon, or the dragon of chaos, and in his evil aspect still. He   30
is resisting with all his might the birth of a new thing, a new era. He
turns against the Christians, since they are the only "good" thing left
on earth.
    The poor dragon henceforth cuts a sorry figure. He gives his power,

and his seat, and great authority to the beast that rises out of the sea, the beast with "seven heads and ten horns and upon his head ten crowns, and upon his heads the name of blasphemy. And the beast which I saw was like unto a leopard, and his feet were as the feet of
5 a bear, and his mouth as the mouth of a lion"—*

We know this beast already: he comes out of Daniel and is *explained* by Daniel.* The beast is the last grand world-empire, the ten horns are ten kingdoms confederated in the empire—which is of course Rome. As for the leopard, bear and lion qualities, these are also
10 explained in Daniel as the three empires that preceded Rome, the Macedonian,* swift as a leopard, the Persian, stubborn as a bear, the Babylonian, rapacious as the lion.

We are back again at the level of allegory, and for me, the real interest is gone. Allegory can always be explained: and explained away.
15 The true symbol defies all explanation, so does the true myth. You can give meanings to either—you will never explain them away. Because symbol and myth do not affect us only mentally, they move the deep emotional centres every time. The great quality of the mind is finality. The mind "understands", and there's an end of it.

20 But the emotional consciousness of man has a life and movement quite different from the mental consciousness. The mind knows in part, in part and parcel, with full stop after every sentence. But the emotional soul knows in full, like a river or a flood. For example, the symbol of the dragon—look at it, on a Chinese tea-cup or in an old
25 wood-cut, read it in a fairy-tale—and what is the result? If you are alive in the old emotional self, the more you look at the dragon, and think of it, the farther and farther flushes out your emotional awareness, on and on into dim regions of the soul aeons and aeons back. But if you are dead in the old feeling-knowing way, as so many
30 moderns are, then the dragon just "stands for" this that and the other—all the things it stands for in Frazer's *Golden Bough:* it is just a kind of glyph or label, like the gilt pestle and mortar outside a chemist's shop.—Or take better still the Egyptian symbol called the *ankh*, the symbol of life etc.?* which the goddesses hold in their hands.
35 Any child "knows what it means". But a man who is *really* alive feels his soul begin to throb and expand at the mere sight of the symbol. Modern men, however, are nearly all half dead, modern women too. So they just look at the *ankh* and know all about it, and that's that. They are proud of their own emotional impotence.

40 Naturally, then, the Apocalypse has appealed to men through the

ages as an "allegorical" work. Everything just "meant something"—
and something moral at that. You can put down the meaning flat.*

The beast from the sea means Roman Empire—and later Nero,
number 666.* The beast from the earth means the pagan sacerdotal
power, the priestly power which made the emperors divine and made   5
Christians even "worship" them. For the beast from the earth has two
horns like a lamb, a false Lamb indeed, an Antichrist, and it teaches
its wicked followers to perform marvels and even miracles—of
witchcraft, like Simon Magus* and the rest.

So we have the Church of Christ—or of the Messiah—being   10
martyred by the beast, till pretty well all good Christians are martyred.
Then at last, after not so very long a time—say forty years—the
Messiah descends from heaven and makes war on the beast, the Roman
Empire, and on the kings who are with him. There is a grand fall of
Rome, called Babylon, and a grand triumph over her downfall—though   15
the best poetry is all the time lifted from Jeremiah or Ezekiel or Isaiah,
it is not original. The sainted Christians gloat over fallen Rome: and
then the Victorious Rider appears, his shirt bloody with the blood of
dead kings. After this, a New Jerusalem descends to be his Bride, and
these precious martyrs all get their thrones, and for a thousand years   20
(John was not going to be put off with Enoch's meagre forty) for a
thousand years, the grand Millennium, the Lamb reigns over the earth,
assisted by all the risen martyrs. And if the martyrs in the Millennium
are going to be as bloodthirsty and ferocious as John the Divine in
the Apocalypse—Revenge Timotheus cries*—then somebody's going   25
to get it hot during the thousand years of the rule of Saints.

But this is not enough. After the thousand years the whole universe
must be wiped out, earth, sun, moon, stars and sea. These early
Christians fairly lusted after the end of the world. They wanted their
own grand turn first—Revenge Timotheus cries!—But after that, they   30
insisted that the whole universe must be wiped out, sun, stars and
all—and a *new* New-Jerusalem should appear, with the same old saints
and martyrs in glory, and everything else should have disappeared
except the lake of burning brimstone in which devils, demons, beasts,
and bad men should frizzle and suffer for ever and ever and ever,   35
Amen!

So ends this glorious work: surely a rather repulsive work. Revenge
was indeed a sacred duty to the Jerusalem Jews: and it is not the
revenge one minds so much as the perpetual self-glorification of these
saints and martyrs, and their profound impudence. How one loathes   40

them, in their "new white garments".* How disgusting their priggish
rule must be! How vile is their spirit, really, insisting, simply insisting
on wiping out the whole universe, bird and blossom, star and river,
and above all, everybody except *themselves* and their precious "saved"
5   brothers. How beastly their new Jerusalem, where the flowers never
fade, but stand in everlasting sameness! How terribly bourgeois to have
unfading flowers!

No wonder the pagans were horrified at the "impious" Christian
desire to destroy the universe. How horrified even the old Jews of the
10   Old Testament would have been. For even to them, earth and sun
and stars were eternal, created in the grand creation by Almighty God.
But no, these impudent martyrs must see it all go up in smoke.

Oh, it is the Christianity of the middling masses, this Christianity
of the Apocalypse. And we must confess, it is hideous. Self-
15   righteousness, self-conceit, self-importance, and secret *envy* underlie
it all.

By the time of Jesus, all the lowest classes and mediocre people had
realised that *never* would they get a chance to be kings, *never* would
they go in chariots, never would they drink wine from gold vessels.
20   Very well then—they would have their revenge by *destroying* it all.
"Babylon the great is fallen, is fallen, and is become the habitation
of devils".* And then all the gold and silver and pearls and precious
stones and fine linen and purple, and silk, and scarlet—and cinnamon
and frankincense, wheat, beasts, sheep, horses, chariots, slaves, souls
25   of men—all these that are destroyed, destroyed, destroyed in Babylon
the great—!* how one hears the envy, the endless envy screeching
through this song of triumph!

No, we can understand that the Fathers of the Church in the East
wanted Apocalypse left out of the New Testament. But like Judas
30   among the disciples, it was inevitable that it should be included. The
Apocalypse is the feet of clay to the grand Christian image. And down
crashes the image, on the weakness of these very feet.

There is Jesus—but there is also John the Divine. There is Christian
love—and there is Christian envy. The former would "save" the
35   world—the latter will never be satisfied till it has destroyed the world.
They are two sides of the same medal.

XXIII

Because, as a matter of fact, when you start to teach individual self-realisation to the great masses of people, who when all is said and done are only *fragmentary* beings, *incapable* of whole individuality, you end by making them all envious, grudging, spiteful creatures. Anyone who is kind to man knows the fragmentariness of most men, and wants to arrange a society of power in which men fall naturally into a collective wholeness, since they *cannot* have an individual wholeness. In this collective wholeness they will be fulfilled. But if they make efforts at individual fulfilment, they *must* fail, for they are by nature fragmentary. Then, failures, having no wholeness anywhere, they fall into envy and spite. Jesus knew all about it when he said: "To them that have shall be given"* etc.—But he had forgotten to reckon with the mass of the mediocre, whose motto is: we have nothing and therefore nobody shall have anything!

But Jesus gave the ideal for the Christian individual, and deliberately avoided giving an ideal for the State or the Nation. When he said "Render unto Caesar that which is Caesar's",* he left to Caesar the rule of men's bodies, willy-nilly: and this threatened terrible danger to a man's mind and soul. Already by the year 60 A.D. the Christians were an accursed sect; and they were compelled, like all men, to sacrifice, that is, to give worship to the living Caesar. In giving Caesar the power over men's bodies, Jesus gave him the power to compel men to make the act of worship to Caesar. Now I doubt if Jesus himself could have performed this act of worship, to a Nero or a Domitian.* No doubt he would have preferred death. As did so many early Christian martyrs. So there, at the very beginning, was a monstrous dilemma. To be a Christian meant death at the hands of the Roman State; since* to submit to the cult of the Emperor and worship the divine man, Caesar, was impossible to a Christian. No wonder, then, that John of Patmos saw the day not far off when *every* Christian would be martyred. The day would have come, if the imperial cult had been absolutely enforced on the people. And then when *every* Christian was martyred, what could a Christian expect but a Second Advent,

resurrection, and an absolute revenge! There was a condition for the
Christian community to be in, sixty years after the death of the
Saviour.

Jesus made it inevitable, when he said that the money belonged to
Caesar. It was a mistake. Money means bread, and the bread of men
belongs to no man. Money means also power, and it is monstrous to
give power to the virtual enemy. Caesar was *bound*, sooner or later,
to violate the soul of the Christians. But Jesus saw the individual only,
and considered only the individual. He left it to John of Patmos, who
was up against the Roman State, to formulate the Christian vision of
the Christian State. John did it in the Apocalypse. It entails the
destruction of the whole world, and the reign of saints in ultimate
bodiless glory. Or it entails the destruction of all earthly power, and
the rule of an oligarchy of martyrs (the Millennium).

This destruction of all earthly power we are now moving towards.
The oligarchy of martyrs began with Lenin, and apparently Mussolini
is also a martyr.* Strange, strange people they are, the martyrs, with
weird cold morality. When every country has its martyr-ruler, either
like Lenin or like Mussolini, what a strange, unthinkable world it will
be! But it is coming: the Apocalypse is still a book to conjure with.

A few vastly important points have been missed by Christian doctrine and Christian thought. Christian fantasy alone has grasped them.

1. No man is or can be a pure individual. The mass of men have
only the tiniest touch of individuality: if any. The mass of men live
and move, think and feel collectively, and have practically no individual
emotions, feelings or thoughts at all. They are fragments of the
collective or social consciousness. It has always been so, and will
always be so.

2. The State, or what we call Society as a collective whole *cannot*
have the psychology of an individual. Also it is a mistake to say that
the State is made up of individuals. It is not. It is made up of a
collection of fragmentary beings. And *no* collective act, even so private
an act as voting, is made from the individual self. It is made from the
collective self, and has another psychological background,
non-individual.

3. The State *cannot* be Christian. Every State is a Power. It cannot
be otherwise. Every State must guard its own boundaries and guard
its own prosperity. If it fails to do so, it betrays all its individual
citizens.

4. Every *citizen* is a unit of worldly power. A *man* may wish to be a pure Christian and a pure individual. But since he *must* be a member of some political State, or Nation, he is forced to be a unit of worldly power.

5. As a citizen, as a collective being, man has his fulfilment in the gratification of his power-sense. If he belongs to one of the so-called "ruling nations", his soul is fulfilled in the sense of his country's power or strength. If his country mounts up aristocratically to a zenith of splendour and power, in a hierarchy, he will be all the more fulfilled, having his place in the hierarchy. But if his country is powerful and democratic, then he will be obsessed with a perpetual will to assert his power in interfering and *preventing* other people from doing as they wish, since no man must do more than another man. This is the condition of modern democracies, a condition of perpetual bullying.

In democracy, bullying inevitably takes the place of power. Bullying is the negative form of power. The modern Christian State* is a soul-destroying force, for it is made up of fragments which have no organic whole, only a collective whole. In a hierarchy, each part is organic and vital, as my finger is an organic and vital part of me. But a democracy is bound in the end to be obscene, for it is composed of myriad dis-united fragments, each fragment assuming to itself a false wholeness, a false individuality. Modern democracy is made up of millions of frictional parts all asserting their own wholeness.

6. To have an ideal for the individual which regards only his individual self and ignores his collective self is in the long run fatal. To have a creed of individuality which denies the reality of the hierarchy makes at last for mere anarchy. Democratic man lives by cohesion and resistance, the cohesive force of "love" and the resistant force of the individual "freedom". To yield entirely to love would be to be absorbed, which is the death of the individual: for the individual must hold his own, or he ceases to be "free" and individual. So that we see, what our age has proved to its astonishment and dismay, that the individual *cannot* love. The individual cannot love: let that be an axiom. And the modern man or woman *cannot* conceive of himself, herself, save as an individual. And the individual in man or woman is *bound* to kill, at last, the lover in himself, or herself. It is not that each man kills the thing he loves,* but that each man, by insisting on his own individuality, kills the lover in himself, as the woman kills the lover in herself. The Christian *dare not love*: for love kills that which is Christian, democratic and modern, the individual. The individual

cannot love. When the individual loves, he ceases to be purely individual. And so he *must* recover himself, and cease to love. It is one of the most amazing lessons of our day: that the individual, the Christian, the democrat *cannot* love. Or, when he loves, when she
5   loves, he *must* take it back, she *must* take it back.

So much for private or personal love. Then what about that other love, "caritas",* loving your neighbour as yourself?

It works out the same. You love your neighbour. Immediately you run the risk of being absorbed by him: you must draw back, you must
10   hold your own. The love becomes resistance. In the end, it is all resistance and no love: which is the history of democracy.

If you are taking the path of individual self-realisation, you had better, like Buddha, go off and be by yourself, and give a thought to nobody. Then you may achieve your Nirvana.* Christ's way of loving
15   your neighbour leads to the hideous anomaly of having to live by sheer resistance to your neighbour, in the end.

The Apocalypse, strange book, makes this clear. It shows us the Christian in his relation to the State: which the Gospels and Epistles avoid doing. It shows us the Christian in relation to the State, to the
20   world, and to the cosmos. It shows him in mad hostility to all of them, having, in the end, to will the destruction of them all.

It is the dark side of Christianity, of individualism, and of democracy, the side the world at large now shows us. And it is, simply, suicide. Suicide individual and *en masse.* If man could will it, it would
25   be cosmic suicide. But the cosmos is not at man's mercy, and the sun will not perish to please us.

We do not want to perish, either. We have to give up a false position. Let us give up our false position as Christians, as individuals, and as democrats. Let us find some conception of ourselves that will allow
30   us to be peaceful and happy, instead of tormented and unhappy.

The Apocalypse shows us what we are resisting, unnaturally. We are unnaturally resisting our connection with the cosmos, with the world, with mankind, with the nation, with the family. All these connections are, in the Apocalypse, anathema, and they are anathema
35   to us. We *cannot bear connection.* That is our malady. We *must* break away, and be isolate. We call that being free, being individual. Beyond a certain point, which we have reached, it is suicide. Perhaps we have chosen suicide. Well and good. The Apocalypse too chose suicide, with subsequent self-glorification.

But the Apocalypse shows, by its very resistance, the things that the human heart secretly yearns after. By the very frenzy with which the Apocalypse destroys the sun and the stars, the world, and all kings and all rulers, all scarlet and purple and cinnamon, all harlots, finally all men altogether who are not "sealed", we can see how deeply the apocalyptists are yearning for the sun and the stars and the earth and the waters of the earth, for nobility and lordship and might, and scarlet and gold, splendour, for passionate love, and a proper unison with men, apart from this sealing business. What man most passionately wants is his living wholeness and his living unison, not his own isolate salvation of his "soul". Man wants his physical fulfilment first and foremost, since now, once and once only, he is in the flesh and potent. For man, the vast marvel is to be alive. For man, as for flower and beast and bird, the supreme triumph is to be most vividly, most perfectly alive. Whatever the unborn and the dead may know, they cannot know the beauty, the marvel of being alive in the flesh. The dead may look after the afterwards. But the magnificent here and now of life in the flesh is ours, and ours alone, and ours only for a time. We ought to dance with rapture that we should be alive and in the flesh, and part of the living, incarnate cosmos. I am part of the sun as my eye is part of me. That I am part of the earth my feet know perfectly, and my blood is part of the sea. My soul knows that I am part of the human race, my soul is an organic part of the great human soul, as my spirit is part of my nation. In my own very self, I am part of my family. There is nothing of me that is alone and absolute except my mind, and we shall find that the mind has no existence by itself, it is only the glitter of the sun on the surface of the waters.

So that my individualism is really an illusion. I am a part of the great whole, and I can never escape. But I *can* deny my connections, break them, and become a fragment. Then I am wretched.

What we want is to destroy our false, inorganic connections, especially those related to money, and re-establish the living organic connections, with the cosmos, the sun and earth, with mankind and nation and family. Start with the sun, and the rest will slowly, slowly happen.

APOCALYPSE: APPENDIXES I, II, III

Note on the texts

The texts in these Appendixes are three uncancelled MS portions of *Apocalypse* – 'nearly 20,000 words' – which DHL wrote in November 1929 and later deleted. Fragments 1 and 2 were part of the MS *Apocalypse* notebook, and Fragment 3, entitled *Apocalypsis II*, was written in a separate notebook. All three of these draft writings are in the possession of the University of Texas at Austin.

The apparatus records editorial changes made for the sake of consistency in italicising titles and in spelling and capitalisation. The following silent emendations have been made:

1   Accidental omissions have been supplied only in the case of incomplete quotation marks and final stops.

2 DHL's capitalisation has been regularised throughout for religious denominations and nationalities, e.g. 'Christian', 'Greek'.

APPENDIX I
APOCALYPSE, FRAGMENT 1

After reading the Old Testament, and then Revelation, one is forced
to the conclusion that the Jews hated their neighbours one and all with
such an obsession of hatred, that Jesus was bound to come with his   5
new gospel: Thou shalt love thy neighbour as thyself.*

Myself I am very grateful to the new translations of the Bible. A
translation like Moffatt's* frees the book from the pompous snoring
of the old Elizabethan language and the parson's voice combined. The
Bible language is wonderful, granted. But like all the much-vaunted   10
Elizabethan English, it tends to be more full of sound than of sense,
and to stupify some part of the intelligence with gorgeous noise. This
gorgeous noise at last becomes almost unbearable, and between it and
the parson's voice and the Sunday School teacher's moral expoundings,
Scripture sounds at last entirely mechanical and empty.   15

But take a simple new translation, and the spell is broken. The
beauty of Isaiah is even greater, now it is more intelligible, the loss
of that Elizabethan gilding gives it its own poetry. And the Gospels
and the Epistles lose that curious theatrical quality which is for us
inseparable from the Elizabethan style, they cease to be something to   20
mouth out, histrionically, and they take on their own true tenderness,
their strange and manly gentleness. After all, how interesting the Bible
is, when we can come to it fresh and find it human and alive, alive
with all the emotions of the human soul, even the smallest and most
unpleasant, as well as the deepest. How strange the religious note is,   25
varying so much and still having sincere intimacy all the time! How
truly beautiful the Psalms, many of them, and the magnificent poetry
of Isaiah! Even the Jewish form of poetry that they call "parallelism",
because the second line re-echoes the first in a parallel image, how
curiously satisfying it can be, once one enters the image-rhythm of it!   30

"Except the Lord build the house, they labour in vain that build it:
except the Lord keep the city, the watchman waketh but in vain..."*

There is the perpetual yet unexpected antiphony, like the strong
heart-beat followed by the weak.

To me, the Bible had gone dead because it was cut and dried: its noise was a fixed noise, its meaning a fixed meaning. And not only was it dead, it was antipathetic. Arriving at manhood, one felt that the Bible had been bullied into one, and by second-rate minds at that. Its whole
5   meaning was second-rate, because it had been expounded by these second-rate orthodox people, parsons and teachers, who would not and perhaps could not extract anything from the book but a sort of glorified grocery-shop morality and book-keeping.

After twenty years and more, after some little study of old literature,
10   of ancient history touching Babylon* and Persia and Egypt, Crete, Mycenae,* and the Ionian sea-board, at last one can come back and discover the Bible afresh, entirely afresh, and rescue it from parsons and Sunday School teachers and Elizabethan theatrical obscurity. It is a question of recovering the true background. Recover the real
15   background, put the book into natural relationship with its time and place and spirit, and it lives again with a fine new life. We have it cut and dried. Set the strange flower on its stem again.

I think the Bible goes so deep in our consciousness, that if the Bible dies, or becomes dead and fixed and repellant to us, then something
20   very important in our responsive soul also goes dead and fixed, and we set into a sort of general resistance. By origin we are Christians, we have been brought up Christians. But what do we mean, after all, by Christians? Religion is a question of ritual and of belief. But as Protestants we have known almost no religious ritual. And what do
25   we believe?

As a matter of fact, we don't know. As far as religion goes, we don't know what we believe. And it doesn't really matter. When you see a churchful of people all repeating the same *Credo,** it is obviously a merely superficial repetition. Look at the faces of these people, and
30   you can see written there very plain and very contrasting beliefs. They are all Christians, and verbally they all believe alike. But actually, their beliefs are as different as beliefs can be. And why not! It must be so.

Religion is not a question of belief, it is a question of feeling. It is a certain deep feeling which seems to soothe and reassure the whole
35   soul. But Christianity is very curious. It seems to have two distinct sets of feeling, one focussing in Jesus and in the command: Love one another!*—the other focussing, not in Paul or Peter or John the Beloved, but in the Apocalypse. And this second sort of Christianity is weird. It is a doctrine of the chosen people, of the elect: it is based
40   on everlasting hatred of worldly power, and of people in power: it looks

for the end of the world, and the destruction of everybody except the *Saved*. And nearly all Christians and teachers of the Bible today teach *this* sort of Christianity, the Apocalypse sort.

And this has really killed the Bible for us. The one thing we loathe is this "salvation" business, and especially the people who are "saved". These horrible "saved" people and all the good godly ones who are *right*, always *right*, they have become so repulsive to us that they have made the Bible itself repulsive, and they have killed all our religious responses in us. And when our religious responses are dead, or inactive, we are really cut off from life, because the deepest part of our consciousness is not functioning. We try to take refuge in art. But to my mind, the essential feeling in all art is religious, and art is a form of religion without dogma. The *feeling* in art is religious, always. Whenever the soul is moved to a certain fullness of experience, that is religion. Every sincere and genuine feeling is a religious feeling. And the point of every work of art is that it achieves a state of feeling which becomes true experience, and so is religious. Everything that puts us into connection, into vivid touch, is religious. And this would apply to Dickens or Rabelais or *Alice in Wonderland** even, as much as to *Macbeth* or Keats. Every one of them puts us curiously into touch with life, achieves thereby certain religious feeling, and gives a certain religious experience. For in spite of all our doctrine and dogma, there are all kinds of gods, forever. There are gods of the hearth and the orchard, underworld gods, fantastic gods, even cloacal* gods, as well as dying gods and phallic gods and moral gods. Once you have a real glimpse of religion, you realise that all that is *truly* felt, every feeling that is felt in true relation, every vivid feeling of connection, is religious, be it what it may, and the only irreligious thing is the death of feeling, the causing of nullity; the frictional irritation which, carried far, tends to nullity.

So that, since essentially the feeling in every real work of art is religious in its quality, because it links us up or connects us with life, you can't substitute art for religion, the two being essentially the same. The man who has lost his religious response *cannot* respond to literature or to any form of art, fully: because the call of every work of art, spiritual or physical, is religious, and demands a religious response. The people who, having lost their religious connection, turn to literature and art, find there a great deal of pleasure, aesthetic, intellectual, many kinds of pleasure, even curiously sensual. But it is the pleasure of entertainment, not of experience. So that they gradually get tired out. They cannot give to literature the one thing it really requires—if it be important at all—and that is the religious response; and they cannot take from it the one thing it gives, the religious experience of linking up or making a new connection. For the religious experience one gets from Dickens belongs to Baal or Ashtaroth,* but still is religious: and in *Wuthering Heights** we feel the peculiar presence of Pluto and the spirit of Hades,* but that too is of the gods. In *Macbeth* Saturn* reigns rather than Jesus. But it is religious just the same.

Now the Bible, we know well, is a great religious book. It is full of God. But not, we find at last, to our unspeakable relief, not the chapel God of the grocery-store keepers. The Jews did a wonderful thing when they focussed the whole religious feeling of man upon One God. But that does not prevent their Bible from being full of all the gods. It is this discovery which a man can make in his maturity, to his unspeakable relief.

The Bible is full of all the gods. Nay, even, the Jahveh* of the Old Testament *is* all the gods, except the dying and redeeming gods. But surely the Jehovah of Genesis and Numbers, Samuel, Psalms, Isaiah, Ezekiel, surely he is all the gods in turn, Dionysic, Apollo-like,* strange like Ra,* and grim like Baal or Bel. You can't make an idol to Jehovah because he has the qualities of all the ancient gods in turn, Ouranos or Kronos or Saturn,* even the old Osiris,* or the mysterious gods of the first Sumerians.* He is One because he is all of them, not because he is different from any of them. He does not sit absolute and apart, while all the other gods topple, mere fallen idols. He is himself all the gods and all the idols, savage and fertile, and even he is all the unknown gods that are yet to come.

To me, it was an immense relief when I read a new translation and realised this. We have been brought up to believe: If this God exists, One and Eternal, then none of the other gods exist, and all the rest is hollow.—But now, having really read the Bible as a *book*, not as a one-sided pronouncement, I realise the very truth of the Bible: If this God exists, One and Eternal, then all the other gods exist too. For all the gods are only "sides" of the One God. We say of a man: Oh, you only know one side of him!—We can say the same of God. We only know one side of him, and a very small side. If we are to know God well, we must know all the gods: which means knowing God on all possible sides.

"Shriek for sorrow, ships of Tartessus
for your haven is no more.—"*

When I was young, and heard the chapel gloating that Babylon was
fallen, and Assyria* was no more, and Persia was but a name, and
Moab* had left not so much as a mark on the ground, I was always   5
profoundly depressed. I felt it would be so wonderful if one could go
to Babylon, or to Nineveh,* or if one could meet the Moabitish women.
But now I find the Bible is full of Moab and Babylon, Nineveh and
Susa,* and that without the gods of Egypt and the gods of the
Chaldeans,* the God of Israel would have been more uninteresting   10
than a block of wood. So much of the splendour of the Bible is Egyptian
splendour, and Babylonian, so much of the beauty, the *reality* comes
from Amalek* and Moab. The Jews were able to make a One God
because they came into contact with so many peoples and so many
civilisations, so many alien gods, each of which lent something to the   15
Jewish mind, and to the Jewish soul. All the old Jewish poetry is the
poetry of adventure with strange peoples and strange gods, and the
Bible is perhaps more profoundly a book of roaming than is Herodotus
or the Odyssey.*

And the influence, of course, is dual. The Jews *loved* roaming, they   20
loved meeting strange peoples, learning from strange cultures, which
meant strange religions. The Jews from the very start down to this
day have always *loved* to be with gentiles, to learn gentile ways and
wisdom. In a sense, they are a people that always has lived and always
will live on the culture of other races. The Jewish mind is simply an   25
amalgam of all the cultures of the ages. And today, wherever there is
a new culture, there will the Jew hasten, fascinated.

So, of course, in the past he was always having to be *whipped* back
to Jerusalem: as he is today. The Jew has such a curious duality. His
real delight is centrifugal: he *loves* to go to strange peoples and to   30
assimilate strange cultures: he always did. But his fear of losing himself
in slavery made him, after Egypt, react savagely against all strange
peoples, and pivot himself on his One God, whose Chosen People he
belonged to.

The Bible contains more of the whipping back to Jerusalem than   35
the excursion into the wonder-world of other races and cultures. The
Jewish prophets hated their neighbours so bitterly because the Jewish
people were all too prone to like their neighbours overmuch, and merge
too easily. Jews on the whole are bored by Jews. Gentiles are much
more interesting. It is obvious from the Book of Daniel and from   40

Esther that the Jews had a most thrilling time in Babylonia, in
Chaldea, and that they learned all there was to be learned from the
Chaldeans. They probably enjoyed Egypt and Babylon, even in
captivity, as they now enjoy New York and London, in freedom:
5 perhaps even more. And the splendid thing about the Bible is the
wideness of its contact and the bigness of its intelligence and its secret
sympathy. It is obvious that the Jews were intensely attracted by Egypt
and Amalek, Moab, Chaldea, Assyria, Phoenicia and Persia. The
attraction appears in the Bible in marvellous poetry of cursing and
10 commination and prophecy of doom, as a rule. But under the words
of hate comes the poetry of the lure.

So now, after all these years of narrow monotheism, and a Bible that
had become a very prison of the soul and the mind, suddenly we realise
that we have been deceived. We have taken the Bible out of its setting,
15 cut it off from the contact with history and the living races it plays
amongst, and set it in unreal isolation, as an absolute. We have been
wrong. We have taken the Old Testament at its own value of a One
God of a Chosen People cursing and annihilating everybody else,
whereas it is a strange and fascinating Odyssey of a whole race
20 wandering among strange races that attracted them intensely, and
threatened to absorb them, would have absorbed them but for the
violent, frenzied resistance of the prophets, from Moses onwards.

The Bible evolved from centuries of vivid contact with strange races
and strange gods. Even Jehovah himself was so evolved. Now we have
25 to put both God and the Bible back into the enormous historical
setting. Everything back into contact. Nothing absolute and detached.
All things in vivid, interweaving contact, the gods of Egypt and
Chaldea with the God of Israel, all understood in contact with one
another.

30 As with the Old Testament, so with the New. Put it back into its
contacts, its vital relationships. The world is vast, the experience of
mankind is vast. Let us get back into contact. We have imprisoned
ourselves unnecessarily in an isolated religion, tethered ourselves to
an isolated god, and listened too long to the language of isolation and
35 exclusiveness. And a state of isolation is a state of falsity and death.

What we need is to get back into contact, into religious contact.
Taking the Bible as our religious basis, we too need to get back into
contact with Egypt and Babylon, we need to know again as the
Chaldeans knew, and the Egyptians. Our consciousness is crippled and
40 maimed, we only live with a fragment of ourselves.

Turning from the Old Testament to the New, we do turn actually
into a new world. It is like coming into the fresh air. It is a strange
thing, the liberating effect of a new feeling in mankind. When Jesus
said: Love one another.—Thou shalt love thy neighbour as thyself.—
Love your enemies.*—he did suddenly open wide a great door from   5
the weary house of strife into the fresh air of a new life.

Again we must get back the context, re-establish the contact with
the "world" of the first century of Christ. It was a world, as we know
ad nauseam, of conquest and of civil war. From 700 B.C. to the year
1 A.D. the great waves of conquest swept over Asia Minor and Eastern   10
Europe. The Jews, from their little Jerusalem, kept being swept away,
though they had, so far, still managed to creep back and restore the
temple.* By the time of Augustus* there was comparative peace. But
the lands of the Mediterranean, especially the east, were a great
churned debris of wreckage, from "conquests" of Assyrians, of Medes,   15
and Persians, of Alexander the Great with his Macedonians, and of
the Roman generals. "How old were you when the Mede* appeared?"
men asked one another in the sixth century before Christ. But by the
end of the century it changed to "How old were you when Darius of
the Persians conquered us?"*   20

Conflict was in the air. From the year 1000 B.C. onwards, the so-called
civilised world has been in a mad whirl of war and conquest. But before
Christ it was even worse than since. The enemy was always either
imminent or present. Destruction and hostility swept over men. Whole
races were shifted, like great herds of cattle, from their own lands to   25
far-off countries. Now that war is almost universally in the air again,
today, we can sympathise somewhat with the men of the last centuries
before Christ, and understand why the Jews hated everybody, and why
the Greeks were so suicidally irritable and quarrelsome. Men were
beside themselves, owing to the centuries of remorseless friction and   30
conquest, they were in a state of chronic irritation amounting to
hysteria. The Jews of Jesus' day were in this condition. The Greeks
were already sinking into hopeless fidgettiness.

It needed the Roman "peace", very much an "armed peace", to
restore a measure of calm. But it needed much more. It needed the   35
new emotion which Jesus brought into the world. "Love one another!
Love your enemies!" The message was a miracle, in that world of
irritation and hysteria. Even today we feel the great soothing and balm
of it. The implication of the message was: Strive no more to be top
dog. Don't struggle any more to master somebody else. Don't fight   40

any more to be first. Be content to be last, and humblest. For in the final kingdom, the last shall be first.—*

This was Jesus' message, familiar to us now, but by no means assimilated or accepted, even today. By no means. Everybody wants to be top dog: and certainly every nation wants to crow loudest on its own muck-heap.

But in Jesus' day, the message was just madness. Man could not *conceive* of anything except the struggle of every man to be top dog. To ninety-nine percent of the people, Jesus' teaching was just creeping and repulsive idiocy. I think, as a matter of fact, it is so to most people today: say sixty-percent, instead of ninety-nine. Yet even in Jesus' day, a few great minds, like Paul's, and the Apostle John's, recognised the fundamental truth of the new teaching, and felt the quickening of the new *feeling*. That was the great point, the quickening of the new feeling. We have to recognise it. If we read the Greek and Roman literature of the first centuries, we feel there is something missing in it, there is a certain staleness. There is nothing of the new breath of life that blows through the Gospels and the great Epistles. The tenderness of Paul in some of the Epistles, expressing his tender concern for his distant brothers, and exhorting them above all things to love one another, not to quarrel, and not to *harden*: this brings a new human relationship into the world, a new sort of love. Perhaps Epicurus* had tried for something similar, but there was a touch of resignation in Epicurus, no vivid hope.

With Jesus, a new thing came into the world. And we can say with confidence, that no further new thing will ever come into the world again, without a further new breath of love, and of tenderness. Another new breath of love, and another new courage of tenderness, coupled with a courage of power, this alone will release us from the weary world that imprisons us. For we are as much imprisoned in war, in conflict, in that mean form of conflict called competition, in the mean fight for money, for a mere living: we are as much shut up in the stale prison of all this, as the men of Jesus' day were shut up in the prison of conquest.

Jesus gave the key-word by which men might slip out of the prison of conquest, individually, or in little communities. But alas, it is a terrible fact of human psychology, that what is true for the individual is not necessarily true for a community such as a nation or an empire. A man may perhaps love his enemy, in the Christian or charitable sense of love, because by so doing, nine times out of ten he can escape from his enemy, or at least escape from the wearisome necessity of keeping up an enmity. But a nation that loves its enemy will be destroyed or absorbed by that enemy. This is a truth that is enshrined in the whole of the Old Testament. The Jews as a nation—or a tribe—tended to be fascinated by alien nations and so make themselves and their nation a victim of the alien people. It nearly happened in Egypt and Babylon, and would have happened easily save for the other profound Jewish instinct of national self-preservation through a religion hostile to all other religions. The prophets and leaders *whipped* the people back into isolation.

Now perhaps we may say that a nation which tends to let itself be absorbed should let itself be absorbed. But men and nations are strange things. Man has needs which are obvious, and deep, obscure needs. A man who is tremendously attracted and tempted by strange races may at the same time have a profound need to adhere to his own race, or nation, at any cost, and even to sacrifice himself to that need. We may say that truth, or right, or religion is greater than race or nation, and superficially, it is so. A priest may sacrifice his nationality entirely to his Church. But this only makes the Church the final enemy of the nation, and, for some men, forces a choice between church or nation.

Truth as a matter of fact is nothing but the profound and compelling feeling of the human heart. The real truth lies in the things we do, not in the things we say or believe.

The great question is, how deep is the need in men to belong to a nation, a self-governing group? It seems as if it were a shallow need. It seems as if we moderns might all of us be citizens of the world; as if, when asked what country we belong to, we might say: The world!—

But I doubt if it is really so. Man has several beings, not only one being. When I get to heaven, no doubt I shall have no passport, I shall be a naked soul indistinguishable from the naked soul of a negro or a Chinaman. But that is a grand abstraction, and abstractions get us nowhere. Here, in the complex being that I am, there lives a me which is simply an individual, just a man like any other man, negro or Tartar. But there lives also a me which is European, which is at home in Europe, which feels and thinks as a European feels and thinks. Further, there is a me which is an Englishman, which has its final group-connection with England, and its fulfilment in *power* in the acts of the English nation. And it is useless to say these things don't matter, the individual alone counts. It is not true.

One of the obscurest but profoundest needs of man is this need to

belong to a group, a group called a church, or a nation, or an empire, and to feel the power thereof. And the chief reason for the profound dissatisfaction of today is that man is unhappy in his collective self. Modern nations no longer give adequate expression to the deeper,
5   collective feelings of the men of the nation. They no longer express our true nature, the nature of power which is in us. Modern nations, in their present activity, have become curiously meaningless, really powerless, in the creative sense, and the men of the nation suffer accordingly, from a sense of meaningless living and of powerlessness.
10   Modern nations need smashing and remaking: the unit is too big, the carcase is too unwieldy, the power is dead.

Hence the great attraction of America. It is a new nation. It has not reached a final form. All things are possible to it. It seems full of power. And therefore men transfer themselves from the old group to the new.
15   A man who goes to America and takes up citizenship does actually sever his old connection, and form a new one. If I go to America and become naturalised, I do, *in myself*, throughout my whole consciousness, undergo a subtle change, and take on a new being. Also I cease from being what I have been, an Englishman.

20   This need for a new group-connection was profound, in the men who embraced Christianity during the first centuries. A man who became a Christian ceased, really, to be a Jew, or ceased to be a Roman. He had discovered a new "nation", the nation of Christians. And the sense of community was intense, in the early church.

25   But Jesus had repudiated all empire on earth. He left it to the devil. The power of the world was Satan's. Render unto Caesar those things which are Caesar's.* A man, a Christian was a *pure* individual, an embodied soul belonging to God, and no more.

This is good Christianity, but it turns out to be fallacy, when
30   applied to mankind at large. The vast bulk of men are not pure individuals, and never will be, for the pure individual is a rarity, almost a kind of freak. The vast bulk of men need to belong to a self-governing group, a tribe, a nation, an empire. It is a necessity like the necessity to eat food.

35   And the psychology of a nation or tribe or empire is not and cannot be the same as the psychology of the individual. The nation is made up of individuals—or rather, of individual human beings. But the psychology of a nation is made up of *certain* basic instincts, *certain* basic needs, *certain* basic aspirations of these individuals, and not of *all* the
40   individual instincts or aspirations. The basic instincts and needs of the

individual which belong to his group soul are almost impossible to determine. They are revealed in action, they cannot rise direct into consciousness because the individual consciousness is individual, and these instincts and needs are really collective. So no one man can embody them or know them. They must be expressed before they can be known. Hence the utter uncertainty of the future.

Jesus, as the pure idealist, wanted to free men from the collective self, the tribal or national self. But strange as it may seem, he might as well have tried to free men from breathing. The problem of the *collective* activity of Christianity was left entirely to be solved by time. And it has never been solved.

Men were tired to death of their old group allegiance, tired to death of being Jews or Greeks or Egyptians or Romans, tired to death of state and nation and empire. Those that became Christians cut the old allegiance. But they immediately founded new groups, new communities, with a new rule of presbyters. And these groups quickly fused into a new State, a Church with a gradually elaborating rule of presbyters and bishops, a new authority and a new *power*. In spite of Jesus, *power* came back. It must be so. In the deeper instinctive self, man is a being of power, and must feel himself powerful, powerful beyond himself, in his community or nation or, in the Christian case, his Church. The Christian Church grew into the Catholic Church, with its supreme Pope as divine as ever Augustus was, or Nero, in the pomp of Rome. The Church became a great power indeed, it established the ritual and religious life of the people, it was building up a fine philosophy, and then, alas, the old, old lust for power and wealth conquered the spirit of love and growth, and by the time of the Borgia popes* the Church was back in the old position of Mammon* or Babylon the great harlot.

Man is a being of power, and then a being of love. The pure individual tries either for sheer power, like Alexander, or sheer love, like Christ. But mankind forever will have its dual nature, the old Adam of power, the new Adam of love. And there must be a balance between the two. Man will achieve his highest nature and his highest achievements when he tries to get a living balance between his nature of power and his nature of love, without denying either. It is a balance that can never be established, save in moments, but every flower only flowers for a moment, then dies. That makes it a flower.

Nevertheless man can be a little more intelligent about himself and his destiny when he realises his dual nature, his nature of power,

which is really collective, and his nature of love, which is individual.

Jesus came to establish the nature of love in the world. The apostles
took up the task. They wanted to do it by avoiding any conflict with
power, and the powers that be. Yet the conflict came. And gradually
the Church itself became the great power, and by the time of the
Reformation it was a power peculiarly devoid of love. So the pendulum
swings.

In that early church of Christians, however, in the first century,
there were plenty of men who became Christians in the belief that here
was the *new* great Power. We have to realise that to a big portion of
early Christians, Jesus was not love at all, he was just the name of a
new power. He signified no tenderness nor gentleness, he signified
rather a semi-magic potency that was going to destroy the world, wipe
out the hated Romans, and establish the new saints in a reign of
glory. As in the beginning of every new movement, Christianity was
embraced by men who were the purest anti-Christ in spirit. There was
an inordinate amount of subtilised sheer hate in the world, in the first
century. A good deal of this sheer hate found its way into the Christian
communities. These Christians of extraordinary subtilised hate are
always revealed by their mad craving to destroy the world and to gain
inordinate power for themselves. To them Jesus, "the Fish"* was
rather a supreme maleficent power that was going to wipe out the whole
phenomenal world, leave only these spirits of pure lust for power to
reign over a void sort of world, than any spirit of divine love. St. Paul
and St. John the Apostle must have had bitter, bitter fights already
with this sort of diabolical Christian, and it is a great wonder the early
Church saved itself and emerged truly as the Church of the breath of
love. Perverted power-lust threatened the early Church as it threatens
every great revolution, and even every idealist movement. Many men
are socialists out of perverted power-lust. And this form of lust is
diabolical, deadly, it is a fearsome form of hate. Even Lenin* was pure
hate, really: but pure. The rest of the bolshevists are usually impure
hate. It comes from the perversion of the nature of power in a man.

And now we can turn to the Apocalypse. For the Apocalypse, the
last book in the Bible, is a book of power. It is a book of power-lust,
written by a man who is a prisoner, denied all power.

Now we must free ourselves from the superficial contempt for power
which most of us feel and express today. We only know dead power,
which is force. Mere force does not command our respect. But power

is not mere force. It is divine like love. Love and power are the two divine things in life. This is what Nietzsche* meant.

But love is only divine when it is in harmonious relation to power: and power is only divine when it is in harmony with love. Jesus plainly said he only came to fulfil, to make complete, the old Law of power.   5
The early Church, and a great Pope like Gregory,* knew and gave perhaps the best example of love in harmony with power, and power in harmony with love. The following popes only too soon lost the love in striving for power, and the antithesis was Francis of Assisi* and similar saints, who wanted to destroy all power in the name of love.   10

In the last century, Shelley sang over and over again of the perfection to which men would arrive when all "power" had been wiped off the face of the earth. But we feel, about Shelley as about Francis, there is a certain basic falseness in it all. We feel, moreover, in both men the same lack of warmth and of real kindly love, in both   15
is the death of love. The death of power is the death of love: and vice versa.

The war against power culminated actually in Lenin. Lenin was pure, as Francis and Shelley were pure. In fact, Francis, Shelley and Lenin are the three great figures of history, men of pure spirit single   20
in their fight against power. Lenin fulfilled what Shelley preached. Lenin was as pure a poet of action as Shelley was of words. And he accomplished the great feat of the Christian ages, he destroyed power in the name of love. Lenin accomplished for the State what Christ preached only for the individual. For the individual, the ideal is love.   25
But you cannot have love as an ideal for a State. Values are different. The State has a lower scale of values. What is love in the individual is well-being in the State. Lenin sincerely wanted the well-being of every individual in the State. He was, in a sense, the god of the common people of Russia, and they are quite right, in the modern sense, to   30
worship him. "Give us this day our daily bread".* And Lenin wanted above all things to give them their daily bread. And he could not do even that. What was love in theory became hate in practice. He loved the people because he saw them powerless—and he was determined that power should not exist on earth. He himself was the final power   35
which should destroy power. It was the Church of Christ in practical politics. And it was anomaly, it was horrible. Because it was unnatural.

Jesus was very careful, really, *not* to assume power, and not to destroy power. The great God of Power, of Might, was the Father.   40

And even Caesar was, in a sense, the Father. Render unto Caesar that
which is Caesar's. And Jesus himself taught us the Lord's prayer.

> "Our Father, which art in heaven, hallowed be thy name,
>   thy kingdom come,
>   thy will be done on earth as it is in heaven—"*

We observe, Jesus himself never said: "*My* kingdom come," nor even:
"*My* will be done on earth as it is in heaven". Jesus truly claimed
no kingdom: the kingdom was the Father's: and the law, the *will* was
the Father's. Jesus only came to supplement or complete this will, to
make the kingdom of the *Father* perfect. Jesus has no kingdom: he
insists all the time that the kingdom is the Father's, it belongs to the
Lord Almighty, the Lord of Hosts, the God of power, to him who gives
life and strength and potency.—And so the Church of Christ *cannot*
have temporal power. But the Church of God can.

Jesus has no "power", and seeks no power. His is the mystery of
love, and it is another mystery. The mystery of love has a great
potency, indeed. But it is not the potency of rule, it is the potency of
no-rule.

Power is a definite and positive thing, an enrichening which comes
to us from Rule, from a Ruler, an Almighty, a Lord of Hosts. Try
to get away from it as we may, ultimately we must come back to the
ancient fact that the universe, the cosmos is swayed by a great Ruler,
an Almighty. There is Rule in the cosmos, there is Mind in the cosmos,
there is even Will in the cosmos. It is a pity Jesus called it "the
Father"—it does so suggest the old gentleman with a beard. But Jesus
spoke in purely human terms. And Jesus was most careful always to
do homage to the Father.

A Kosmokrator* there is, in spite of all our efforts at denial. There
is a great and terrible Ruler of the cosmos, who gives forth life, and
takes back life. The Kosmokrator gives us fresh life every day. But
if we refuse the Almighty, the Ruler, we refuse the life. And whoever
cuts us off from the Almighty cuts us off from life. Whoever gets
between me and the Lord of Life, the Kosmokrator, Lord of Hosts
and giver of might, source of our strength and power and our glory
as far as we can be glorious, whoever gets between me and this, or
Him, if you like, is my enemy, and *hates* me. So that St. Francis of
Assisi, and Shelley, and Lenin all three hated men who lived in the
might and splendour of life, who ruled and accepted rule. And since
all common men live and want to live in the might and the splendour

of life, Francis, and Shelley, and Lenin hated all common, upstanding, free and dauntless men. This is peculiarly and viciously true of the socialists everywhere: they hate all free, upstanding and dauntless men.

The most free, the most upstanding, the most dauntless men are happy, splendidly happy to accept the rule of a real man of power, who draws vitality from the cosmos. And they are unhappy, wretched when cut off from rule and from power, and forced to be democratic.

Now the fact that the Lord's prayer says first of all: Thy kingdom come, shows that men first and foremost want *rule*, the sense of power, power in the rulers above them. They want it even before they want bread. The common man wants to be consummated in the splendour and might of the rulers above him. It is a primary, paramount need, old and yet still unrecognised. When rulers have no cosmic splendour and might, then the common man tears them to pieces. It is a crime that a ruler should be impotent and without cosmic splendour, it is a great crime against the manhood of men. What does a man care about good food and good plumbing, if his life is inglorious and meaningless! Men like Lenin and the socialists, and Shelley and the "spiritists" would steal away from man his most precious treasure of all, his sense of solid splendour in life, his share in the glory of the cosmos. For first and foremost the cosmos is glorious, and man is part of the cosmos.

But the might, and the splendour, and the glory must all be tempered by love. Which means, we must be willing to submit, upon necessity, to the death of our individual splendour and might, as individuals we must upon occasion be willing to be weak and insignificant, humble, meek, mournful, poor in spirit, in order that a greater, a completer glory may come among men. For one man cannot be truly glorious unless all men, according to their degree, are glorified. This is the supreme truth that men like Caesar,* or like Napoleon,* have failed to grasp.

Before Jesus, before the period in which Jesus came, men sought only glory and might, let it cost what it would. Every man sought his own splendour, no matter what other men might suffer. Or if individual men were not quite so overweening, nations were. Every nation sought its own glory, at the cost of all its neighbours.

But already in the sixth century before Christ came the first signs of the other necessity in man, the need to die in the immediate self, and be re-born in a greater self. Men had been very blind to one another. It needed an experience as of death to make them aware, a little more aware of one another, and of the other man's needs.

It was in the sixth century men began, almost universally in the "known" world, to practice the cults of the dying god. It was then that the Orphic mysteries* began. The dying god may have symbolised the death and re-birth of vegetation, of corn, the rousing again with spring of the phallic power of fertility, throughout "nature". But it meant much more than this. It meant also, from far-off centuries, before Plato,* long before Jesus, the need man felt of death, the death-wish, so that a man might experience mystically, or ritually, the death in the body, the death of the known desires, and a resurrection in a new self, a more spiritual or highly-conscious self. The great death-wish of the centuries following the sixth century B.C., which brought the tragic conception into life, and which has lasted to this day, was the wish for escape from the old way of consciousness, the way of Might and of Cosmic Power, into a new way of consciousness, the way of knowledge. Man has two supreme forms of consciousness, the consciousness that I AM, and that I am full of power; then the other way of consciousness, the awareness that IT IS, and that IT, which is the objective universe or the other person, has a separate existence from mine, even preponderant over mine. This latter is the way of knowledge: the loss of the sense of I AM, and the gaining of knowledge, or awareness, of the other thing, the other creature.

About 600 B.C., the wish for pure knowledge became dominant in man, and carried with it the death wish. Men wanted to experience death, and come out on the other side, and know what was on the other side of death, all the time while they were still alive. This great wish for death and the adventure through death into the beyond took on many different shapes in many different religions. The Olympians perhaps knew nothing of it. But into the Olympian religion came the Orphic mystery and the Dionysic ecstasy, ways of getting out of the body and of obtaining experience beyond, in the beyond of this world: ways of knowing as the gods knew, which is the same as knowing what lies beyond death. For the gods lie beyond death. That world where the gods live is the world that men call death, and that world where men live is the world of the death of the gods.*

In all known countries sprang up the strange rituals called mysteries, which were first and foremost the ritual in which a man experienced death, and went through the dark horror of Hades, to rise again in a new body, with a new consciousness and a new glory, god-like. These mysteries went far beyond any fertility cult, though they might embody

that too. The ear of corn that was born was also the new body of a
man with its new consciousness, god-like.

In Greece it was the Orphic mystery, the mysteries of Dionysos,
Iacchos, the Eleusinian mystery:* in Egypt it was the mystery of Osiris
and Isis:* in the near East, the mysteries of Tammuz,* the mysteries   5
of Attis:* and in Persia, the mystery of Mithras.* In India, Buddha
took his mystery to a different conclusion, to Nirvana.* But it was in
the same spirit, with the same nostalgic wish for death in the body,
and in the old way of consciousness, and the complete passing away
of the old self into a final state of complete being, called Nirvana. With   10
the Hindus, something the same happened. But with them it was a
way through death to a new *power*, a new control of the vitalistic forces.

So the whole world went religious mad, if we may dare to say so,
about the same time. The Greeks who resisted the Orphic and
Dionysic "madness"—to use their own words—none the less took a   15
similar road, seeking the loss of self and the gaining of *pure knowledge*.
The pure knowledge that the Ionian Greeks began to thirst for, in the
sixth century B.C., is not ultimately very different from Buddha's
Nirvana or even St. John's New Jerusalem. Pure knowledge, pure
science, Nirvana, Pradhana,* the sheer ecstasy of Iacchos, the transport   20
of the initiate re-born of Isis, or re-born at Eleusis, or re-born from
the blood of the Mithraic bull, all these are *states of consciousness* which
are almost identical. The modern physicist is on the brink of Nirvana,
the man who follows Einstein* right through achieves in the end a state
of ecstasy which is the culmination of the way of knowledge. There   25
is a short-cut, through ritual, through yoga practice. And there is the
long, long way from Thales and Anaximander* down to Einstein. But
the final state of consciousness achieved is almost the same, in each
case. *And it is the goal*, in each case. The modern physicist is on the
brink of the culminating ecstasy, when his search for *knowledge* will   30
consummate itself in the final and inexplicable *experience*, which will
be mystic jargon if put into words. All roads lead to Rome: and all
search for knowledge, *whatever the knowledge*, leads to the same result,
the mystic experience of ecstasy in re-birth, the experience of Nirvana,
the achievement of the state of Pradhana, one or the other of the   35
ultimate experiences which are all alike, but reached by different roads.

Men achieved, in the fifth century B.C., by ritual, what men are now
at last achieving by science, the science of physics. Ritual comes first:
then dogmatic religion: finally science. And they all three at last
achieve the same end, the same state of consciousness. Einstein himself   40

is in the same state of consciousness, essentially, as an Orphic initiate was in, four centuries before Christ.

So, following the fulfilment of the experience by ritual, came the recording of the mystic experience. Now every Mystery was secret, profoundly secret. The ritual might never be revealed, nor even the experience. Every initiate must experience the Mystery for himself, in his own body. He must die his own death. At the same time, the priests of each religion did apparently elaborate a theory or an explanation of the Mysteries, and this, divulged to the initiates, must have passed into the common consciousness in exoteric forms. Anyhow we know enough of the Eleusinian Mysteries to know roughly what they were about: about the mystery of death, and the passage through Hades, and the re-birth in a higher world, or state: a glory. But unfortunately no pagan apocalypse remains to us, only a Mithraic fragment.* For the rest, every Apocalypse is Jewish, and by far the most famous is that of John of Patmos. But there are others: the Apocalypse of Enoch, and the visions in the Book of Daniel are also counted as apocalypse. An Apocalypse is really a vision, a revelation of heavenly things, and it takes the place of the older form of prophecy, in which the voice of God was heard, while God remained unseen, or seen only in a burning bush.

The Apocalypse of John is unique. It is undeniably Jewish, intensely Jewish, though written in the name of Christ. At the same time, there is something very unjewish about it, and it is, we might say, entirely unchristian. At the very beginning, it suggests the esoteric symbols of the pagans, and as we read on, we realise that here is a document that has a scheme far too complex for a Jewish revelation. This is an esoteric document, elaborate, complex, and concealed, and there is nothing Christian in it but the name of Christ. For Christianity brought first and foremost a new feeling into the world, rather than a new idea: a feeling of brotherly or spiritual love, as contrasted with the old carnal love. And it was not, as with Epicurus and the Greeks of his school, a feeling of affection tinged with resignation and hopelessness, the affectionate tolerance of those who have really lost hope. It was a fresh and triumphant feeling, that through brotherly, spiritual love man would be saved throughout eternity. Brotherly love without any form of desire was in itself a new feeling. But that God Himself, or at least, the Son of God, was such a lover, the supreme desireless lover, this was a new religious conception. And that the resurrection would be an entering into immortality in the great desireless love of Christ, this

too was a new conception, a new inspiration. We can judge the
Christianity of any work, or any individual, by the presence or absence
of this "pure", desireless love, selfless, esteemed as divine. And we
can find none of it in the vengeful chapters of John's Apocalypse. John
of Patmos wants his revenge, final, heaven after. Neither the pagans
nor the Jews nor even the Christian gnostics* grasped the new feeling
and the new concept of desireless, immortal love, a love which was
basically a love of the other man, a love of the neighbour, loving one's
neighbour being conceived as part of the divine desireless love of
Christ. Even the mind of Plato contained no such concept, and his
emotional self knew no such feeling. Plato wished sincerely for the
human "good". He did not realise that what humanity needed was
a little "pure" love. He still thought it wanted Rule: wise rule,
benevolent rule, but still, loveless rule.

The pagan religions, the Jewish religion never got beyond the great
conception of power. In the beginning, the cosmos itself was the great
Power that Is. The cosmos was alive, and its power was a great living
effluence. Looking into the sky was like looking into the eyes of some
mighty living creature, or being: and even today, we cannot look into
the eyes even of a cat or a baby without quivering from the naked
contact with life and the power of life. The universe was all power,
and man derived power from the cosmos. At his maximum, he was
full of power, and like a bridegroom, vivid with potency. So that,
towards the end of the great pagan era, though long before Christianity
or Plato, cosmic power came to be conceived as phallic power, and the
act of marriage was the consummation of man's divinity. But this was
only towards the *end* of the pagan era: or shall we say, with the Greeks,
towards the end of the barbaric era. The almost universal phallic
worship of the last centuries before true history begins, the worship
which left the phallic stones standing everywhere in southern Europe,
was perhaps the last phase of the great cosmic worship of power. Power
was in the cosmos, power was in the sun and moon, power was in the
phallos. Our anthropologists abandon the sun-myth for the fertility-
myth, and they will no doubt abandon the fertility-myth for something
else. But any way, they have at last accepted the army of phallic stones
that even yet stand erect and forbid the honest anthropologist to ignore
them.

When the cult of dying gods came into the ancient worship of cosmic
power, the two great aims of worship did not change essentially. The
aim of the worship was still the acquiring of the splendid phallic power

or fertility which man recognises as his best and fullest physical state, and further, the acquiring of the higher power which, when attained, gives man his immortality. To have the fullest phallic potency man must undergo a temporary winter-death and transit through Hades,
5   like the plants. This is an old cosmic truth lost sight of today, yet lingering in the fertile nations. And again, to enter into that higher power wherein man has his immortality, a man must die an even deeper death, a death of the consciousness, and emerge with a new consciousness. So that from the dual mystic death he emerges with
10 a new body and a new consciousness or spirit, and the consummation of the initiation is based on the "marriage" of these two, the re-union.

So I think we can safely say, the old pagan Mysteries all consisted in a death, first of the body and then of the spirit or consciousness: a passage through the underworld of the dead, in which the spirit or
15 consciousness achieved death step by step: then a sudden emergence into life again, when a new body, like a babe, is born, and a new spirit emerges: then the meeting of the new-born frail spirit with the Great Spirit of the god, which descends from heaven for the consummation: and then the final marriage again of a new body and new spirit.

20 None of this, as we see, is Christian exactly. It is too physical and too self-glorious. It is, if you like, a grand self-glorification which Christianity absolutely discouraged. Christianity is based above all on *communal* love, and communion must be a communal act. Even Pentecost* is not individual—the Spirit descends on the members of
25 the Church, while they are together, not upon some special *initiate*. In Christianity, a man might never really forget his neighbour, for the very love of Christ was a love of the neighbour. In Christianity, a man lost his own *self* for ever, and became only a vessel of the divine love.

This obliteration of self *entirely* was obnoxious to all pagans, and
30 even Jews; and the self-glorification consummated in the pagan and Jewish ritual was obnoxious to all Christians. To the pagans, as to the Jews, the lack of a certain pride and assumption in a man was repugnant. To the Christians, pride and assumption were the devil. Even the Epicureans, who practised a sort of affectionate resignation
35 and a sort of humility, were really very unpopular in the pagan world. The Stoics,* with their pride, their insolence almost in enduring misery or misfortune, carried on the old pagan spirit, and won the day with the pagans. The great split had started long before Christ, between the way of pride and power, and the way of mildness and
40 gentleness. Christianity made the breach absolute.

Now on which side of the breach is John of Patmos? First we must
be clear that John of Patmos is not the same man as the Apostle John,
John the beloved disciple, John who wrote the Fourth Gospel. The
Fourth Gospel is perhaps the greatest of Christian documents, and
John the Apostle is one of the great religious spirits of all time. John
of Patmos is quite another man. He is said to have been already an
old man when he was exiled from Ephesus to Patmos by the Roman
magistrates of the city of Ephesus, for some offence against the Roman
State, perhaps refusing to perform the ritual act of worship to the
Emperor. For the date when Revelation is supposed to have been
finished is fairly late, about 96 A.D., after the Christians had been
recognised by Rome as a hostile sect. Again, because of the peculiar
and ungrammatical, "bad" Greek in which Revelation is written, later
critics have decided that John of Patmos did not know much Greek,
that he had probably emigrated quite late in life from Galilee to
Ephesus, that his natural language was Aramaic, but that in a religious
connection he even *thought* in Hebrew. Hence his Revelation is a
mental translation from good old Hebrew into bad Greek. All of which
is very plausible except the bad Greek: which is so peculiar and special
in its form, that one cannot help suspecting that John of Patmos
invented his own lingo for his own highly esoteric work, his Revelation
which was a sheer mystification to anyone who didn't have the key.
So that we absolutely cannot swallow the idea that John of Patmos was
a rustic old Rabbinical Jew who emigrated late from Galilee, and
stammered naïvely in bad Greek, and got himself exiled for some years
to Patmos, for some naïve fault or other. Revelation is a sophisticated
work if ever there was one.*

And is it in the Christian spirit of meekness and gentleness that it
is written? The reader of the Apocalypse can answer for himself. But
since the book begins with the seven famous "messages" to the seven
churches in Asia, and since each message ends with a promise of
reward, if we look at the seven rewards we can roughly judge what
the man who wrote the book wanted. The rewards are:

1. To him that overcometh will I give to eat of the tree of life, which
    is in the midst of the paradise of God.*
2. He that overcometh shall not be hurt by the second death.*
3. To him that overcometh will I give to eat of the hidden manna,
    and will give him a white stone, and in the stone a new name
    written, which no man knoweth saving he that receiveth it.*
4. And he that overcometh, and keepeth my works unto the end,

to him will I give power over the nations: And he shall rule them with a rod of iron; as the vessels of a potter shall they be broken to shivers: even as I received of my Father. And I will give him the Morning Star.*

5. He that overcometh, the same shall be clothed in white raiment, and I will not blot out his name out of the book of life, but I will confess his name before my Father and before his angels.*

6. He that overcometh will I make a pillar in the temple of my God, and he shall go no more out: and I will write upon him the name of my God, and the name of the city of my God, which is new Jerusalem, which cometh down out of heaven from my God: and *I will write upon him* my new name.*

7. To him that overcometh will I grant to sit with me in my throne, even as I also overcame, and am set down with my Father in his throne.—*

This is a mysterious scale of promises which goes very high indeed. For "he that overcometh" shall at last sit in the throne alongside of the Messiah and even of Almighty God, sharing the throne even of the Lord of Hosts. The very thought is enough to make one tremble, and disclaim any such awful ambition. For whatever our conception of Almighty God may be, and even if we cannot form any conception, and are content with a last wild feeling of awe and delight, still the presumption of sharing the eternal throne frightens us and shocks us. I am not and never shall be equal to Almighty God, or able to sit on a throne beside him. My very soul tells me this. My very soul tells me that if the Kosmokrator, the Unknown, at last gives me the kiss of acceptance, that is my happiness.

Jesus himself did not expect to sit on the throne of the Father. The angel of Annunciation promised Mary: "He shall be great, and shall be called the Son of the Highest: and the Lord God shall give unto him the throne of his father David: And he shall reign over the house of Jacob for ever: and of his kingdom there shall be no end.—"*

Or again: "And Jesus said unto them: Verily I say unto you, That ye which have followed me, in the regeneration when the Son of Man shall sit in the throne of his glory, ye also shall sit upon twelve thrones, judging the twelve tribes of Israel".*—And it is David who says: "The Lord said unto my Lord, sit thou on my right hand. Until I make thy foes thy footstool".*—And even this does not seat Jesus upon the throne of the Father, even in David's poetic song. And Paul goes on

plainly to say of Jesus: "God hath made that same Jesus, whom ye
have crucified, both Lord and Christ".*

The seventh promise, to the Church of Laodicea, is quite clear, and
quite definite. Moffatt's translation gives: "The conqueror I will allow
to sit beside me on my throne, as I myself have conquered and sat   5
down beside my Father on his throne".* It is a stupendous, and, we
must feel, non-Christian promise. It is however pagan: for an initiate
might sit down with Dionysos or with Isis, in the full consummation
and glory of initiation. But both Dionysos and Isis, also Mithras and
Attis, they are all mediator gods, who go between heaven and earth;   10
they are not Almighty God himself. It is strange even for a man to *think*
of sitting down beside Almighty God: somehow terrifying.

Now lest there seem an element of sentimentality or falsity in this
feeling, let us ask ourselves again, do we really *believe* in Almighty God,
anyhow? Are not the words cant words, nowadays?   15

From the last far corner of the soul comes the confession: There
is Almighty God.—With the reason, we think: Ah, in the cosmos of
the astronomists, where then is this Almighty God?—But the reason
answers herself: The cosmos brought forth all the world, and brought
forth me. It brought forth my mind, my will, and my soul. Therefore   20
there must be that in the cosmos which can bring forth all things,
including mind and will and feeling. Therefore there must be that in
the cosmos which contains the essence, at least, or the potentiality, of
all things, known and unknown. That in the universe which contains
the potentiality of all things, contains the potency also of thought and 25
act and feeling and will, along with the rest. And this terrific and
frightening and delighted potency I call Almighty God. I think of it,
and am filled with fear—fear of my own crass presumptousness,   and
filled with a sense of delight and liberation. If there is Almighty God,
I care about nothing else. There is Almighty God, and I am delighted,   30
the whole burden of my fear shifts over.

There is Almighty God. The next question, still more serious, is
how to come into living contact.

How did men in the past come into Contact? The way of Jesus is
good, but we want a greater way, a more ample contact. I do not want   35
to be safe in the arms of Jesus. I am not safe in the arms of Jesus,
for my soul cries out to seek Almighty God. And I will seek down any
avenue.

The seven promises to the seven churches ought to be the real clue
to the Apocalypse. But as a matter of fact, taken in detail the work   40

is incomprehensible. Only roughly can we gather what it means. But from the start, it is obvious it cannot be taken at its face meaning. The words are not intended to mean just what they say. They are intended to have a wrapped-up meaning, or perhaps a whole series of wrapped-up meanings: three or four separate meanings wrapped up in the same sentence, like creatures tied up in a cloth. And it is now impossible for us to unfold the cloth and let out all the meanings. Because John of Patmos tied the knots too tight, for one thing, and for another, we feel that the manuscript had been tampered with, messed about, before it became really public.

Anyhow we know from the first chapter that we are reading a book quite different from any other Christian book of the New Testament. In fact, it is difficult to believe that John of Patmos had ever read any of the Gospels or of the Epistles, or even that he knew anything of the canonical life-story of Jesus. The Jesus of Revelation is simply incomprehensible from the Gospel point of view. The Gospels, especially the Fourth, are so very careful to insist

[The MS fragment ends here in mid-sentence]

APPENDIX II
APOCALYPSE, FRAGMENT 2

The tenderness of Paul in some of the Epistles, expressing his tender concern for his distant brothers, and exhorting them above all things to love one another, not to quarrel, and not to *harden*: this brings a new human relationship into the world, a new sort of love. Perhaps Epicurus* had tried for something similar, but there was a touch of resignation in Epicurus, no vivid hope. The Epicureans felt that the gods cared no more about the world of man. The Christians taught that God cared supremely: but that man showed his love of God by loving his fellow-men.

Now the pagans of Jesus' day did not care very much about their fellowmen. The world was full of religion, even religions of dying gods who rose to life and gave new life also to men. But in the mysteries, the initiate gained a new life, a re-birth, a "glory" for himself, and he was supposed to keep it to himself. He must not even tell anybody. The aim of the mysteries, of initiation, was to make a man glorious along with the God, Isis,* Osiris, or Orphic Dionysos, or Mithras:* to make a man glorious, to take him through the symbolic death, and so free him from the terrors of actual death, which would be the "second death" of the initiate: and also, by teaching him to die in the immediate or greedy self, and to rise in a higher or nobler self, thus free him from the chain of "mistakes" which the pagans did not call "sins", as we do.

Thus the pagans were religious, and their religion was also moral: the Stoic* severely so. But there was no very definite sense of sin. And also there was no particular concern about the other person. The Christians transferred some of the Jewish passion of "a Chosen People" into their brotherly love, Christians fell at once into communities and "churches", Christian love was collective, and the duty of every Christian in saving himself was to help save his neighbour. *Every* soul was precious, and so every man should concern himself in saving every soul. The pagans did not think that every soul was precious—far from it—and it was a man's business to save himself alone. His other duties were duties of citizenship, moral duties, not concerned with the soul.

177

The first great split between Christianity and paganism came in here: in the intense feeling of community which Christianity at once inspired in the early "Churches", a new collective oneness, apart from, and even hostile to race or State or local culture. It was partly a transfer of the Jewish feeling of the Chosen People, watched over by God, to peoples who were not Jewish.

The second great difference was the great split which the Christians made with the Cosmos. The Christian saw nothing in the world but the soul of man, the love of Christ, and sin. The sun ceased to matter, or the moon, and harvest and spring-time were of no concern. It was not till after the Dark Ages that the Catholic Church brought back into human life the great rhythm of the seasons, and re-established the great pagan festivals of Christmas, Easter, Midsummer, and the Day of All the Dead,* which set the calendar of the year and the calendar of the soul in harmony again. Then later Christianity reverted in Protestantism, and particularly Puritanism, to the old abstraction which cared for nothing but the soul of man, and sin, and summer and winter were lost, the sacred moments of the equinoxes were forgotten, the great festivals became times of eating only, the cosmic connection was less than a myth.

But in Jesus' day the connection with the cosmos was still strong, in all the old religions, even the Jewish. Jesus came from Galilee, not from Judea. Galilee was an open land of mixed races, subject to every influence. It had none of the shut-in intensity of fanaticism of Jerusalem and Judea, so blackly Jewish. Jesus came from a spiritually free country, probably even a kindly country. The peasants and artizans were perhaps mostly Jews, speaking, presumably Aramaic. And these, of course, focussed in the synagogues, just like the Jews in Europe. But most of the higher workmen and shop-keepers and the property-owning classes of Galilee must have been Greek-speaking, and by race Greek or Asiatic or Egyptian, almost anything. They had their summer villas on the Lake of Galilee, just as rich people have villas on the Italian Lakes. And apparently they lived without friction. Nay, one feels they must even have been friendly, kindly, even as the English or American owners of villas on Lake Como are mostly kindly towards the Italian peasants and fishermen today. Jesus grew up in no unfriendly atmosphere in Galilee. We feel it in all the Gospels. And we feel the change, when he goes into Judea among the Jews. Indeed, his rather beautiful trust of his fellow men in Galilee only makes the Jews of Jerusalem more dangerous to him, later on. It may be that

the rich pagan Greeks of Galilee were Epicurean by tendency, gentle
in manners and indulgent to their inferiors, and that this gentleness
helped to beget Christianity. For it is not words that beget new things,
it is feeling. And without knowing one word of Epicurean doctrine,
Jesus may have been profoundly influenced by Greek Epicureans,   5
merely by contact with their refined gentleness and tolerance, and their
unassuming affectionateness of people of old breeding or culture. It
is old culture that counts, not old breeding. And one cannot help
feeling in Jesus the result of that diffident kindliness which is
characteristic of old and tried culture. But in Jesus, a religious young   10
Jew of the working-class, the diffidence is burned out and the
kindliness kindled to love by religious passion.

The Greek world of Jesus' day was tired. There was too much to
cope with. There had been too much war, too much disaster. And there
was now too much consciousness. Into the Greek-speaking world was   15
gathered the consciousness of every living culture, every extant
religion, whether Hellenic or Egyptian, Chaldean or Persian or Roman
or even, probably, Hindu. The Greeks knew of *all* the religions: as
we do today. They knew of all the cults and philosophies, all the
problems, all the solutions. And it was too much for them. They knew   20
too much, and it paralysed them, dissipated their energy. Jesus
probably spoke some Greek, even if not much. We presume he
naturally spoke Aramaic, a language which spread over the Near East.
He was preserved by his Jewishness and his synagogue from enquiring
after strange gods. Yet he must have been familiar with the pagan   25
temples, temples to Isis, temples to Mithras and Bacchus.* They must
have been part of his landscape, as must the pagans carrying flowers
and sacrifice to the gods, and the open-air ritual of sacrifice. Jesus must
have seen it all, all his life, familiar and not unfriendly. We cannot
feel that he hated it: surely it had its beauty for him too. He was a   30
country boy, not bred up in the narrowness of a city set. In the country
things which are are accepted more naturally. And probably it was
the charm of the small pagan temples in the Galilean countryside
which made him resent so hotly the trafficking in the great temple of
Jerusalem.   35

The temples were there, the pagan worship was in the air. How
should Jesus be insensitive to it! It is only stupid, mechanical people
who are not aware of things felt by others. Jesus may not have known
anything definite about the Mysteries of Mithras, or Isis, or the Orphic
Mysteries. Yet since some of them were practised in his neighbourhood   40

how could [he] be unaware of them, and of their supposed significance?
A great nature like that of Jesus is sensitively *aware*. And who is going
to tell me that he was totally unaware of Dionysos and the Orphic
Mysteries, or the mysteries of Isis or Mithras? for the temples of these
deities must have stood by the Sea of Galilee. Only a stupid nature
is unaware of things that are vital to others. Could I be unaware of
a Catholic procession if I met it in the street, or fail to ask what it was
about?

And in the same way that he must have known something of the
pagan Mysteries, even by breathing them in the air, since he lived in
a pagan province, Jesus must have known also something of the ancient
star-lore, and the ancient symbols. The old, old Chaldeans of the oldest
Babylon began reading the stars, and the Jews very often read with
them, from the earliest days. The stars were in the Jewish consciousness,
despite the fact that the scribes expurgated them so often. You can't
easily make a people unaware of something which it is profoundly
aware of. Even by turning the chief stars into archangels, you don't
escape them entirely.

The stars are very remote to us: thinly scattered in enormous,
enormous space: comparatively, so lonely and few. But that is how we
see them objectively, scientifically. The first way of seeing the stars
was purely subjective.

It seems to me, man has had, as far as we can tell, three great phases
of consciousness, each carrying its own culture. The first was a far-off
phase of purely collective consciousness, when men thought and felt
instinctively *together*, like a great flock of birds or pack of wolves. They
did not think single thoughts or feel single feelings, but their great
thoughts and their great feelings were tribal, felt all at once by a mass
of men, but culminating or focussing in some leader.

This feeling-in-unison is profound and is religious. At its highest,
it is purely religious: taking "religious" to mean the feeling of being
in connection. And at its deepest, the early *unison* consciousness of man
was aware of the cosmos, and aware of the immediate connection
between itself and the vast, potent, terrible cosmos, that lived with all
life. Naked tribal man breast to breast with the naked cosmos, pouring
his consciousness collectively into the cosmos, and in ritual, in naked
superb ritual alone taking from the cosmos life, vitality, potency,
prowess, and power: *pouvoir*, *Macht*, might. The tribe or nation
culminated in one man, the leader or chief, the tip of the great
collective body. And this tip of the tribe touched the very heart of the

cosmos, the core of the sun, and drew down the life of the potent heavens to man, potent yet yearning man.

This was the condition of pre-historic, or shadow-historic civilised man. It was the civilisation of the tumulus and the pyramid, pyramidical to symbolise the broad basis of the people culminating in the living tip of the leader or hero. It was a culture absolutely religious, for *all* was religious, every act was performed in connection with the great cosmos, and at the same time, there were no gods. Man, tribal or collective man was nakedly breast to breast with the cosmos, and the need for God had not arisen in the human soul.

It did not arise till man felt himself cut off from the cosmos, till he became aware of himself apart, as an apart, fragmentary, unfinished thing. This is the Fall, the fall into knowledge, or self-awareness, the fall into tragedy and into "sin". For a man's sex is his fragmentariness. The phallos is the point at which man is broken off from his context, and at which he can be re-joined. In his awareness of sex, which is awareness of separateness and fragmentariness, lies man's sense of shame and sin.

How man came to be cut off in consciousness from the cosmos we do not know. But we can see that it is the same thing as knowledge: knowledge is only possible in a separation of subject and object. We can also see that it is tragedy. And we can see that it may be called "sin", since it is a "fall" from unison or at-oneness.

We can also see that it makes a God, or gods necessary to the consciousness. There must be an intermediary between man and the "lost" cosmos. There must be an intermediary consciousness which understands both sides, both the great, creative, incomprehensible cosmos and the soul of man. In short, the cosmos must have a great man in it—a soul, or God.

Then follows the great history of the gods, the overthrow of Ouranos the Demiurge or Creator by Kronos the Kosmokrator, then the overthrow of the Kosmokrator or Ruler of the Cosmos by Zeus the Thunderer or Father who speaks to his children. And finally, the potential overthrow, or at least supplementing of Zeus by Dionysos, semi-substitution of Jesus for the Father, the Spirit for the Almighty.*

This is the history of man's repeated "falls" in self-consciousness: from Creator to Ruler, from Ruler to Father, from Father to Son, and from Son or Spirit to mind alone, godless once more. The last state is the same as the first, godless. But now, instead of being naked vital man breast to breast with the vital cosmos, it is naked, disembodied

mind losing itself in a naked and disembodied universe, a strange Nirvana.* This is the final condition of science, of modern physics and modern physicists. Really to "understand" the last theories in physics needs a mystic *experience* like that of the ecstatic saints, or like that
5 of Nirvana, or the state of *samadhi** in Brahmin saints, or the ecstatic state of an Orphic initiate.

These are the three states of man,* cosmic-religious, god-religious, and philosophic-scientific. Jesus was the last manifestation of the god-religious state. We are at the end of the philosophic state. What
10 next? We don't know.

The tribes that exist as tribes on earth today are only degenerate fragments of the great old cosmic-religious humanity. So also were the cave-men; degenerate fragments, left isolated by some geological cataclysm. These are not the human beginnings at all, but fag ends
15 of a previous human greatness.

Similarly the pagan religions of Jesus' day were the vast decadence of the Zeus or Father stage of religion, mingled with strange echoes of all the other past, the Kosmokrator, the Creator, and even the naked Cosmos.

20 Now when man first "fell" into knowledge or self-consciousness, I believe the first thing he did was to lie down and gaze at the stars.* Then he felt himself back in his old oneness: he was again at one with the mighty and living cosmos. But alas, now he was doomed to view it objectively.

25 So I believe the stars are the very oldest religion. And I believe the oldest of all old historical civilisations, the great River civilisations of the Euphrates, the Nile, the Indus were all primarily "star" civilisations, cosmic in the astronomical sense.

This star-cult never died. It outlived all the gods, and lingers even
30 today. In Jesus' day it was immeasurably degraded and mixed up with horoscopy and witch-craft. But it was star-cult still, the heavens were still terrific and marvellous, the planets were still tremendously potent Rulers.

And did Jesus know absolutely nothing of star-cult? Impossible. To
35 an imaginative, vivid nature, impossible. The Jews had been shifted twice into Babylonia.* They had learned all they could of Chaldean star-lore. The Jewish priests, scribes, lawyers who fixed the law of Moses in the Pentateuch,* about 400 B.C. apparently, they no doubt suppressed all the star-lore they could from the Scriptures. Later
40 scribes, editing later books, from Isaiah and Ezekiel down to Daniel

no doubt suppressed still more. But enough remains to take us
continually to the ancient Babylon, long before Belshazzar's.* And the
"wheels" of Ezekiel* are surely Anaximander's wheels. They are very
much botched, but there they are surely Anaximander's wheels. Now
Anaximander was an Ionian Hellene or Greek born just before the year   5
600 B.C.* He is one of the most shadowy fathers of science, but his
wheels of the heavens are stupendous, and fascinating to this day. And
Ezekiel, or Ezekiel's transcriber has got them all mixed up with the
vision of the Almighty, which the Prophet saw at the beginning of his
prophetic days.   10
     Now Anaximander is supposed to have invented the wheels, but
surely the Chaldeans, the Babylonians invented them, after thousands
of starry years, against Ionian decades. Modern science hates to go one
step beyond the Greeks: but it seems to me that Chaldea taught Ionia
before Ionia could stammer in Greek. Why be afraid of the great   15
ancient pre-Greek world! It goes deeper and deeper into time.
     The Jews always had a lot of star-lore up their sleeve—lots of pagan
lore, really. The savage old orthodox priests of the Jerusalem temple
fixed the law, and suppressed stars and strange gods, but throughout
the centuries Jews have thought and dreamed outside the Mosaic law.   20
     Jesus was such a dreamer: but the early Christian fathers were good
suppressers. Already the apostles Paul and John had realised that
Christianity must be a cult to itself—they were Jews—; and they were
both educated in pagan lore, so they knew how to suppress all they
wished to suppress. Paul was not only a Jew, he came from a city   25
of Stoics* and was a good deal a Stoic, and ancient Puritan. The
Apostle John reads strangely like a chastened pagan. It is obvious that
both he and St. Paul know the Orphic Mysteries—or at least, a good
deal about them. Both men knew by instinct what they wanted to
suppress from the new religion. And this was: first, star-lore, for   30
star-lore had become a burden, a superstition of horoscopy and "fate";
then, blood-rites, for these had become tangled up with magic; then,
the peculiar apotheosis of the individual* which was the glory of the
pagan initiate; then, the cult of "powers", for the pagan initiates were
supposed to acquire all sorts of powers; then, the cult of vision and   35
prophecy, which tended to break up a brotherhood; and finally, all the
pagan symbolism possible, for it tended to set men on the old paths.
     The early fathers, from the Apostles downwards, tended to suppress
all these things. Yet in the second century A.D., having cast out the
old pagan and starry devil bit by bit, they let him in whole again at   40

the very last minute, and there he is, the old demon, sitting at the very end of the Bible, in the Apocalypse. But then the door was slammed, and the work of destruction went on wholesale. The Christians destroyed all pagan evidence, and the destruction was carried on even
5   to our day. Fifty years ago, in remote Catholic villages, or Puritan villages, every strange-seeming book or manuscript was carried to the parish priest or clergyman, and if he smelled anything that wasn't Christian, he promptly burned it. Nineteen hundred years of burning! Almost everything is lost, and we have to go by hints.
10   The Apocalypse was almost lost. The eastern Fathers,* in Antioch and Byzantium and Alexandria, they fought hard to exclude Revelation from the Bible. Naturally! for in those old countries they knew what it was about. But the more barbarous Latin Fathers of Italy and Africa wanted it included, first, because it was supposed to have been written
15   by the great Apostle John, second because it was such a good hammer against the Roman Empire, identified with Babylon. Well, it turned out just as good a hammer against the Roman Church, and it turned out that John of Patmos was not the Apostle John at all, but quite another man.
20   There were three Johns: John the Baptist, who had really a great following with curious doctrines lasting long after Jesus' day;* then John the Apostle, who wrote the Fourth Gospel and some Epistles: then John of Patmos, called the Divine.
         John of Patmos is supposed to have been already an old man, when
25   he composed his Revelation on the island of Patmos. There had been other Jewish apocalypses before his: even the later part of the Book of Daniel is an apocalypse. An apocalypse is a revelation of what lies beyond this world: really, it is a journey into heaven. John's Revelation is obviously this.
30   The work is written in curious, ungrammatical, almost enigmatical Greek.* Modern critics have supposed that John of Patmos, like Jesus, was a native of Galilee: that he emigrated late in life to Ephesus: that he gave offence to the Roman government in Ephesus owing to some religious difference, and that he was exiled to Patmos for a term of
35   years, returning, however, at last to Ephesus, and living, according to tradition, to a great old age.
         But there seems no reason at all for supposing that John came from Galilee, or that he was rustic and unlettered, arriving from the country in the city of Greeks when he was already old. The writer of Revelation
40   was no naïve spirit from the rural countryside. He was a Jew of Jews,

and surely a city Jew who had spent most of his years in reading "religion" and discussing it. Surely he was one of those Jews of the Dispersion* who remained intensely Jewish, but who none the less interested himself in the cults of the pagans: a sort of new Jew fascinated by the mysteries and the symbolic ritual and perhaps, more remotely, by the many forms of sorcery extant in the pagan world of Ephesus. There is a touch of the sorcerer about him, and his mind is, perhaps, partly the mind of the conjuror.

One thing is certain: he is very little of a true Christian. He had almost none of the new spirit of "loving his fellow-man in Christ", which was the clue to the other, greater John the Apostle, and to St. Paul. Neither is he a "prophet" as Jesus was. He is that new thing, a "seer" who sees terrific and occult visions, and his processes are the processes of magic and of occult science.

It may be this Apocalypse is older than the date usually assigned to it from internal evidence: viz. 96 A.D. It certainly is much older in spirit and design: though that is no test of date. One cannot help feeling, after reading the work several times, that it is not Christian at all: which means, that its author knew nothing of the Gospels or the great Epistles, nor of the Apostles, but that merely the *name* of Jesus is put in, in place of the old word Messiah.* The work is certainly Messianic: but the Messiah is that strange semi-magical figure of Jewish imagination, a terrific magical apparition that should turn the world inside out. The Messiah is never for a moment the "gentle Jesus". There seems to be even no inkling of such a Jesus. Time after time appears the terrific vision of the Son of Man, and the Son of Man is always a slightly monstrous marvel-apparition which is the same as that of the Almighty and very like that of the pagan Time Spirit and Demiurge and Kosmokrator.* But it has nothing whatsoever to do with the Jesus of the Gospels. Neither has the Lamb that shall save the world. The Lamb is entirely esoteric, and Jewish-pagan. And, if we must admit it, a trifle ridiculous.

It is possible that the accepted date of 96 A.D. is correct, for the finishing of the Apocalypse. It is also possible that the destruction of the Temple referred to may be the second destruction, by Herod Antipas,* and not the Third, by Titus; and that therefore the Apocalypse may be considerably earlier, say even 50 A.D., and previous to the Gospels and the Epistles. It may be, the Apostles knew the Apocalypse, before the Gospels were written. And if they did, it would certainly point them a road to be avoided at all costs.

We must believe that St. John the Apostle and St. Paul, both of
them Greeks by culture, had not only a sure *instinct* what to avoid in
current religion, but also a highly educated philosophical knowledge
of what was dangerous. Brought up as they were in the welter of
5 religions, beset by the innumerable semi-magical cults and sects, they
did as men must do who want fresh air for the soul, they set their faces
against magical cult and esoteric cult, absolutely. St. John did indeed
leave the miracles: but there was no magical practice connected with
them. The idea is that pure belief will heal. And he even introduced
10 the story of the wine at the marriage at Cana,* and this is very
suggestive of Orphic ritual. But he wanted, no doubt, to establish *at
the very first* that Jesus *had* the miracle-working powers, that they were
part of the divine nature: and then to proceed to the new doctrine:
where Jesus says: I have not taught in secret; what I have taught, I
15 have taught openly—*

For the rest, there is an astonishing absence of any suggestion of
magic, of transformation or transmigration,* and of star-influence, in
the New Testament, and this must be because St. Paul especially, being
of stoical education, set his face against such things. We cannot help
20 feeling that by the time the Gospels had achieved their present form,
all the loose ends of paganism possible had been removed from them
by Christian teachers who knew well what they were doing.

And we cannot help feeling that the same happened, more ineffec-
tually, to the Apocalypse. St. Paul would surely have suppressed the
25 book. But it appealed, and appeals today powerfully to the lower strata
of religious imagination, bordering on sorcery and magic. The early
Christians could not forego it. So that what happened, probably, is
that his unknown "editor"* of whom the critics complain was not an
editor at all, but that for years the manuscripts of the Apocalypse were
30 expurgated and amended, bit by bit, to remove the more glaring
paganisms and to substitute a more Christian note. The seven letters
to the seven churches have surely been cooked up in this way, till they
are almost meaningless. The seven rewards may be more or less
original: they suggest a certain scheme of rewards attending on the
35 conquest of the seven natures of man by the "spirit": but even they
are confused. There has been deliberate confusion made in the
Apocalypse, no doubt by Christian scribes and teachers up to the year
150 A.D. or thereabouts, and for the definite purpose of covering up
the pagan trail in the book. And when finally one manuscript was
40 chosen by the Fathers as authoritative, it would be one in which the

original thread was sufficiently broken and tangled to make the scheme
irrecoverable. Since the scheme is no longer there, it is no longer to
be recovered entire.

But at least sections of the Apocalypse seem to be intact. Myself,
I feel the whole work as John of Patmos left it was probably quite 5
complete; but afterwards, it had to be watered down, and doctored
up, to make it fit the Christian scheme. And the greatest havoc was
played at the beginning and at the end of the book: the middle fared
rather better.

Even as it is, anyone who is at all acquainted with the old use of 10
symbols must feel at once that here we have an esoteric work, a secret
"plan" of regeneration: really, the description of the processes of
initiation into a higher form of life, through the way of mystic death,
the journey through the underworld or Hades, the re-emergence of
the spirit into the new light of a higher world, or heaven, then the 15
re-birth of the body (perhaps as a babe) and then the "re-birth" of
the spirit through fusion with the Saviour, and finally, the re-marriage
of the new body with the new spirit in the deathless glory of the gods:
or heaven.*

Orthodox critics have a very ingenious interpretation of the scheme 20
of Revelation. They look on the book as "prophecy", following the
rather feeble historical-prophecy method of the latter part of the Book
of Daniel. The Apocalypse is supposed to be the prophecy of what
will happen to the Church of Christ. First, there is the early Church
under Roman persecution: persecution increases and increases till the 25
blood of the martyrs is *all* shed, and the Church is *destroyed*: this may
be under the Romans, or, if you are a modern Protestant, the Church
of Christ is now *almost* destroyed by the Babylon of Mammon,
commerce, luxury etc., after a run of two thousand years. When the
blood of all the martyrs is shed, then Christ will appear again, and 30
destroy the world, kings, emperors and all. After that, follows the
millennium, when the saints and the martyrs are resurrected and, from
their numerous thrones, actually govern the earth: emperors, kings and
princes are no more, but the saints rule, and do not allow commerce
or any woe. This goes on marvellously for a thousand years, and then 35
all is over. The world is finished. Souls are summoned from paradise,
earth and hell, to be judged. This is the Last Judgment, and the Second
Death of the wicked. But the righteous do not suffer the Second Death
at the Last Judgment. They rise to the new jewel-city of Jerusalem.

This interpretation is as good as one can get, taking the point of 40

view of the Church, and taking the book as it stands. But the book
seems hopelessly messed up at the end, and also at the beginning. And
the "Church" interpretation leaves a good deal of the middle of the
work meaningless.

5   We have to admit that while John of Patmos did no doubt have a
Church in mind, a "body" of Christian men: he was too much a Jew
of the Chosen People to escape the collective idea: at the same time
he had the idea of the individual redemption or regeneration of the
body and spirit perhaps even more deeply in mind. The Apocalypse
10   equates rather better to the individual than to the Church. The
individual dies the mystic death. Now this is not done in a moment.
It is a process of seven stages. Man has seven "natures", seven
"levels" of being, seven dynamic centres of consciousness. These
centres are conquered one by one, by the higher consciousness or spirit.
15   It is like seven "stages of the Cross".* Man conquers his "nature"
in seven stages, by seven great degrees.

This *conquest* of the natural man is in the reverse of the *growth* of
the natural man. Man grows up stage by stage, from babe to child,
from child to adolescent, from adolescence to manhood, from manhood
20   to husband, from husband to fatherhood, from fatherhood or ruler of
the household, to mature authority in the clan or State. This is a mere
shallow instance of the seven stages of man's development, and his
seven levels of consciousness.

When he starts the great self-conquest which constitutes the mystic
25   death, he travels in the reverse direction of life and growth: that is,
he goes counter-sunwise, widdershins. He conquers himself first as an
elder, or magistrate, an authority in the world, then as a father or ruler
of young life, then as a bridegroom or sexual being, then as an
adolescent, with the adolescent curiosity and egoism, then as a boy,
30   with a child's calm assurance of self, and finally as a babe, or
physical-functioning entity. He conquers his nature stage by stage, in
the reverse direction of growth. At each stage there is a death. At the
seventh stage, or it may be the *sixth*, there is a final death; and then
follows a liberation of some sort, a re-emergence of the true ego, the
35   irreducible witness, and then a process of re-birth and a marriage.

In the old psychology, man considered himself really as a dual entity,
a creature of soul and spirit, anima and animus,* blood and "water".
The body was a third thing, caused by the fusing of the blood and
the "water", the anima and animus, the soul and spirit: and so, as
40   the soul and spirit separate, the body disappears. In the "trinity" of

a human entity, it is the body itself which is the "ghost", being merely
the manifestation of the "marriage" of the great "two", the blood and
water, the moist and the dry, the soul and the spirit.

Hence a full Mystery would contain a dual death: of soul and spirit.
But since soul was really conceived of as being the blood itself, we tend   5
easily to say, the death is of the body and the spirit, and the resurrection
is of the body and the spirit. Whereas truly, the death is of the soul
and spirit, and on consummation of this death, the body (the world)
dissolves: and the resurrection is of the soul and spirit, and when these
two rise and fuse again, new, the new body descends upon them—the   10
new Jerusalem. The new Jerusalem, esoterically, is the new body of
a re-born man. It is also the new body of the community, the Church
of Christ, the Bride.

This may seem all nonsense to modern minds. But it is the honest
and passionate attempt of man to understand his own mysterious and   15
complex nature, and I must say, it seems to me even now more
satisfactory, more *dynamic* than our so-called science of psychology.
Of course I don't mean to say that as I put it, crude and bald, it is
very significant. But if we really try to grasp the pagan symbolic
psychology, in its great range and its great depth of understanding—   20
symbolic understanding—it does make our modern conception of the
human being look small and trashy. And we really *are* smaller and
sillier, as understanding emotional beings, than the pagans were. We
are cleverer mentally. But physically, emotionally, vitally we are
smaller and sillier than the intelligent pagans of St. John's day.   25

Besides, if we take the very earliest "scientists", we do not jeer at
them for saying the very things the old religions say. "Water is the
material cause of all things", says Thales,* and modern scientists
refrain from jeering. But it needs a close study of the pagan conception
of the universe in the sixth century B.C. to know what was really meant   30
by water.* And at the same time the scientists hate it when Thales
is supposed to have said: All things are full of gods.*—They consider
he never would have said it. Yet it seems exactly the thing a
"scientific" mind might have said at the end of the seventh century,
and leads us in to a profoundly interesting and revealing study of what   35
Thales can have meant by "gods".* Anaximander taught that all
things come into being owing to the "strife" of opposites, the moist
and the dry, the cold and the wet. *As soon as there is creation, there
is duality.* This appears to be one of the very oldest and deepest notions,
of religion and science alike. The third thing is the Boundless, the   40

Infinite, which is increate. The great wheels of the heavens, of
Anaximander, are great rings of fire enclosed in dark envelopes of air
(or cloud): the whole universe is made up of these two, the hot and
the cold, the moist and the dry. And these elements, in the body, are
blood and water, soul and spirit. And the body, the third thing, is an
apparition from the boundless, the infinite. "All things are earth and
water, that come into being and grow", says Xenophanes.* "All things
are an exchange for Fire", says Herakleitos.* And again: "Fire lives
the death of air, and air lives the death of fire".*

All this "impious pagan duality" was taken over by philosophy from
religion. In fact all the oldest ideas were taken over from religion. Then
they were pulled to pieces, or unravelled, by philosophy, and science
began.

But man has two ways of knowing the universe: religious and
scientific. The religious way of knowledge means that we accept our
sense-impressions, our perceptions, in the full sense of the word,
complete, and we tend instinctively to link them up with other
impressions, working towards a whole. The process is a process of
association, linking up, binding back (religio) or referring back towards
a centre and a wholeness. This is the way of poetic and religious
consciousness, the instinctive act of synthesis. "O my love is like a red
red rose"* is an act of synthesis and fusing of the love and the red
rose, a movement towards a unison through poetic association. This
is a religious act, a binding back (religio) or connection, but it is
spontaneous. In definite religion the perceptions are referred back
consciously till they reach the clue which holds all things together,
God.—"Lord, thou hast been our dwelling place in all generations—".* There we have ourselves and our generations and our
dwelling-place all suddenly fused in the Lord. It is poetry, but it is
specific, religious poetry. All poetry is religious in its *movement*, let its
teaching be what it may. And we can just as safely say, that no religion
is truly religious, a binding back and a connection into a wholeness,
unless it is poetic, for poetry is in itself the movement of vivid
association which is the movement of religion. The only difference
between poetry and religion is that the one has a specific goal or centre
to which all things are to be related, namely God; whereas poetry does
the magical linking-up without any specific goal or end. Sufficient that
the new relations spring up, as it were, that the new connections are
made.

Science is only the contrary method, the opposite working of the consciousness. Yet how strange the contraries are. The scientific instinct breaks up or analyses the direct impression: that is the first step: and then logical reason enters, and makes inferences. Religion starts from impressions accepted whole and referred back to other impressions. Science starts from questioning an impression, and comparing it, *contrasting* it with another impression.

At dawn we see the sun, red and slow, emerge over the horizon and beginning to sparkle: religion and poetry at once say: like a bridegroom coming forth from his chamber:* or like the gold lion from his lair: something similar. But the scientific spirit says: What *is* the shining thing? Does it really rise up from behind the hill every day?—and if so, how does it get back behind the hill, in order to be ready for the next dawn? How does it *work?*—

There we see the two processes of the human consciousness. Whenever I see the sun going down, I shall say to myself: The sun is leaving us: he is looking back at us and departing: he is setting over the edge of the world, taking his way into another place.—That is the inevitable feeling of every man who looks at the sun setting, be he the greatest scientist living. And it will be the feeling of every man, while men remain men. It is our *immediate* awareness of sunset. To remove or "correct" this awareness, we have deliberately to change our state of mind, and say: No, the sun is not sinking. It is the earth which is turning round and cutting with her sharp edge, called the horizon, over the face of the really motionless planet, the sun.—There we have our second or cognitive awareness of sunset: and we believe the second awareness to be the "truth".

But it is obvious there are two forms of truth. To our senses, the red sun slowly sinks like a drowning thing. This is the truth, and perhaps the more vital truth, since it is our everyday *experience*. On the other hand, we know by a long, long chain of inference that sunset is caused by the earth's diurnal rotation on her axis. This is the other truth, the truth of explanations. To obtain the realisation of this second truth we have to cut off our sense-impressions of sunset. But also, in our sense-impression of sunset, we have to forget other sense-impressions, other phenomena, which somehow contradict this "sinking like a drowning thing" impression.

There we are, with two sets of truth, because we have two ways of consciousness. Nothing on earth will prevent us from *feeling*, and from knowing by feeling, that the sun at evening sinks down like a drowning thing. And nothing on earth will now alter our knowledge, our

knowledge by inference, that the sun does not sink at all, but that the
earth turns her back on him. At least, I suppose nothing will ever alter
this "fact".

   So there we are, dual in consciousness. And as in this matter of
5   sunset, one stream of consciousness excludes the other. When I see
the sun sink I *can't* see him stand still while the earth spins round to
hide me from him. It can't be done. When I *know* that the earth spins
round at sunset and carries me away from the motionless sun, it is
impossible for me to *see* the sunset: my senses are abstracted, and must
10   be. If they weren't, I should see a red sun slowly merging down behind
the world's horizon, taking his way to other skies. Contradictions!

   The impious duality of the pagans returns full upon us, when we
realise how dual is our consciousness itself. Man is a creature of dual
consciousness. It is his glory and his pain. Because though the two
15   streams of consciousness can never be identified with one another,
though we are divided between them, very often torn between them,
still we are whole and integral beings in which the two streams can
be harmonised and reconciled, each being left to its own full flowing.
There *need* be no war-fare. Why should I not have two entirely
20   different sunset-conceptions, or two ways of sunset-knowledge, since
both are natural to me?

   If we can accept the *unquestioning* way of consciousness, the way of
direct impression, which proceeds from affirmation to affirmation, we
shall be much better able to understand the older form of the pagan
25   consciousness. Long before Christ, the questioning method of consciousness had arisen, in India and in Ionia particularly. But everywhere
it had to struggle against the older form of consciousness, to which
the "question" was obnoxious, or even impious, when applied to vital
things or concepts. It was impious to question the gods. The feeling
30   lasts to this day, and will always last, since the primitive consciousness,
shall we say the primal way of consciousness in man is the unquestioning
way of affirmation, and movement from affirmation to affirmation by
way of image. Even the scientists of the last century *saw* all their
science, built up their systems of images in answer to the scientific
35   questions. Lord Kelvin* couldn't grasp anything unless he could make
an image of it: a model, he said. And Darwin* *saw* his evolution
theories, like a seer, in successive images. The images came in answer
to his questions, but images they were, none the less, built up from
bones and fossils. Even our very view of the cosmos, the earth going
40   round the sun and the planets obeying their own laws of motion, even

this is only a mental image re-constructed from our visual image of the heavens. It is a composite photograph instead of a direct photograph.

But today, science, even the science of physics, is said to have moved beyond the image, the atom is now imageless and utterly unimaginable. Therefore, to most minds, to mine certainly, it has turned into nothingness. The modern atom is to my mind a desperate nothingness, and science has really ceased to be. I give it up. The physicists today seem to me to be in a state of mind of supreme *contemplation*, they have gazed upon the atom, like a Buddhist on the navel, till they are translated into a state comparable to Nirvana or Samadhi,* or the mystic ecstasy of the initiate, and there we must leave them.

So that whether we follow the way of affirmation or the way of question, we proceed from image to image. The motion is the only thing that is different: the mind can only come to rest upon an image. But in the way of affirmation, image adds itself to image in a humming unison like a swarm of bees, till at last the individual consciousness consummates itself, the swarm is completed upon the clue, the God-idea, the humming unison of the consciousness rises to a pitch where it transcends, and the whole consciousness swoops into a pure state of conscious awareness which is at the same time like a swoon of pure oblivion, and the crisis of the religious consciousness is reached. Even a great poem brings the same supreme state of at-oneness, in its own degree.

But the process of question, the process of philosophy and science, even exact science like physics, at last reaches the same state, or a state exactly comparable. Anyone who knows the condition of supreme religious consciousness knows that the true modern physicist and mathematician—it is now the same—is in a precisely similar state of mind or soul, or has passed through such a state, and builds his science on a description of this state: imageless, unimaginable. Both the religious and the scientific states of mind are at last imageless and unimaginable, to be known only by transcription: and modern physics are an attempt to transcribe such a state.

Both ways end in the same place, the absolute somewhere or the absolute nowhere. But the method of approach is different. There is the method of association and unison, and the method of contrast and distinction. The whole way of spiritual, rational, and mental consciousness is a way of contrast. The Son of God is himself a question directed against the Father, and a complement in opposition.

The point of all this is that there need be no quarrel between our two ways of consciousness. There *is* a quarrel, there always has been, perhaps there always will be, since human nature is *ab ovo** quarrelsome. But there need not be.

5   So let us leave the way of question, and try to take again the older way of affirmation. We shall find that our mind now definitely moves in images, from image to image, and no longer is there a logical process, but a curious flitting motion from image to image according to some power of attraction, some *sensuous* association between images.

APPENDIX III
APOCALYPSIS II

probably began the Psalm: Ah, why is there such antagonism to
God?—He would have said almost all in those few words. But he would
at the same time have lost almost all the emotional reactions. So there
we are.

The language of the remote ancients—and not so very remote,
either—is to me incomprehensible, or nearly so, even when it is
translated into our own speech. The Psalms are really antipathetic to
the modern mind, because the modern mind is so abstracted and
logical, it cannot bear the non-logical imagery of the Hebrew hymns,
the sort of confusion, the never going straight ahead. But there *was*
no straight ahead to the ancient mind. An image, an emotional
conception completed itself, then gave place to another, and sometimes
even the emotional sequence is puzzling, because the images started
different trains of feeling then, from those they start now.

We can understand the terrific delight of the early Greeks when they
really found out how to think, when they got away from the concrete
and invented the abstract, when they got away from the object itself
and discovered laws and principles. A number was once *actually* a row
of pebbles. There was no *seven*, only seven pebbles or counters. To
the early Pythagoreans three was a perfect number, because when you
divided it, it left a central guardian, with one number on either hand:
a perfect balance. Whereas four—the even numbers were imperfect,
because when you divided them it left a gap in the middle. This, we
see, is just three pebbles in a row, or four pebbles in a row. And
arithmetic sprang into being when Pythagoras—or whoever it was—
thought of arranging the pebbles in squares and in triangles, instead
of in rows, long rows. An arrangement of pebbles in squares immediately gave the idea of multiplication, and the arrangement of a
triangle on a base of four gave the dekad, the ten: made up of
$1+2+3+4$: and this became the number that was called the
"natural" number.* "All the Hellenes and barbarians count up to ten,
by nature, and then begin again".*

Pythagoras lived in the fifth century B.C.—and until his day,

apparently, arithmetic slumbered in the bosom of the eternal. The
delight men took in discovering actual number, the laws of number,
and so escaping from the inevitable pebbles, was intense. It was so all
through the field of consciousness. The enormous and tyrannous
5   heavens of stars and Rulers were now examined objectively, to see how
they *were governed* instead of how they ruled. Till now, till about
600 B.C., when the *real* change in the direction of man's consciousness
definitely set in, the cosmos had consisted of Powers and Rulers. Now,
it was to be proved subordinate and subject in itself to a greater rule.
10   There was a new wild instinct on earth: to prove that all the great
Rulers were subject to One Rule. The rule of kings was over, in the
consciousness of man. The immediate connection with the cosmos was
broken. Man and the cosmos came out of touch, they became, in a
sense, enemies. Man set himself to *find out* the cosmos, and at last to
15   dominate it. Henceforth the grand idea was no longer the living sway
of the cosmos over man, through the rule of kings. Henceforth it was
the dominion of man over the cosmos, through the collective effort of
Mind. Men must love one another, so that collectively Man could
conquer the cosmos. And the conqueror was Mind. And Mind was
20   One and indivisible.

This terrific *volte face* of the human consciousness had a dual effect
on man himself. It thrilled him with the highest happiness, or bliss,
the sense of escape from the cosmos and from the body, which is part
of the cosmos, into Mind, immortal Mind. And at the same time, it
25   filled him with a great ennui and a great despair, as he felt death inside
himself, the death of the body. Plato, who thrills with the greatest thrill
of all, perhaps, is ultimately filled with a great pessimism. The thrill
of the discovery of the laws of mind, the laws of thought, logic,
grammar, made men wild with intoxicated delight. Socrates, in Plato,
30   is simply drunk with the triumph of being able to reason. Drunk! In
some of the dialogues we see Socrates disgustingly false and tricky,
tricking his opponent with arguments palpably specious and puerile,
so that we wonder the opponent swallowed such stuff. Then we
remember that argument, real dialectic was such a new thing on the
35   face of the earth, that when the purest nonsense was arrived at logically,
or with apparent logic, it was mutely accepted. A great deal of the
argumentative side of early Greek philosophy—and later—results in
pure nonsense.* But it was mental, *rational* nonsense, so it was found
acceptable. Irrational truths became nonsensical, and rational nonsense
40   became truth. So it was in the field of pure philosophy, *human*

philosophy. Even Plato's *Ideas* are really rationalised nonsense. But they are still accepted, under the convention of: Reason at any price, the Ideal, cost what it may!

It is obvious to us now that Reason is only a function, like any other, and the Idea, even the Platonic Idea, argue as we will, is only an abstraction from direct sensual experience. However brilliant the conclusion drawn from certain premisses, the premiss itself is drawn from an experience of the senses. All our consciousness starts with sensual experience, call them perceptions or what you will, and ends with abstractions from this experience, conceptions or ideas or whatever we like.

Everything is based on sense-experience; in our consciousness, the atom, the electron itself is experienced, perceived or felt by the senses, or it is nothing at all. Spirit, as far as it is *experience*, is only a more subtle form of sense-experience. And even God, as far as he is real, is our experience of the senses. The whole great basis of our consciousness is sensual, and this field of consciousness is immense, illimitable. But man sets limits to his sensual consciousness, and then he atrophies and dies.

There is the sensual consciousness, enormous and potent: and then there is Mind. Mind is the function of abstraction from sensual experience, and in abstraction it established another world of reality for man. If we make a square of pebbles, with four pebbles on each side, it contains sixteen pebbles. It will always be so, forever: and the same whether it is pebbles or people or houses. $4 \times 4 = 16$. Now then, which is reality—the square of pebbles, or the eternal law that the square of four is sixteen? Which is the real eternal, the sixteen pebbles lying on the ground in a square, or the immutable law or idea, $4 \times 4 = 16$? Wherein do you see God, in the sixteen pebbles on the floor, or in the intangible truth, $4 \times 4 = 16$? Which "rules", the law, or the substantial object?

The answer is, of course, that neither rules. The "laws" don't "govern" the universe. The "laws" of the universe are only the more subtle properties of "things". It is a law of pebbles, that $4 \times 4 = 16$. It is also a law of houses and men, $4 \times 4 = 16$. Indeed it is a law of all things. For all things it is true, $4 \times 4 = 16$. The law is without exception. There is no exception to the rule. The rule rules all things, for $4 \times 4 = 16$ yesterday and today and forever. This then is the eternal Ruler. Such are the immutable, eternal and unanswerable Rulers of the universe: such Laws. And since they are things of the mind, they must proceed from a great Mind. Hence the one eternal and infinite Ruler of the universe is a supreme Mind, and the Supreme Mind rules by uttering eternal Ideas, or Laws. This is the Logos, and the Platonic Idea, and the modern conception of God. To this supreme Mind the body must submit, even unto death. And this is Jesus. For the body that is sacrificed to Mind will rise up a new body, to a new life. When Mind triumphs, then sin and sorrow, confusion and strife will pass away. Or when the Spirit triumphs: Spirit being the great impulse of yielding to Mind, the Spirit of self-sacrifice and rising beyond the body: then all men will be good, and heaven will be on earth.

Plato believed that the only happiness for man was the rule of Mind over the body. That is, he believed in a philosopher-king, one of the old tyrants—in the Greek sense—governed and swayed by reason, by philosophy, by the eternal Mind. The king governing, but himself governed by Mind: this would produce a perfect state. Well, Plato was adviser to a king, a tyrant, and it was a terrible fiasco.* Mind ruling over a king didn't seem to work. In fact, during history, the kings that have been ruled by mind, either their own or somebody else's have usually made the greatest mess: or left the greatest mess behind. The necessary quality in a king seems to be character, of which Mind forms only a part.

So, kingdoms ruled by Mind are nearly as unhappy as kingdoms ruled without mind. So—it is kingdoms that are wrong, and rule which is the mistake. Let there be no kings, no rulers, and no rule, but let every man be governed from within by the Spirit. Now spirit, we know, is the will to submit, to sacrifice the self to Mind, or to Law, or to the other person. The Mind says that Sweet Reason shall rule, and the body cries its glad assent. And this is Shelley. All physical kings and rulers are evil. There shall be no rule, but the rule of "love"—which means submission, submission to the sweet reason of the spirit.

The process is one long process: the destruction of the last vestige of the rule of kings, the destruction of all the great Rulers from the consciousness of man, the separation of man from the cosmos, from the old cosmic sway, and finally, the reversal of the Rule of the ages: the rule of Man, collectively, over the cosmos, the rule of Mind over Matter, the rule of the Son of Man, which is of course the spirit or mind of man, over all the world. This is to bring the grand Millennium.

We are very near this Millennium. The ancient rule of kings has fizzled down to almost nothing. There are no ruling men: men are collected in masses, and the masses occasionally come into collision.

The triumph of Mind over the cosmos progresses in small spasms: aeroplanes, radio, motor-traffic. It is high time for the Millennium.

And alas, everything has gone wrong. The destruction of the world seems not very far off, but the happiness of mankind has never been so remote.

Man has made an enormous mistake. Mind is not a Ruler, mind is only an instrument. The natural laws don't "govern", they are only, to put it briefly, the more general properties of Matter. It is just a general property of Matter that it occupies space. $4 \times 4 = 16$ is not "reality": that is to say, it has no existence in itself. It is merely a permanent property of all things, which the mind recognises as permanent: as sweetness is a property of sugar. Ideas are not Rulers, or creators: they are just the properties or qualities recognised in certain things. The Logos itself is the same: it is the faculty which recognises the abiding property in things, and remembers these properties. God is the same. God as we think him could no more create anything than the Logos could create anything. God as we conceive him is the great know-all and perhaps be-all, but he could never *do* anything. He is without form or substance, he is Mind; he is the great *derivative*. God is derived from the cosmos, not the cosmos from him. God is derived from the cosmos as every idea is derived from the cosmos.

The cosmos is not God. God is a conception, and the cosmos is *real*. The pebble is real, and $4 \times 4 = 16$ is a property of the pebble. Man is real, and Mind is a property of man. The cosmos is certainly conscious, but it is conscious with the consciousness of tigers and kangaroos, fishes, polyps, seaweed, dandelions, lilies, slugs, and men: to say nothing of the consciousness of water, rock, sun and stars. Real consciousness is touch. Thought is getting out of touch."

The crux of the whole problem lies here, in the duality of man's consciousness. Touch, the being in touch, is the basis of all consciousness, and it is the basis of enduring happiness. Thought is a secondary form of consciousness, Mind is a secondary form of existence, a getting out of touch, a standing clear, in order to come to a better adjustment in touch.

Man, poor man, has to learn to function in these two ways of consciousness. When a man is *in touch*, he is non-mental, his mind is quiescent, his bodily centres are active. When a man's *mind* is active in real mental activity, the bodily centres are quiescent, switched off, the man is out of touch. The animals remain always in touch. And

man, poor modern man, with his worship of his own god, which is
his own mind glorified, is permanently out of touch. To be always
irrevocably in touch is to feel sometimes imprisoned. But to be
permanently out of touch is at last excruciatingly painful, it is a state
5   of being nothing, and being nowhere, and at the same time being
conscious and capable of extreme discomfort and *ennui*.

God, what is God? The cosmos is alive, but it is not God.
Nevertheless, when we are in touch with it, it gives us life. It is forever
the grand voluted reality, Life itself, the great Ruler. We are part of
10   it, when we partake in it. But when we want to dominate it with Mind,
then we are enemies of the great Cosmos, and woe betide us. Then
indeed the wheeling of the stars becomes the turning of the millstones
of God, which grind us exceeding small, before they grant us
extinction. We live *by* the cosmos, as well as in the cosmos. And
15   whoever can come into the closest touch with the cosmos is a bringer
of life and a veritable Ruler; but whoever denies the Cosmos and tries
to dominate it, by Mind or Spirit or Mechanism, is a death-bringer
and a true enemy of man. St. John, in the Apocalypse, is working for
the dominion of Mind over the Cosmos: that is the Millennium. First,
20   the *whole* Church of Christ, the Logos or Mind, will be martyred by
the Rulers of the world. Then Christ will come again, and the martyrs
shall be themselves princes, princes, princes over all men, for a
thousand years: for all Rulers will have been destroyed and cast into
hell. Finally, after these thousand years of Millennium and rule of
25   Martyrs, the grand end shall come, the end of the cosmos entirely, and
the Last Judgment.

How they long for the destruction of the cosmos, secretly, these men
of mind and spirit! How they work for its domination and final
annihilation! But alas, they only succeed in spoiling the earth, spoiling
30   life, and in the end destroying mankind, instead of the cosmos. Man
cannot destroy the cosmos: that is obvious. But it is obvious that the
cosmos can destroy man. Man must inevitably destroy himself, in
conflict with the cosmos. It is perhaps his fate.

Before men had cultivated the Mind, they were not fools.

EXPLANATORY NOTES

EXPLANATORY NOTES

A Review of *The Book of Revelation* by Dr. John Oman

41:4 **The Apocalypse.** The Book of Revelation, the last book of the New Testament, written by John of Patmos. 'Apocalypse' (from Greek 'uncovering', 'disclosure') is divine revelation made known in a dream or vision; also the literature devoted to such revelation – in particular the Jewish and Christian writings which purported to discern the mysteries of creation, the cosmos, and the End of Days.

41:20 **the four Prophets of the Old Testament.** The three 'Greater' Old Testament prophets are Isaiah, Jeremiah and Ezekiel. Daniel is here added to them, presumably for his apocalyptic writings.

42:5 **L. H. Davidson.** A variant of DHL's pseudonym 'L. H. Davison' first used – at the request of Oxford University Press – on the title page of *Movements in European History*, 1921. See Nehls, i. 471.

Introduction to *The Dragon of the Apocalypse* by Frederick Carter

45:5 *Dragon of the Apocalypse.* DHL first read in June 1923 an early version of this book, which was published in 1926 as *The Dragon of the Alchemists*. He was then at Chapala, Mexico where he lived from May to July 1923 (see letter to Frederick Carter, 15 June 1923 where he describes his tussle with the local post office to obtain Carter's MS). In 1929, Carter sent a later and much revised version of the original MS to DHL and this became *The Dragon of the Apocalypse*, later published under the title *The Dragon of Revelation* for which DHL wrote this introduction (see also Introduction to the present volume).

46:37 **macrocosm.** The 'great world' or universe as distinct from the 'little world' or microcosm, i.e. from man as an epitome of the universe.

47:25 **Millennium.** The belief in a future 'millennium', a thousand-year period of blessedness. See Revelation xx.

47:29 **New Jerusalem.** The belief that immediately after death – which is a putting off of the material body – man rises again in a spiritual or substantial body, in which he continues to live to eternity. The Second Coming of Christ to establish a New Church on earth which will stand forever, was seen representatively by John of Patmos in his vision of the holy city, the New Jerusalem, descending from God out of heaven, prepared as a bride adorned for her husband.

47:40 **And I saw...A white horse!** Revelation xix. 11 (AV) ['...behold a...'].

48:17 *Pilgrim's Progress.* An allegory in the form of a dream vision by John Bunyan (1628–88) published in 1678.

48:17 **Dante.** Dante Alighieri (1265–1321), Italian poet, born in Florence, Italy. DHL is referring to the *Divina Commedia*, Dante's greatest work, comprising the *Inferno*, *Purgatorio* and *Paradiso*.

48:37 **Mr. Facing-both-ways...Janus.** Mr. Facing-both-ways is a character in Bunyan's *Pilgrim's Progress*. Janus was the Roman god of entrance gates and of beginnings whose Festival was held in the first month of the reformed calendar, Januarius. The closing of the monumental gates of the Temple of Janus in the Forum signified peace, their opening, war. Janus was represented with two faces, each looking in the opposite direction from the other.

49:8 **Kronos.** The Greek word *Chronos* means 'time'. The similarity of 'Chronos' to 'Kronos' led to identification, also with Aion (AEon), Time. Kronos was originally a Canaanite deity, a fertility god and lord of heaven, but in Greek mythology as Cronos or Chronus he was the youngest of the Titans, offspring of Heaven and Earth. He was the father of the Olympians Hestia, Demeter, Hera, Hades, Poseidon and Zeus, who later supplanted him. See 109:27n.

50:17 *Sanahorias.* Spelt *Zanahorias*.

50:30 **sodom-apples.** The 'fruits of Sodom' which vanish into ashes (see Deuteronomy xxxii. 32).

51:11 **Chaldean.** The ancient land of Kaldu was a part of southeast Babylonia. Because of the ancient association of Babylon with astrology and astronomy, the word Chaldean became a designation for oriental astrologers, magicians, and practitioners of occult arts. See Genesis xi. 28, Jeremiah l–li. In Daniel iv. 7 and v. 7 the Chaldeans are mentioned as magicians and astrologers.

51:17 **Baal.** Bel or Baal was the name of the Assyrio-Babylonian chief god, sometimes equated with En-lil and Marduk. For the story of 'Bel and the Dragon' see the Old Testament Apocrypha.

51:28 **Euphrates, Mesopotamia.** One of the rivers of Eden (Genesis ii. 14). In the Old Testament the Euphrates is generally known as 'the river'. The promise made to the Israelites that their territory should extend to 'the great river' (Genesis xv. 18) was fulfilled through the conquests of David (2 Samuel viii. 3 and x. 16–19; 1 Kings iv. 24). The alluvial plain between the Euphrates, the longest river of western Asia, and the Tigris constituted Babylonia or Mesopotamia, one of the cradles of civilisation, now modern Iraq.

52:9 **a strong man to run a race?** See Psalms xix. 4–5.

52:14 **Belshazzar's day.** The son of Nebuchadnezzar (king of Babylonia 605–562 B.C. who first captured Jerusalem, built the walls of Babylon and perhaps the famous 'Hanging Gardens'). Belshazzar was the last king of Babylonia and was killed in the sack of Babylon by Cyrus in 538 B.C.

52:31 **Artemis and Cybele.** Strictly speaking, Selene was the moon goddess in Greek mythology, while Artemis was the virgin goddess of nature, although originally a mother deity (non-Hellenic in character) of lakes, rivers, woods and wildlife. She was the daughter of Zeus and sister of Apollo and became identified with the Roman goddess Diana. Cybele was the Great Mother of Phrygia, the Anatolian name of the ancient Mediterranean goddess of nature, of the mountains, forests and of earth and fertility. Cybele was identified by the Greeks with Rhea as the wife of Chronus and mother of Zeus. Neither Artemis nor Cybele were originally moon goddesses.

53:17   **Astarte?** Also Ashtart or Ashtoreth, was the mother goddess of Phoenicia. She was the deity of sexual activity, fertility, maternity and war, and erroneously identified as a moon goddess. She is shown with horns in Phoenician art, but these are cow horns representing fertility, not those of the moon.

54:39   **Chapel, to Band of Hope and to Christian Endeavour.** DHL attended the Congregationalist Chapel in Eastwood and belonged to the Band of Hope temperance union. See Ada Lawrence and G. Stuart Gelder, *Young Lorenzo: Early Life of D. H. Lawrence* (Florence, 1931), p. 57. The Christian Endeavour organisation originated in the USA in 1881 and quickly spread to Britain. Inter-denominational and international, it is essentially a young people's movement and encourages active participation and service in the local church.

55:7   **"I was...the Alpha and the Omega".** Revelation i. 10 (AV) ['...I am Alpha and Omega...']. These are the first and last letters of the Greek alphabet, 'the beginning and the end', originally said of the Divine Being.

55:10   **"Alleluia...reigneth".** Revelation xix. 6 (AV).

55:13   **"And he treadeth...of Almighty God".** Revelation xix. 15 (AV).

55:21   **Moffatt's.** James Moffatt, *The New Testament: A New Translation* (1913). See Introduction to the present volume, p. 12.

55:28   **Assyria.** Assyria, which dominated the Fertile Crescent during the twelfth to seventh centuries, was a Semite state partaking of the general culture of Mesopotamia.

55:29   **the Seleucids.** The dynasty founded by Seleucus Nicator (one of the generals of Alexander the Great) which reigned over Syria from 312 to 65 B.C. and subjugated a great part of western Asia.

55:30   **Pompey and Anthony.** Gnaeus Pompey (106–48 B.C.), the famous Roman general who, with Julius Caesar and Crassus formed the first triumvirate in 60 B.C. but was defeated by Caesar in the ensuing civil war in 49–48 B.C. Mark Antony (c. 83–30 B.C.) and Octavian (later Augustus Caesar) defeated Brutus and Cassius at Philippi after the murder of Caesar and divided the Roman Empire. Antony ruled the eastern half but his marriage with Cleopatra was a cause of his later break with Octavian and in the civil war which followed Antony was defeated. He committed suicide in 30 B.C.

55:32   **Homer.** The Greek epic poet, traditionally the author of the *Iliad* and the *Odyssey*, who is thought to have lived some time before 700 B.C.

55:34   **Ur.** The city where, according to the God of Genesis, Abraham settled. It stood on the Persian Gulf near one of the mouths of the Euphrates and was the seat of three Sumerian dynasties, of which the first came to an end about 3575 B.C. and the third about 2300 B.C.

55:34   **Nineveh.** This populous and ancient city of Assyria lay on the east bank of the Tigris and flourished under Sennacherib c. 700 B.C. and later in the seventh century under Ashurburnipal who founded the great library. It was sacked in 612 B.C. by Babylonians, Scythians and Medes and never recovered its past glory.

55:34   **Sheba to Tarshish.** Sheba (Genesis xxvi. 30) is probably the Biblical town of Beersheba. Tarshish, or Tartessus, a region in southern Spain, grew proverbially wealthy through its trade with Phoenicians and Carthaginians, and with Brittany and southwest Britain for tin.

56:2   **Mithraic.** Originally Persian, the worship of Mithras, god of light and truth, became a Roman mystery cult with secret rites and stages of initiation through which the god's devotees had to pass. From the second half of the first century A.D. it spread throughout the Roman Empire.

Apocalypse

59:3   **Apocalypse.** See 41:4n.

59:10   **nonconformist.** See n. 73, p. 16 of the Introduction.

59:27   **Band of Hope or Christian Endeavour.** See 54:39n.

59:29   **Sunday School teacher.** The teacher's name was Rimmington, though both DHL in 'Hymns in a Man's Life', *Phoenix II* 600 and Jessie Chambers in *D. H. Lawrence: A Personal Record*, 1935, p. 17, call him 'Remington'.

60:9   *War and Peace.* The epic novel by Leo Tolstoy (1828–1910) written between 1865 and 1872.

61:8   **pie-pie.** Slang for pious, sanctimonious.

61:16   **"And I saw...was called"—.** Revelation xix. 11 (AV) ['...sat upon him was...'].

61:20   *Pilgrim's Progress.* See 48:17n.

61:22   **Euclid..."The whole is greater than the part".** Many generations of schoolboys knew geometry only as 'Euclid' because the teaching of that branch of mathematics was based on the *Elements* of Eucleides, a Greek mathematician, who taught at Alexandria about 300 B.C.

61:27   *Faerie Queen.* The poem by Edmund Spenser (1552–99). *The Faerie Queene* published 1589–96.

61:40   **"And before the throne...and is to come—".** Revelation iv. 6–8 (AV). Cf. Ezekiel i. 5 and i. 10.

62:9   **the wadings in blood...the Lamb.** See Revelation vii. 14; xiv. 20; xvi. 3–4; xix. 13.

62:10   **"the wrath of the Lamb".** Revelation vi. 16–17 (AV).

62:12   **all the Bethels.** From Hebrew, 'House of God'. Formerly the chief sanctuary in Palestine of the Israelite (i.e. non-Judaean) tribes. See Genesis xxviii. 10–22. A Bethel is the name used, especially by certain Methodists and Baptists, for a place of religious worship such as a chapel.

62:13   **all the Salvation armies.** The Salvation Army, founded by W. Booth in 1865, is an extensive international Christian organisation for evangelistic and social work.

62:21 **Pentecost chapel.** The Pentecostal Movement began in the first years of the twentieth century among believers who sought a baptism in the Holy Spirit accompanied by speaking with tongues similar to instances recorded in Acts of the Apostles.

62:23 **MYSTERY...THE EARTH.** Revelation xvii. 5 (AV). Babylon, one of the greatest cities of the ancient world, was once the capital of the Chaldean empire. After the conquest of Jerusalem by Nebuchadnezzar in 597 B.C. the Jews were deported to Babylon; hence 'Babylon' is synonymous with captivity, bondage. It is also the mystical city of the Apocalypse, whence in modern times applied polemically to Rome or the papal power, and rhetorically to any great and luxurious city.

62:34 **"Babylon the great...bird—".** Revelation xviii. 2 (AV).

63:6 **Pharisee.** The Pharisees were a Jewish religious group. In the Gospels they appear as the chief opponents of Christ, whom they attacked, e.g., for forgiving sins, breaking the Sabbath, and consorting with sinners. Christ repeatedly denounced their purely external observance of the Law, their multitude of formalistic precepts which even they could not keep, and above all their self-righteousness.

63:15 **a city that "had...in it".** Revelation xxi. 23 (AV).

63:19 **brimstone.** Frieda Lawrence recalls DHL humorously acting out a revival meeting of this sort. See Nehls, i. 171.

64:5 **Primitive Methodist Chapels.** The Primitive Methodist Church came into being in 1811 in connection with, but for the most part outside, the Wesleyan Methodist Church. It is 'primitive' in that it professes to represent the earliest form of church order.

64:18 **Congregationalist.** Congregationalism rests on the independence and autonomy of each local church and professes to represent the principle of democracy in Church government from its belief in Christ as the sole head of His Church. All the members of the Church, being Christians, are 'priests unto God'. See 'Hymns in a Man's Life', *Phoenix II* 600.

64:28 **Beauvale Chapel.** DHL occasionally attended this Chapel in Eastwood, Nottinghamshire. See *Letters*, i. 23.

64:33 **"Lead, kindly Light"!** A hymn by [Cardinal] J. Newman. For DHL the hymn seemed to represent sentimentality: 'I am glad our Scotch Minister on the whole avoided sentimental messes such as "Lead, Kindly Light", or even " Abide With Me"', 'Hymns in a Man's Life', *Phoenix II* 600.

65:2 **Love one another!** John xiii. 34 (AV) ['...love...'].

66:5 **"internal evidence".** DHL had been reading R. H. Charles's two-volume work, *A Critical and Exegetical Commentary on the Revelation of St. John* (1920) who established this date: 'The date of J^ap [John's apocalypse] can be established by external and internal evidence' (Charles, i. xci).

66:11 **Ephesus.** In New Testament times, one of the largest cities of the Roman world, the capital of the Proconsular Province of Asia, and a great port and commercial centre. Its fame rested largely on the great temple to Artemis (or Diana, as the Romans called her), one of the 'Seven Wonders of the World'. See Acts xix.

66:18   **The author of the Fourth Gospel.** Charles confirms this. See Charles, i. xxii.

67:7   **Temple of Jerusalem.** A national shrine of the Jews at Jerusalem. The first Temple dates from the reign of Solomon (*c.* 970–930 B.C.). It was destroyed by the Babylonians in 586 B.C. and re-built in 520 B.C. This structure (the 'Second Temple') suffered desecration at the hands of Antiochus Epiphanes in 167 B.C.

67:14   **Millennium.** See 47:25n.

68:13   **Buddha.** 'The Enlightened', the title given by the adherents of one of the great Asiatic religions, thence called Buddhism, to the founder of their faith, Sakyamuni, Gautama or Siddhartha, who flourished in northern India in the fifth century B.C.

68:13   **Plato** (*c.* 427–348 B.C.), the great Athenian philosopher who became a pupil and devoted admirer of Socrates whose teachings he recorded in his *Dialogues*. Benjamin Jowett's classic translation of the *Dialogues*, which DHL read, appeared in 1871. See 96:23n.

68:20   **Francis of Assisi** (1181?–1226), founder of the Franciscan Order, and saint.

68:23   **Lenin.** Vladimir Ilyich Ulyanov (1870–1924), the Russian politician who established the dictatorship of the Communist Party in 1917.

68:25   **two or three men come together.** Cf. Matthew xviii. 20.

69:5   **Abraham Lincoln** (1809–65), President of the United States (1861–5).

69:6   **President Wilson.** Woodrow Wilson (1856–1924), President of the United States (1913–21).

69:19   **the late Tsar.** Tsar Nicholas II (1868–1918), the last emperor of Russia (1894–1917), abdicated after the February 1917 revolution. He was imprisoned and on 16 July 1918, together with his whole family, was shot by order of the local Soviet authorities.

69:37   **with a kiss.** See Matthew xxvi. 48; Mark xiv. 44; Luke xxii. 48.

71:6   **any rule of "Beasts".** See Revelation xiii.

73:4   **"superiority" goal.** A cancelled part of the MS reads: 'What Adler calls a "superiority goal" is, if we come down to the individual nature of man, a primal, almost an instinctive impulse to become a master, a lord, and a splendid one.'
   Alfred Adler (1870–1937) was an Austrian psychiatrist who broke with Freud in 1911 to found a separate school of individual psychology. He emphasised the role of organic inferiority in determining the structure of personality. In his view, an attitude of inferiority develops when an individual feels deficient in comparison to others. Adler postulated a basic striving for superiority or self-assertion which leads a person with an attitude of inferiority to seek to compensate.

73:27 "**John to the seven churches...even so, Amen**". Revelation i. 4–7 (Moffatt) ['...*the faithful witness, the first-born...prince over kings of earth...has loosed us from our sins...a realm of priests for his God...ever: Amen. Lo, he is coming on the clouds, to be seen...who impaled...all the tribes of earth shall wail because of him:...*'].

73:27 **Moffatt's translation.** See 55:21n.

73:28 **authorised version.** The Bible of 1611, also called the King James version, normally capitalised as Authorised Version.

73:30 **wandering by the lake.** See Matthew iv. 18ff and Mark ii. 10ff.

74:16 "**On the Lord's day...seven golden lampstands—**"". Revelation i. 10–ii. 1 (Moffatt) ['..."Write your vision in a book, and send it to the seven churches, to Ephesus and Smyrna and Pergamum and Thyatira and Sardis and Philadelphia and Laodicea." So I...*One who resembled a human being, with a long robe,* and *a belt of gold...his head and hair were white as wool,* white *as snow; his eyes flashed like fire, his feet glowed like finely burnished bronze, his voice sounded like many waves,...the sun in full strength*...saying, "*Be not afraid; I am the First and the Last, ...am I alive...what is to be hereafter. As for the secret symbol*...lampstands—the ...thus:—These...lampstands:...*'].

74:17 **the sword of the Logos.** The Word of God. See Hebrews iv. 12.

74:21 "**My heart is sad...and watch**". Mark xiv. 34 (Moffatt) ['..."*my heart is sad,* sad even to...'].

74:24 **the visions of Ezekiel and Daniel.** See Ezekiel i. 26–8 and Daniel vii. 9–10 and x. 5.

75:14 **holocaust.** Gilbert Murray, whose *Five Stages of Greek Religion* DHL had read, points out that a holocaust was part of a ritual of placation in which 'every shred of the victim was burnt to ashes, that no man might partake of it. We know quite well the meaning of that form of sacrifice: it is a sacrifice to placate or appease the powers below, the Chthonioi, the dead and the lords of death' (29).

75:17 **Chthonioi.** The Chthonian deities were Greek gods or demi-gods who dwelt in the underworld, as opposed to the Olympian or heavenly gods. They were connected with both fertility and the dead and probably derive from earlier Aegean religion.

76:21 **Helios.** In Greek mythology, the sun or the sun-god, often confused in later classical times with Apollo. Helios was the son of the Titan Hyperion, and Thea, and the brother of Selene, goddess of the moon.

76:22 **Chaldeans.** See 51:11n.

77:18 **Artemis...Cybele...Astarte.** See 52:31n and 53:17n.

77:39 **Venus?** The MS originally read 'Vega'. DHL would have been aware of the mystic importance of Vega as the pole star of a previous cycle 13,000 years ago from his reading of Frederick Carter. See 'The Ancient Science of Astrology' in the *Adelphi*, April 1924, 997–1005.

77:40 **Aldebaran.** A red star of the first magnitude. It forms the bull's eye in the constellation Taurus.

78:2 **He who is not with me is against me!** Matthew xii. 30 (Moffatt).

78:11 **fate and destiny, a prison.** DHL found this information in Gilbert Murray: 'The various Hermetic and Mithraic communities...are full of the influence of the seven planets and of the longing to escape beyond them...The religion of later antiquity is overpoweringly absorbed in plans of escape from the prison of the seven planets' (180).

78:30 **katabolism.** Destructive metabolism. Cf. 'The Hands of God', *Complete Poems* 699.

79:28 **the Book of Daniel** is believed to have been a product of the Hellenistic age, written around the middle of the second century B.C.

79:29 **the Apocalypse of Enoch.** In December 1929 DHL had been reading the Book of Enoch, one of the more important Jewish pseudepigrapha, i.e. writings ascribed to some other than their real author, generally with a view to giving them enhanced authority (see letter to Carter, 15 December 1929). The Book of Enoch was written by several authors and embodies a series of revelations on such matters as the origin of evil, the angels and their destinies, and the nature of Gehenna and Paradise. It is one of the few historical memorials of the religious development of Judaism from 200 B.C. to A.D. 100.

79:34 **Antiochus Epiphanes.** King of Syria from 175 B.C. (d. 163 B.C.). The epithet 'Epiphanes' means 'illustrious'. His policy of attaining political unity by propagating Greek culture met with violent resistance from the Jews. In 169 B.C. he attacked Jerusalem and defiled the Temple.

81:9 *King of Kings and Lord of Lords.* Revelation xix. 16 (AV). ['...KING OF KINGS, AND LORD OF LORDS...'].

81:16 **Pompey or Alexander or Cyrus.** All three, surnamed 'the Great', are here synonyms for earthly power and conquest.

For Pompey see 55:30n.

Alexander (356–323 B.C.), son of Philip II of Macedon, became king of Macedon in 336 B.C. He was one of the great conquerors of history, and a military genius who in ten years overran the Persian empire, invading Egypt, Turkestan and India, and initiated the second great outward expansion of Greek civilisation.

Cyrus II (reigned c. 559–530 B.C.), the Persian emperor who built the Achaemenid empire of Iran, the greatest empire the world had then seen. After his conquest of Babylon he allowed the Jews then exiled there to return to Judah.

81:32 **the Aegean civilisation.** This expression is used to denote a fairly homogeneous cultural area, comprising Crete, Cyprus, the Cyclades, the Greek mainland and, sometimes, adjoining coastal areas of Asia Minor and Syria in the pre-Hellenic period (before 1200 B.C.). The Aegean religion was characterised by the cult of a goddess connected with fertility and death.

81:33 **a book of a pagan Mystery.** DHL absorbed this notion of a single ancient book of pagan mystery from Frederick Carter, who recalls: 'Of all the writers dealing with the origins of this Apocalypse he preferred Dupuis' version in the *Religion*

Universelle. Not that Lawrence had read Dupuis, but I had, and gave him a synopsis of the argument. This was to the effect that in it existed the only document that had come down to us of all the secret cults, the sole survivor giving a full description of the Mithraic initiation with its symbols and figures. He liked this notion of an exposition derived from one cult and preserved as canonical and inspired by its foe. But his critical sense made him doubtful of it' Carter 53.

81:37 a Christian work. DHL has adapted Charles's account in the *Commentary* on the Old Testament sources of Revelation, its writing and subsequent editing, to fit his own notions. See Charles, i. xxii–xxiii.

82:4 the trampling...the horses. Cf. Revelation xiv. 19–20.

82:7 "Come, Lord Jesus, Come!" Revelation xxii. 20 (Moffatt) ['...Amen, Lord Jesus, come!...']; (AV); ['...Amen. Even so, come, Lord Jesus...'].

82:16 the post-David period. David (probably d. *c.* 970 B.C.), first king of the Judean dynasty.

82:19 Assyrian. See 55:28n.

82:21 Ezekiel's great vision. Ezekiel, prophet of the Old Testament, is said to have been active in the early sixth century B.C. His descriptions of his visions of the Divine throne and glory became the basis for an entire branch of Jewish mysticism and also greatly influenced apocalyptic writings and Revelation.

82:23 the Time Spirit. DHL was probably remembering Frederick Carter's definitions: 'There are certain ancient images of Time, Mithraic and Gnostic, and Orphic...the figure usually named AEon, sometimes called Abraxas, and there is an Orphic version named Phanes' (*The Dragon of the Alchemists*, p. 45); and 'Great AEon,...originally an Iranian or Babylonian conception of the Great Figure of Time and Night' (*The Dragon of Revelation*, p. 29).

82:25 Anaximander, the Greek astronomer and philosopher (*c.* 610–540 B.C.), disciple of Thales. He taught that the first principle, or primary substance, is eternal and indestructible matter (the Boundless or the Infinite) containing within itself all contraries, such as heat and cold, moist and dry, and that the phenomenal universe has been evolved through the separation of these contraries and the creative union of those elements which have an affinity for each other.

82:30 Anaximander's wheels in Ezekiel. DHL had been profoundly influenced by John Burnet's *Early Greek Philosophy* and derived this and other pre-Socratic accounts of the phenomenal universe from him. Burnet quotes an ancient Greek commentator on Anaximander: 'The heavenly bodies are a wheel of fire, separated off from the fire of the world, and surrounded by air. And there are breathing-holes, certain pipe-like passages, at which the heavenly bodies show themselves. That is why, when the breathing-holes are stopped, eclipses take place. And the moon appears now to wax and now to wane because of the stopping and opening of the passages' (66–7). Burnet goes on to explain that 'We do not see the wheels of fire as complete circles; for the vapour or mist which formed them encloses the fire, and forms an outer ring except at one point in their circumference, through which the fire escapes, and that is the heavenly body we actually see' (68).

83:8 **the four Creatures.** These are the cherubim, originally Assyrian or Akkadian in origin. The notion of winged, multiple-headed beasts serving as guardians of temples and palaces must have been general in many near-Eastern countries and influenced or coloured the accounts in Genesis and other Old Testament books.

83:13 **Michael and Gabriel.** In Biblical and post-Biblical lore Michael ranks as the greatest of all angels, whether in Jewish, Christian, or Islamic writings, secular or religious. He derives originally from the Chaldeans by whom he was worshipped as a god. Gabriel is the second highest-ranking angel. The name Gabriel is also of Chaldean origin and was unknown to the Jews prior to the Captivity. Michael and Gabriel are the only two angels mentioned by name in the Old Testament.

83:22 **Demiurge.** This English form of the Greek word δημιουργός meaning 'craftsman', was used of the Divine Being by Plato in his account of the formation of the visible world, and so by Greek Christian writers simply of God as the Creator of all things. The Gnostics used the word disparagingly of the inferior deity to whom they ascribed the origin of the material universe, distinguishing him from the supreme God. In its English form the word is commonly used in reference to this Gnostic doctrine. Cf. 'The Body of God' and 'Demiurge', *Complete Poems* 691 and 689.

83:30 **"but our author...in mind".** This is unfair to Charles, who is making a linguistic point on the text, not one on sources. He writes: 'But, whatever may be the original derivation of this conception, it could hardly be present to the mind of the Seer in the present passage, else we should have γοὺς ἑπτὰ ἀστέρας and not ἀστέρας ἑπτά The number seven, in itself sacred, determined the number of the Churches (i. 20), and thus by a coincidence the number of the stars as seven. See Jeremias, *Babylonisches im Neuen Testament*, 24–26. But the seven stars may be the seven planets', Charles, i. 30.

84:31 **Archdeacon Charles.** Charles's exhaustive and scholarly analysis of and commentary on Revelation is primarily concerned with its sources in the Hebrew of the Old Testament, the Pseudepigrapha and Greek sources. He is keenly aware of the pagan derivation of much of the Old and New Testaments but it lies outside most of his study. 'There are certain statements and doctrines in the Apocalypse which could not have been written first hand by a Christian. These are in some cases of Jewish origin, but others are ultimately derived from Babylonian, Egyptian, or Greek sources' Charles, i. clxxxvi.

85:22 **Orphic.** Several variations in ancient Greek cosmogony were ascribed to the 'Orphics'. These were people who, uniting elements from the cult of Apollo and from Thracian reincarnation beliefs, thought that the soul could survive death if it were kept pure, and elaborated a partly individual mythology, with either Dionysus or Orpheus as a central figure, to illustrate this theory. Some adherents of these beliefs were calling themselves 'Orphics' by the fifth century but the formation of an exclusive religious sect with a definite body of relevant sacred literature came later, in the Hellenistic and Roman periods, about the third century B.C.

85:29 **the dispersion.** The Dispersion of the Jews, or Diaspora, had its beginnings in the Assyrian and Babylonian deportations (722 and 597 B.C.). Originally confined to parts of Asia, especially Armenia and Iran, it later spread throughout the Roman Empire to Egypt, Asia Minor, Greece, and Italy. The Jews of the Dispersion remained in close touch with their home country, paying the Temple taxes and keeping their religion and the restrictions of the Law, though Hellenic culture penetrated into their thought.

86:18 **Nero, or Nero redivivus.** Nero, the last Roman emperor (A.D. 54–68) of the Julio-Claudian dynasty, was proverbial for his tyranny and brutality. The belief that Nero would return to earth as a Satanic monster, as the dragon of Revelation xiii and the beast of xvii, was widespread.

86:39 **their pettifogging work.** Charles comments that John of Patmos 'did not live to revise his work...This task fell...into the hands of a very unintelligent disciple...He intervened repeatedly, rearranging the text in some cases, adding to it in others...' Charles, i. xxii–xxiii.

87:11 **Rheims Cathedral.** Reims, Cathedral of Notre-Dame, one of the finest examples of French classical gothic construction, was begun in 1211. It suffered badly during the First World War, but was restored with meticulous care and re-opened in 1927. Possibly DHL is referring to the outcry over its near-destruction.

87:26 **Minoans.** The name given by Sir Arthur Evans to the Bronze Age civilisation of Crete (*c.* 3000–1000 B.C.) revealed by his excavations at the Palace of Minos at Knossos.

87:26 **Etruscans.** These were the earliest historical occupants of the area approximating to Tuscany in modern Italy, and Rome's principal early rivals for the hegemony of central Italy. They formed a confederation of politically independent city-states and were at the height of their power *c.* 500 B.C., but were finally conquered and absorbed by the Romans. DHL's fascination with their culture is recorded in his *Etruscan Places* (1932).

87:27 *Urdummheit.* DHL had been reading Gilbert Murray's *Five Stages of Greek Religion.* Murray writes: 'The progress of Greek religion falls naturally into three stages, all of them historically important. First there is the primitive Euêtheia or Age of Ignorance, before Zeus came to trouble men's minds, a stage to which our anthropologists and explorers have found parallels in every part of the world. Dr. Preuss applies to it the charming word "Urdummheit", or "Primal Stupidity". In some ways characteristically Greek, in others it is so typical of similar stages of thought elsewhere that one is tempted to regard it as the normal beginning of all religion, or almost as the normal raw material out of which religion is made' (16).

87:36 **Thales.** A Greek philosopher and scientist, Thales of Miletus (640–546 B.C.) was one of the Seven Wise Men of Greece and the founder of Greek geometry, astronomy and philosophy. In mathematics he founded the geometry of lines and thus is credited with introducing abstract geometry. In philosophy, he taught that water, or moisture, was the one substance from which the world was formed.

87:37 **Pythagoras.** The Greek philosopher and mathematician, born in Samos (hence known as the 'Samian Sage'), Pythagoras is said to have travelled widely in search of wisdom. He settled (*c.* 530 B.C.) in Crotona, a Greek colony in southern Italy. Around him, inspired by his teaching, developed an association devoted to reformation of political, moral and social life. To Pythagoras are ascribed the doctrine of metempsychosis and the teaching that earthly life is only a purification of the soul. He left no writings; all that is known of his doctrines comes from his disciples.

88:12   *Neufrecheit*. German. Neu = new; frechheit = brazenness, impertinence.

88:36   'The interest in the (Antichrist) legend...fanatics.' Charles is pointing out the extraordinary historical resilience of Revelation. Each age applies the prophecies of Antichrist and the End to itself. The passage from Bousset's article in the *Encyclopedia of Religion and Ethics*, ed. James Hastings (1925), pp. 578–81, reads: 'In the centuries that followed the Reformation, the doctrine that the Pope was Antichrist gradually receded into the background. It was, of course, still resolutely held by Protestant scholars, particularly by commentators on the *Apocalypse* even in our own times. But it came to be more and more only learned pedantry, and the belief no longer possessed the power of forming history. With this last phase the interest in the legend entirely disappeared, and it is now to be found only among the lower classes of the Christian community, among sects, eccentric individuals, and fanatics' (581).

89:4   **Caesarism.** The system of absolute government founded by Caesar; monarchial absolutism.

89:18   'those who are destroying the earth'". See Revelation xi. 18 (AV). The whole of the previous quotation, which is ended by this reference to Revelation, is from Charles, i. 86.

90:7   **Euphrates.** See 51:28n.

90:7   **Indus.** The Indus Valley Civilisation in northwest India dates from the early part of the third millennium B.C.

90:10   **Mycene.** An ancient Greek city-state in the Peloponnese, first occupied by Greek-speaking peoples *c*. 2000 B.C. and most powerful in the sixteenth to thirteenth centuries when it loosely controlled mainland Greece and the Aegean, as suggested in Homer's *Iliad*.

90:19   **Rameses,** a variant of Ramses, the name of twelve kings of the xixth and xxth dynasties of ancient Egypt.

90:19   **Assiburnipal,** a variant of Ashurbanipal, king of Assyria (669–626 B.C.).

90:20   **Darius.** Darius I (558?–485 B.C.), king of Persia (521–485 B.C.), greatly extended the Persian empire, built Persepolis, and began the great war between the Persians and the Greeks. His army was defeated at Marathon and he died shortly thereafter, leaving the execution of his schemes to Xerxes. Darius is referred to in Daniel v. 31ff.

91:23   **Herakleitos.** Heraclitus of Ephesus, a Greek philosopher who flourished *c*. 500 B.C., wrote a work 'Concerning Nature' in which he maintained that all things are in a state of flux, a ceaseless conflict of opposites, coming into existence and passing away, and that fire, the type of this constant change, is their origin. Heraclitus had a great influence on DHL's thought.

91:23   **Empedokles** (*c*. 493–433 B.C.), the Greek philosopher and statesman, was a disciple of Pythagoras and Parmenides. He postulated that the universe was a plenum composed of four kinds or 'roots' – fire, air, water and earth – which mingle and separate under the contrary impulses of Love and Strife, thus causing the creation and passing away of all 'mortal things'. These ideas, and the notion that generation and decay are nothing but the compounding and dissolution of eternally unchanging 'elements', had a great fascination for DHL.

91:23   **Anaxagoras.** This Greek philosopher (*c.* 500–*c.* 428 B.C.) taught that all natural objects are composed of infinitesimally small particles, or seeds, containing mixtures of all qualities, and that mind or intelligence acts upon masses of these particles to produce the objects we see. See 'Anaxagoras', *Complete Poems* 708.

91:24   **Socrates and Aristotle.** DHL is drawing an idiosyncratic distinction between these two philosophers and the pre-Socratics above. Although DHL affected to disagree with Aristotle he had something in common with his metaphysics, since Aristotle also regarded the soul and body as inseparable elements in the living being.

92:5   **sphinx conundrum.** The sphinx was a mythological creature with a human head and the body of a lion. It was sent to Thebes by Hera, Queen of Heaven, to ask the Thebans the riddle about the three ages of man. They failed to solve it, and after each effort the sphinx carried away and devoured one of them, including Haemon, the son of King Creon, until Oedipus solved the riddle. The sphinx then committed suicide or was killed by Oedipus.

92:26   **Hector,** in Greek legend, was the eldest son of Priam and Hecuba, and the most valiant of the Trojans who fought against the Greeks. He was slain by Achilles in revenge for the death of Patroclus, whom Hector had killed; and his body was tied to the chariot of Achilles and dragged to the Greek ships.

92:26   **Menelaus,** King of Sparta, was the son of Atreus and the younger brother of Agamemnon. He was the successful suitor of Helen, but was robbed of her by Paris, the son of Priam. Thereupon he assembled the princes who had been the suitors of Helen and who had bound themselves to defend her, and the expedition against Troy began.

95:8   **before the birth of the Child.** See Revelation xii. 5.

95:24   **And all this is God.** See 'God is Born' and 'The Body of God', *Complete Poems* 682 and 691.

95:26   **what the old Greeks meant by god, or** *theos.* DHL derived the ideas in this paragraph from Gilbert Murray: 'We must notice the instinctive language of the poets, using the word θεός in many subtle senses for which our word 'God' is too stiff, too personal, and too anthropomorphic. Tὸ εὐτυχεῖν 'the fact of success', is 'a god and more than a god'; τὸ γιγνώσχειν φίλους 'the thrill of recognizing a friend' after long absence, is a 'god'; wine is a 'god' whose body is poured out in libation to gods; and in the unwritten law of the human conscience 'a great god liveth and groweth not old' (27).

96:11   **eschatological...scientists.** DHL uses 'scientist' here in the original sense of a man who possesses knowledge in any department of learning. 'Eschatology', the doctrine of the last or final things – as death, resurrection, immortality, the second coming of Christ, the last judgment etc. – is strictly a theological term. The editor of the Florence first edition substituted 'philosophers' for 'scientists'. See pages 130 and 134 where DHL equates scientists with philosophers.

96:19   **Hesiod.** The Greek poet (*c.* 800 B.C.) whose writings comprise (1) the *Works and Days*, collections of practical and religious maxims, a calendar of unlucky days, etc.; (2) the *Theogony*, giving the origin of the universe out of chaos and the history of the gods, an important work to the comparative mythologist.

96:23   **Professor Jowett's Plato.** Benjamin Jowett (1817–93), Regius Professor of Greek from 1855 to 1893 at Balliol College, Oxford, is best known for his translation of the *Dialogues* of Plato (1871).

96:26   **chlamys.** A short oblong mantle fastened with a clasp in front or at the shoulder.

97:11   *epos.* Greek. Early oral narrative poetry celebrating incidents of heroic tradition; a series of events worthy of epic treatment (*OED*). DHL uses this word incorrectly to suggest a cycle or period of time.

97:14   **The "world" is established...in sevens.** DHL derived some of the number symbolism he uses here from Charles's *Commentary* and from Frederick Carter, e.g. 'Seven is peculiarly the moon's number. Twelve is the formal ordering of the sun's passage through the year, which is divided into four quarters of the seasons' (*The Dragon of the Alchemists*, p. 52).

97:28   **twenty-four elders...temple.** See Revelation iv. 4–6.

97:38   **the eastern Fathers,** e.g. Origen, Basil, St John Crysotom, from centres such as Alexandria, Constantinople, Antioch, as against the western fathers such as Augustine, based in the cities of north Africa and Rome.

98:8   **Christian iconoclast.** A breaker or destroyer of images; one who took part in the movement in the eighth and ninth centuries to put down the use of these in religious worship in the Christian Churches of the East; hence, applied analogously to Protestants in the sixteenth and seventeenth centuries and to Oliver Cromwell (1599–1658), Lord Protector of England (1653–8).

98:13   **"Iris too is a cloud".** DHL took this from Burnet who quotes Xenophanes (the Greek poet, *c.* 576–480 B.C.): 'She that they call Iris is a cloud likewise, purple, scarlet and green to behold' (120); and continues: '"Iris too" is a cloud, and we may infer that the same thing had been said of the sun, moon, and stars; for the doxographers tell us that these were all explained as "clouds ignited by motion"' (121). DHL's application of this to the Almighty is obscure, since Xenophanes is writing about the formation and working of the universe, not about its god.

98:15   **sardine stone.** See Revelation iv. 3. This stone is thought to be jasper or topaz; also 'sard', 'sardius', a variety of carnelian varying in colour from pale yellow to reddish orange.

98:15   **the commentators.** See Charles, i. 113–14.

98:19   **a new era.** DHL was drawn to the concept of the great dance of the heavens, cf. 'Dawn is no longer in the House of the Fish' in 'Astronomical Changes', *Complete Poems* 616. He absorbed some of these notions from Carter's *The Dragon of Revelation*, e.g. 'Now we are near the point of change once again, this time from the Fishes to the Waterpourer. Two thousand years ago the sun left his Equinoctial sign, the Ram, and entered the Fishes. From which came without doubt the singular use of the symbol of the fish by the earlier Christians. The use of the earlier Jewish image of the slain Lamb of Passover was not adopted until later on by the Church. It was, in fact, the symbol of another age, an earlier one and as such a regression ...Before the days of the Lamb, the Bull opened the year, and before that, the Twins' (26).

98:19   **The Fish.** (Greek ἰχθύς) In Christian art and literature the fish is the symbol of Christ, also sometimes of the newly baptised and of the Eucharist. It came into use in the second century, but neither its origin nor its meaning have so far been completely elucidated. The symbol may be of pagan origin or derived from the acrostic ΙΧΘΥΣ = Ιησοῦς Χριστός Θεοῦ Υἱός Σωτήρ ('Jesus Christ, Son of God, Saviour) or the acrostic from the symbol.

98:25   **Thunder...creation.** Cf. 'Silence' and 'Kissing and Horrid Strife', *Complete Poems* 698 and 709.

98:26   **Logos of the beginning.** See John i. 1 and Revelation xix. 13.

98:33   **Then before...seven Spirits of God.** See Revelation iv. 5.

99:10   **The Almighty has a book in his hand.** See Revelation v. 1.

99:17   **how the book is to be *opened*...broken.** See Revelation v. 2. DHL is forgetting John Oman's *Book of Revelation* which he had reviewed in 1924. Oman writes about first-century books: 'The roll was the fashionable form of a book till a much later date than this. But the fastening of leaves together into a kind of notebook was an immemorial custom...It is now...known that as early as any date likely to be assigned to Revelation, the folded sheet was used, and even one sheet laid inside another, with these quires sewn together through the fold. Books even of ordinary literature were on sale by this time in this form' (33–4).

99:21   **The Lion of Judah...with seven horns.** See Revelation v. 5–6.

99:32   **the sacrificed god...the Apocalypse is based.** In a letter to Frederick Carter dated 29 October 1929 DHL explains: 'I agree with Eisler – or I mean, I feel he's right – the Zodiac was the year's rhythm of sacrifice and attainment of the *Mana* of the creatures – the great effort of pre-spiritual man was to get to himself the *powers* – the *honours and powers and might* – the Mana – of the vivid beasts – and the Mana of all was consummated in Man – or God. This is John's idea too – the association of the vivid attributes of the great Creatures into the human One Might and Power (or divine)'.

Dr Robert Eisler wrote several works on early Christianity and pagan cults and astrology. See *Orpheus the Fisher: Comparative studies in Orphic and early Christian cult symbolism* (1921) p. 27.

99:33   **Mithras.** The cult of Mithras, an ancient Aryan god of light and truth, which spread over the empire of Alexander the Great, is said to have reached Rome in 67 B.C. All creatures were supposed to have sprung from the bull which he had overcome and sacrificed before he ascended to heaven, where he guaranteed a blessed immortality to those who had been initiated into his mysteries – by baptism, purification by honey, and the use of bread, water and wine consecrated by priests called 'fathers' who enjoined a high moral code. The similarities with Christianity are striking, but Mithraism was almost completely superseded by Christianity in the fourth century.

99:37   "Wash me...whiter than snow—". A chorus writted by E. R. Latta to the Salvation Army hymn 'Blessed be the fountain of blood' composed in 1899 by Samuel H. Hodges. Cf. Revelation vii. 14.

100:4   hecatomb. A great public sacrifice (properly of a hundred oxen); a large number of animals offered or set apart for sacrifice.

100:10   by their bite ye shall know them. Cf. Matthew vii. 20.

100:11   "as it were slain". Revelation v. 6 (AV) ['...as it had been slain...'].

100:24   There follows a paean...the drama begins. Essentially an exposition of Revelation v. 8–14. The reference to Joseph and the sheaves is to Genesis xxxvii. 5–8.

101:2   the famous four horsemen. See Revelation vi. 1–8.

101:17   the seven seals...transfigured. DHL derived the idea of Apocalypse as a manual of spiritual development from James Pryse whose *The Apocalypse Unsealed* he had read. Pryse wrote that the process of transcendental self-conquest lay in the controlled awakening of the seven principle ganglia or *chakras* (centres of psychic energy in the astral body at its point of contact with the physical body). The seven seals are these seven major *chakras* and their opening is the drama of self-conquest and mystic re-birth. See Introduction, pp. 5–6.

101:21   the famous four horsemen...the four dynamic natures of man and the three "higher" natures. According to Pryse (*Apocalypse Unsealed*), 'the body has four principal life-centres' (14) and the four horses correspond to these four divisions. The drama has seven stages, 'four (the conquests of the *chakras*) relate to the four somatic divisions, and the other three to the mental, psychic and auric principles' (70–1).

101:33   The sons of God...says Enoch. See 1 Enoch vi–vii and 2 Enoch xviii. 1–6. Cf. Genesis vi. 1–4.

102:37   *mana*. Gilbert Murray defines mana as 'that primitive word which comprises force, vitality, prestige, holiness, and power of magic, and which may belong equally to a lion, a chief, a medicine-man, or a battle-axe' (34). Cf. 'Mana of the Sea' and 'Lord's Prayer', *Complete Poems* 705 and 704.

103:4   the bended bow of the body, like the crescent moon. In the apocalyptic Zodiac described by Pryse the body of cosmic man is bent like a bow.

103:15   Pythagoras show his golden thigh. Pythagoras had a golden thigh given him by the gods, and showed it to Abaris the Hyperborean priest during the celebration of the Olympic games. Traditionally the thigh was the seat of male strength, firmness, majesty. It is sometimes a euphemism for the phallos, e.g. Genesis xxiv. 2.

103:28 "Take this bread of my body with thee". Reminiscent of the words spoken by Christ to his disciples at the Last Supper. See Matthew xxvi. 26; Mark xiv. 22; Luke xxii. 19.

104:1 **The orthodox commentators.** Charles gives a summary of these views. See Charles, i. 155ff.

104:2 **Titus or Vespasian.** Vespasian (A.D. 9–79), first of the Flavian emperors of Rome (A.D. 69–79), was succeeded by his eldest son Titus (A.D. 39–81) who reigned A.D. 79–81.

105:6 **meretrix.** A harlot.

105:10 "every mountain...out of their places". Revelation vi. 14 (AV).

106:3 **Creation...is four.** Cf. 'The Two Principles', *Phoenix II* 225–37 where DHL speaks of the basic 'fourfold division of the cosmos' and the 'fourfold activity [which] is the root activity of the universe'; and 'all creation depends upon the fourfold activity' (233). In ancient times the world was seen as a square, 'at each angle of which were the supports of the heaven's pillars or mountains. These four quarters have their iconographic symbols in the four living creatures' (Carter, *The Dragon of the Alchemists*, pp. 52–3).

106:6 **four winds...the four angels of the winds.** Traditionally the west wind was the good wind. The angels of the four winds are: Uriel (south), Michael (east), Raphael (west), Gabriel (north).

106:8 **mystic wind from the east.** This is the sirocco, the wind of God.

106:18 "Salvation...to the Lamb". Revelation vii. 10 (AV) ['...unto the Lamb".']

106:22 "Blessing...Amen."— Revelation vii. 12 (AV) ['...and might, ']

106:25 "went through the great tribulation". Revelation vii. 14 (AV) ['...they which came out of great tribulation...'].

107:10 **Mysteries of Isis.** Isis, the principal goddess of ancient Egypt, sister and wife of Osiris and mother of Horus, typified the faithful wife and mother. According to legend there was a statue of her which bore the inscription: 'I am that which is, has been, and shall be. My veil no one has lifted'. Hence, *to lift the veil of Isis* is to pierce the heart of a great mystery. DHL had read *Isis Unveiled* by the theosophist Mdme. Blavatsky. Cf. *The Escaped Cock*. DHL's familiarity with pagan initiation rites may have come from his reading of Gilbert Murray who tells of Apuleius' initiation to Isis (182).

107:15 **Buddhist monk.** Although the *TCC* has Hindu the MS reads Buddhist. There is no proof that DHL himself made this change since it occurs on page 65 of the *TCC*, the one page which is typed on different paper (presumably to replace the original which was lost) and which has no corrections in DHL's hand.

107:16 "third eye". It is believed that all men possess a third eye which is the focus of great occult power. The position of the third eye is said to be in the middle of the forehead, just above the point where the eyebrows meet.

107:18   **Uraeus.** A representation of the sacred asp or serpent, employed as an emblem of supreme power and worn on the head-dress of ancient Egyptian divinities and sovereigns, the uraeus also symbolises the sublimated serpent raised (the power of *kundalini*, see Introduction, pp. 5–6), and thus becomes a symbol of strength transformed into spiritual power.

107:27   **there is silence...half an hour.** Revelation viii. 1 (AV) ['...there was silence in heaven about the space of half an hour.'].

108:16   **Seven angels...of God.** The seven angels of the Presence, traditionally represented by the seven planets. They are named in 1 Enoch.

109:23   **"harrowing of Hell".** The medieval English term for the defeat of the powers of evil at the Descent of Christ into Hell after His death. It was a favourite theme of art and drama in the Middle Ages.

109:27   **the Gea-Ouranos-Kronos-Zeus series of Myths.** In Greek mythology, Gea, the earth goddess, was born of Chaos and was the first of the heavenly beings. From her came Uranus, the heavens, and Pontus, the sea. Mating with Uranus, she produced many offspring, and, jealous of the rights of these children, made the sickle with which Chronus, her youngest son, castrated Uranus. Chronus mated with his sister Rhea to produce Hestia, Demeter, Hera, Hades, Poseidon, and Zeus but, warned that one of his children would supplant him, swallowed his offspring as they were born. However, Rhea hid Zeus and instead gave Chronus a stone to swallow. At last, with the aid of the Titans, Zeus overthrew Chronus and obtained the regency. The same sort of sequence is found in the mythology of other lands of the Mediterranean ancient world.

109:38   **"two woes".** See Revelation ix. 3–12.

110:7   **horses, horses.** This sentence is odd but in both *MS* and *TCC* DHL writes 'horses, horses,'.

110:20   **Apollyon.** The Greek form for the Hebrew Abaddon, meaning 'destroyer'. In Revelation ix. 11 he is the angel of the bottomless pit, and in Revelation xx. 2 he 'laid hold on the dragon, that old serpent, which is the Devil and Satan, and bound him a thousand years'. According to the foregoing, Apollyon is a good angel, servant and messenger of God; but in occult and, generally, in noncanonical writings, he is evil. In Bunyan's *Pilgrim's Progress* Apollyon is the devil.

110:24   **two more still to come.** Cf. Revelation ix. 12.

111:4   **"Loose the four angels...Euphrates".** Revelation ix. 14 (AV).

111:5   **four corners.** See 106:3n.

111:17   **The horses...they do hurt.** DHL is paraphrasing Revelation ix. 17–19 (AV) ['...and the heads of the horses were as the heads of lions; and out of their mouths issued fire and smoke and brimstone. By these three was the third part of men killed, by the fire, and by the smoke, and by the brimstone, which issued out of their mouths. For their power is in their mouth, and in their tails: for their tails were like unto serpents, and had heads, and with them they do hurt.']. DHL uses the grammatically incorrect 'issues' (line 13) and 'comes' (line 15) in *MS*.

112:6   **two apocalyptists...cavalry of the east.** Charles explains: 'In the riders and the demonic steeds there is a combination of two quite different ideas. Gunkel ...well observes: "In the representation of the second host two different traditions stand side by side: according to the one, the creatures spit forth fire, smoke, and brimstone, and have therefore a strong mythological character; according to the other, they are squadrons of cavalry clothed in corresponding colours, fiery red, smoky blue, and sulphurous yellow"' Charles, i. 253.

112:11   **"lake of fire burning with brimstone".** Revelation xix. 20 (AV).

112:15   **Sheol and Gehenna.** According to Charles the lake of fire is not Gehenna. 'Gehenna was originally regarded as a fiery and final place of punishment for men; and this meaning it retained in Judaism, so far as the Gentiles were concerned. Sheol, which was originally a dark, cheerless, non-fiery abode of the departed, began as early as 100 B.C. to acquire the fiery character of Gehenna, and in Luke xvi. 23 it acquires another characteristic of Gehenna, i.e. the departed in Hades are punished in the presence of the righteous...The final place of punishment prepared for the fallen angels has thus become also the final abode of wicked men' Charles, i. 240–2.

113:3   **Salt...bitter.** Anaximander's doctrine which DHL found in Burnet's *Early Greek Philosophy.* Burnet writes: 'Anaximander started...from the strife between the opposites which go to make up the world; the warm was opposed to the cold, the dry to the wet. These were at war, and any predominance of one over the other was an "injustice" for which they must make reparation to one another at the appointed time' (53–4). '"The sea is what is left of the original moisture. The fire has dried up most of it and turned the rest salt by scorching it"' (64). 'The gradual drying up of the water by the fire is a good example of what Anaximander meant by "injustice"' (65). Cf. also 'Salt', 'The Four', and 'The Boundary Stone', *Complete Poems* 705, 706.

113:4   **leviathan.** In the Enoch parables, the primitive sea-dragon and monster of evil. In Biblical lore (Job xli. 1) leviathan is the great whale.

113:8   **the bitter, corrupt sea, as Plato calls it.** DHL has misunderstood. The reference is to *Laws,* iv. 705, and reads: 'It is agreeable enough to have the sea at one's door in daily life, but, for all that, it is, in very truth, a briny and bitter neighbour. It fills a city with wholesale traffic and retail huckstering, breeds shifty and distrustful habits of soul, and so makes a society distrustful and unfriendly within itself as well as toward mankind at large.' It is not known which translation of Plato's *Laws* DHL used, but the sense of the passage would remain roughly the same.

113:13   **"neither see nor hear nor walk".** Revelation ix. 20 (AV) ['...which neither can see...'].

114:10   **the seven creative thunders.** Cf. 'Silence', *Complete Poems* 698.

114:20   **this great "angel"...oath of the gods.** A paraphrase of Revelation x. 6 (AV) ['...sware by him that liveth for ever and ever, who created heaven, and the things that therein are, and the earth, and the things that therein are, and the sea, and the things which are therein, that there should be time no longer.'] In Greek mythology, however, the gods were bound by their oath on the river Styx, which flowed nine times round the infernal regions.

114:33   Orthodox commentators. See John Oman, *Book of Revelation*, p. 112 and Charles, i. 281–3.

114:34   Moses and Elijah...mount. Christ appeared transfigured in a vision with Moses and Elijah on the Mount (variously thought to be Mount Tabor, Mount Hermon or the Mount of Olives) to Saints Peter, James and John. The event was described by the Evangelists (see Matthew xvii. 1–13; Mark ix. 2–13; Luke ix. 28–36) and was significant because it showed the testimony of the Jewish Law and Prophets to the Messiahship of Christ.

115:4   "Adonai", the God of the earth. This is the plural of Semitic 'adon', lord; in Hebrew religion the most usual substitute for the wonderful, hidden name of God. See 156:17n.

115:11   "Come up hither". Revelation xi. 12 (AV). The passage is a paraphrase of Revelation xi. 4–12 (AV).

115:22   the Tyndarids, Kastor and Polydeukes. Castor and Pollux, the twins of Greek mythology and legend were the sons of Tyndareus and Leder in Homer, although other tradition says that Pollux and Helen were children of Zeus and immortal while Castor was mortal. When Castor died, Pollux, the immortal twin, begged Zeus to be allowed to share his brother's fate. As a result, the brothers, either together or alternatively, lived one day in the earth and the next among the gods of Olympus. They are also said to have been placed among the stars as the constellation Gemini, the Twins. They were protecting deities of sailors, travellers, of the laws of hospitality, of oaths. The myth of the twins seems to be universal, not merely Indo-European in origin.

115:35   Dioskouroi. The sons of Zeus, Castor and Pollux. Burnet notes that St Elmo's fire was given this name: '"The things like stars that appear on ships...which some call the Dioskouroi"' (122). They sometimes tend to be confused with the Cabiri. See 116:11n.

116:5   Tritopatores. These were mysterious deities of Attic cult and said to be the forefathers or ancestors of mankind. They were often referred to as lords of the winds and gate-keepers to whom were offered such expiatory sacrifices as are due to the spirits of the underworld. There is no evidence, however, that they were ever associated with the Dioskouroi or the Twins.

116:11   the Samothracian cult...the Kabiri. The Cabiri were non-Hellenic deities, probably Phrygian in origin, whose cult was established at many places in Greece, most notably at Samothrace, where mysteries were celebrated. The Cabiri formed a pair and, originally of chthonian origin and concerned with fertility, were later confused with the Dioskouroi, possibly because they also protected sailors. DHL could have been familiar with these rather obscure deities from his reading of Goethe, where they are mentioned in *Faust*, or from Jung's *Psychology of the Unconscious* (1916), p. 130ff.

116:21   homunculi. Plural of Latin 'homunculus'; a diminutive man, manikin, pigmy.

116:27   balancers. Cf. 'Walk Warily' and 'Kissing and Horrid Strife', *Complete Poems* 707 and 709.

117:10 A creature of dual and jealous consciousness...duality. Cf. 'On Being a Man', *Phoenix II* 616–22 where DHL writes of 'the self which darkly inhabits our blood and bone, and for which the ithyphallos is but a symbol. This self which lives darkly in my blood and bone is my *alter ego*, my other self, the homunculus, the second one of the Kabiri, the second of the Twins, the Gemini. And the sacred black stone at Mecca stands for this: the dark self that dwells in the blood of a man and of a woman' (619).

117:32 "Sodom" and "Egypt". Revelation xi. 8. Figuratively, any town or towns regarded as exceptional centres of vice and immorality; an allusion to the cities Sodom and Gomorrah which God destroyed. See Genesis xviii, xix.

117:36 "rejoice...send gifts to one another". Revelation xi. 10 (AV) ['And they that dwell upon the earth shall rejoice over them, and make merry, and shall send gifts one to another'].

117:37 a pagan Saturnalia...Babylon. In ancient Roman times the Saturnalia, or Festival of Saturn, was held in December and observed as a time of general unrestrained merrymaking, extending even to the slaves. The Hermaia was a similar festival in Crete in honour of the god Hermes and the Sakaia feast-day in Babylonia was similarly a time of license, feasting and revelry.

118:7 "Two, two...green-O!—" A very old folksong that has appeared in many forms in ancient and modern languages from Hebrew onwards. In England the most common titles are 'The Twelve Apostles' and 'The Ten Commandments', or, from the refrain, 'Green grow the rushes, O!'.

118:13 "The kingdoms of this world...and ever".— Revelation xi. 15 (AV) ['...Lord, and...Christ; and...'].

119:6 Even orthodox commentators admit...unjewish. A little misleading since Charles writes: 'Scholars have sought the source of this chapter variously in Babylonian, Persian, Greek, and Egyptian myths. It is not, however, directly and wholly from any one of these, but from an early international myth.' He goes on to give a very detailed account of these possible origins, Charles, i. 310.

119:31 "And there appeared...cast out with him"— Revelation xii. 1–9 (AV) ['...And she...the third part...a thousand and two hundred and threescore days...cast out...'].

120:32 the Scarlet Woman. See Revelation xvii. 4–5. The harlot is often interpreted as ancient Babylon or the city of Rome, doomed to destruction. For various interpretations of her significance and that of the 'Beast' on which she rides, see Charles, ii. 54–87. See also 62:23n.

121:37 Diana of Ephesus. According to legend this statue fell from heaven. She is represented with many breasts and with trunk and legs enclosed in an ornamental sheath. The temple of Diana at Ephesus was one of the Seven Wonders of the World, with a roof supported by 127 columns. Diana was an ancient Italian goddess identified with Artemis. See Acts xix. 24–35.

123:18 Esau. Jacob and Esau were the twin sons of Isaac and Rebecca in the Bible. Esau, the elder, was a hunter, Jacob a dweller in tents. Esau, coming in faint from the field, sold his birthright to Jacob for a mess of pottage (Genesis xxv). Jacob, personating Esau, obtained Isaac's deathbed blessing (Genesis xxvii).

123:27 **Samson.** A Hebrew hero (probably eleventh century B.C.), enemy of the Philistines and traditionally the last of the great 'judges' (see Judges xiii. 2 – xvi. 31) who was endowed with great strength which enabled him to perform remarkable feats (e.g. slaying a lion and moving the gates of Gaza).

123:28 **David slew Goliath.** David (probably d. *c.* 970 B.C.), first king of the Judean dynasty, who according to tradition slew the Philistine giant Goliath with a pebble and a sling in battle. See 1 Samuel xvii.

124:3 **Libido or *Elan Vital*.** Libido is the energy of instinctive desires, especially, according to Freud, those connected with sexual activities. However Jung saw the libido as the source of all creative impulses, spiritual as well as physical, a notion much closer to DHL's beliefs. *Élan vital* or 'life force' was a phrase introduced by the philosopher Henri Bergson (1859–1941) to denote the force of creative evolution underlying all activity in the universe.

124:9 **When Moses set up the brazen serpent.** See Numbers xxi. 4–11 (AV). 'And they journeyed from mount Hor by the way of the Red sea, to compass the land of Edom: and the soul of the people was much discouraged because of the way. And the people spake against God, and against Moses, Wherefore have ye brought us up out of Egypt to die in the wilderness? for there is no bread, neither is there any water; and our soul loatheth this light bread. And the LORD sent fiery serpents among the people, and they bit the people; and much people of Israel died. Therefore the people came to Moses, and said, We have sinned, for we have spoken against the LORD, and against thee; pray unto the LORD, that he take away the serpents from us. And Moses prayed for the people. And the LORD said unto Moses, Make thee a fiery serpent, and set it upon a pole: and it shall come to pass, that every one that is bitten, when he looketh upon it, shall live. And Moses made a serpent of brass, and put it upon a pole, and it came to pass, that if a serpent had bitten any man, when he beheld the serpent of brass, he lived.'

124:22 **Lindberg.** Charles Augustus Lindbergh, the American aviator (1902–74), made the first solo non-stop transatlantic flight from New York to Paris, 20–1 May 1927 in his monoplane *The Spirit of St. Louis*.

124:23 **Dempsey.** William Harrison ('Jack') Dempsey (1895–), the American heavyweight boxer, won the heavyweight championship of the world on 4 July 1919.

125:6 **It is the same dragon...in controlled motion.** DHL would have found this in Pryse who writes in *The Apocalypse Unsealed* that this latent power or *kundalini* can be roused to activity by man's spiritual will to act as a perfecting force: 'As it passes from one ganglion to another its voltage is raised, the ganglia being like so many electric cells coupled for intensity' (16); and 'the action of the serpent force results in the opening of the mystic third eye' (21).

125:15 **Moses...redemption of men.** DHL's reading of Carter would have reminded him of the dual nature of the serpent. Carter writes: 'The double sense of the serpent image as emblem both of wisdom and evil, lends a contributory

significance to the mystery of the Cross, and to the strange saying of Jesus Christ:—
  "As Moses lifted up the serpent in the wilderness,
  even so must the Son of Man be lifted up."
Such a declaration, thrice made in the mystical Evangel (St John iii. 14; viii. 28;
xii. 32), defines its importance in the thought of the writer. And so the serpent is
not only the image of the Tempter in Eden, but is again that of the Deliverer from
the evil serpents, poisonous and creeping' (*The Dragon of the Alchemists*, 48).

125:21 **agathodaimon...kakodaimon.** Good spirit and evil genius, respectively.
DHL was indebted to his reading of Jung for the idea of the serpent associated with
the hero, the *libido*, which, conquering itself, gives birth to itself again. 'The hero
is himself a serpent, himself a sacrificer and a sacrificed. The hero himself is of *serpent
nature*; therefore the redeeming principle of the world of that Gnostic sect which
styled itself the Ophite was the serpent. The serpent is the Agatho and Kako demon'
See C. G. Jung, *Psychology of the Unconscious*, p. 417.

126:16 **Laocoön.** In Greek legend, Laocoön was a Trojan priest of Apollo who
attempted to dissuade the Trojans from bringing the Wooden Horse into the city.
As he was about to sacrifice to Apollo, two sea serpents emerged on the beach and
encircled Laocoön's two sons. The father, too, as he tried to rescue them was gripped
in their coils and killed. Taking this as an omen, the Trojans breached the walls and
drew the horse into the city. DHL had been familiar with Lessing's Laocoön since
his early days through an extract in Richard Garnett's *International Library of Famous
Literature* (1899), ix. 4170–80. There is a striking reproduction of the Vatican
sculpture facing p. 4170.

127:1 **Andromeda.** In Greek mythology, the daughter of Cepheus, king of
Ethiopia, and of Cassiopeia. Her mother boasted that she was more beautiful than
the Nereids, and Poseidon, at the nymphs' request, sent a monster to ravage the
country. At the direction of an oracle, her parents had Andromeda chained to a rock
as a sacrifice to end the monster's ravages. Flying back from the slaying of the Gorgon,
Perseus saw her, fell in love with her and slew the monster. Cepheus then gave
Andromeda in marriage to Perseus. The concept of the constellation Andromeda,
however, is far older than the classical story. The Maiden Chained was known to
the Chaldeans and the Babylonian story of Marduk and Tiamut as told in their
creation epic may have been the basis for the later Andromeda legend.

127:8 **the modern police-woman.** The Women's Police Service originated as
a voluntary force in 1915. In autumn 1918 the official women's force was established
by the Metropolitan Police Commission.

127:20 **touch like a spring-time breeze.** An example of how DHL's repetitive
style encouraged errors of transmission. The typist repeated two lines, and the error
was perpetuated in the Florence edition.

128:5 **It was the colour of glory.** Cf. 'For the Heroes are Dipped in Scarlet',
Complete Poems 688.

128:25 **men wore soft gold for glory.** Cf. letter to M. C. Chambers, 24 April 1928·
'I'm sure for thousands of years men loved gold for its own golden life, its yellow

life-stuff, and drew power from it: and that's how it came to have its value, which mankind can't get over. But the real value is religious, not monetary.'

128:34 **Nebuchadnezzar.** See 52:14n.

129:10 **the Gold Age...the Steel Age.** In Greek mythology the four ages of man were: (1) the Golden, or the age of Chronus-Saturn, when happiness and fertility were universal and men lived in pure innocence without evil or sin; (2) the Silver, when men ceased to revere the gods, knew evil and fell to killing each other; (3) the Bronze, in which a powerful race of cruel, hard men lived who used metal tools and weapons and constantly fought; (4) the Iron, the age of sin in which Zeus let loose the Deluge which drowned everyone except Deucalion and Pyrrha. The present age, variously called the age of Stone and the Steel Age, is the last and most degraded period in the existence of the human race.

129:15 **The great red dragon.** Charles discusses the symbolism of the seven-headed dragon, 'ultimately derived from Babylonian mythology', Charles, i. 317.

129:25 **"to shepherd mankind with an iron flail".** Revelation xii. 5 (Moffatt) ['...to *shepherd* all *the nations with an iron flail...*'].

130:5 **the numbers seven, four and three...the ancient mind.** In traditional numerology seven was the number of creation, the cosmos, space, and was represented by a square plus a triangle. The Pythagoreans equated the world with four and the deity with three.

130:20 **And the number three...condition of being.** This is from *Early Greek Philosophy* again where Burnet quotes the Pythagoreans: 'When the odd is divided into two equal parts, a unit is left over in the middle; but when the even is so divided, an empty field is left, without a master and without a number, showing that it is defective and incomplete' (288); and 'In the division of numbers, the even, when parted in any direction, leaves as it were within itself...a field; but, when the same thing is done to the odd, there is always a middle left over from the division' (289).

130:24 **the Boundless...primordial creation.** Burnet explains that this 'Boundless' substance was 'an endless mass, which is not any one of the opposites we know, stretching out without limit on every side of the world we live in. This mass is a body, out of which our world once emerged, and into which it will one day be absorbed again' (58). The two 'opposites' are not strictly speaking 'elements' at all, a notion which came later with Empedokles.

131:10 **Anaximenes with his divine "air".** Anaximenes, who flourished *c.* 546 B.C. was either a younger associate or a pupil of Anaximander. He also said that the underlying substance of the universe was one and infinite but unlike Anaximander he maintained it was determinate, not indeterminate, and that it was a form of vapour, or 'air'.

131:18 **the first Pythagoreans...Limit in Fire.** 'Pythagoras identified the Limit with fire, and the Boundless with darkness...Parmenides in discussing the opinions of his contemporaries, attributes to them the view that there were two primary "forms," Fire and Night. We also find that Light and Darkness appear in the Pythagorean table of opposites under the heads of the Limit and the Unlimited respectively' Burnet 109.

131:21 **Herakleitos...every day.** Burnet quotes Heraclitus: 'All things are an exchange for Fire' and 'The sun is new every day' (135). Heraclitus taught that the primary substance is Fire and that this is in constant flux so that 'All things are in motion like streams' (146). The notion of 'exchange' is illustrated in what happens when fire takes in fuel and gives out heat and smoke instead (147). Although there is perpetual flux, things appear relatively stable since 'the aggregate bulk of each form of matter in the long run ,remains the same, though its substance is constantly changing' (150).

131:22 **"The limit...bright Zeus".** Heraclitus, quoted in Burnet 135.

131:26 **Night lives...the death of Night.** A paraphrase from Heraclitus: 'Fire lives the death of air, and air lives the death of fire; water lives the death of earth, earth that of water' Burnet 135.

131:30 **"escaping the wheel of birth".** Burnet points out that Orphicism was 'mainly based on the phenomenon of "ecstasy"....It was supposed that it was only when "out of the body" that the soul revealed its true nature. It was not merely a feeble double of the self, as in Homer, but a fallen god, which might be restored to its high state by a system of "purifications"...and sacraments...the main purpose of the Orphic observances and rites was to release the soul from the "wheel of birth," that is, from reincarnation in animal or vegetable forms. The soul so released became once more a god and enjoyed everlasting bliss...Philosophy is itself a "purification" and a way of escape from the "wheel"' (81–3).

132:24 **The morning star...one on shore.** Cf. *The Plumed Serpent* where Quetzalcoatl is the Lord of the Morning Star who stands between the day and the night in the creative twilight.

132:25 **We know...flood.** Burnet writes: '...in the sixth century darkness was supposed to be a sort of vapour, while in the fifth its true nature was known' (109); and 'It was Empedocles...who first discovered that what we call air was a distinct corporeal substance, and not identical either with vapour or with empty space' (74).

133:5 **Three...the Almighty.** See Carter, *The Dragon of the Alchemists*, pp. 52–3.

133:13 **the wheels of the revolving heavens.** See Ezekiel, i. 15–23.

133:34 **Cherubim.** Originally Assyrian, the cherubim were pictured as huge, winged creatures with leonine or human faces, bodies of bulls or sphinxes, eagles, etc. They are the first angels to be mentioned in the Old Testament (Genesis iii. 24). In Ezekiel (x. 14) four cherubim, each with four faces and four wings, appear to the Hebrew prophet. In rabbinic and occult lore, the cherubim are prevailingly thought of as charioteers of God, bearers of his throne, and personifications of the winds. In Revelation (iv. 8) they are living creatures who render unceasing praise to their Maker. See also Carter, *The Dragon of the Alchemists*, p. 49.

134:8 **"Four for the Gospel Natures".** This might be a local variant, or possibly DHL misremembers. The English Folk Dance and Song Society maintains that all Christian versions of this ancient folksong, usually known as 'The Ten Commandments' or 'The Twelve Apostles', agree to the reading 'Gospel makers', 'writers' or 'preachers', never 'natures'. See 'St. Matthew', 'St. Mark', 'St. Luke', 'St. John', *Complete Poems* 320, 323, 325, 328; and the preface DHL wrote in 1929, 'The

Evangelistic Beasts', *Phoenix* 66. See also 'The Two Principles', *Phoenix II* 225–37, where DHL writes: 'In religion we still accept the Four Gospel Natures, the Four Evangels, with their symbols of man, eagle, lion, and bull, symbols parallel to the Four Elements, and to the Four Activities, and to the Four Natures' (233). The symbols of the four evangelists are angel (Matthew); eagle (John); lion (Mark); and bull (Luke).

134:13   At first...Fire. According to Burnet, however, the earliest Ionian cosmologists of about the sixth century B.C. established only one primary substance.

134:19   Anaximenes said all was water. Incorrect. This was Thales. Anaximenes gave the name 'air' to the one and infinite substance.

134:19   Xenophanes said all was earth and water. 'All things are earth and water that come into being and grow', quoted by Burnet 120.

134:25   Water gave off...the watery earth. According to Burnet, Xenophanes believed that sun, moon and stars were 'clouds ignited by motion' (122). The sun, then, is an ignited cloud, 'a collection of sparks from the moist exhalation' (122).

134:30   Herakleitos...an element. Burnet writes: 'Anaximander had taught that the opposites were separated out from the Boundless, but passed away into it once more, so paying the penalty to one another for their unjust encroachments. It is here implied that there is something wrong in the war of opposites, and that the existence of the opposites is a breach in the unity of the One. The truth Herakleitos proclaimed was that the world is at once one and many, and that it is just the "opposite tension" of the opposites that constitutes the unity of the One' (143).
   It was Strife that separated out the primary substance into all its manifestations and it was through Strife, the creative principle as DHL rightly identifies it, that the world exists. Heraclitus himself said: 'Homer was wrong in saying: "Would that strife might perish from among gods and men!" He did not see that he was praying for the destruction of the universe; for, if his prayer were heard, all things would pass away...' Burnet 136. DHL's 'Strife', *Complete Poems* 714, expresses this idea. However, DHL is here mistaken in calling Fire an element – it is the One, the Boundless. The notion of elements arose with Empedokles (see below 134:35n).

134:35   the Four Roots. 'Hear first the four roots of all things', Burnet 205. According to Burnet these four roots 'seem to have been arrived at by making each of the traditional "opposites" – hot and cold, wet and dry – into a *thing* which is real' (228). Cf. 'The Four', *Complete Poems* 706.

134:39   "Fire and Water...breadth". Burnet 208. Burnet also explains: 'The function of Love is to produce union; that of Strife, to break it up again. Aristotle, however, rightly points out that in another sense, it is Love that divides and Strife that unites. When the Sphere [of the cosmos] is broken up by Strife, the result is that all the Fire, for instance, which was contained in it comes together and becomes one; and again when the elements are brought together once more by Love, the mass of each is divided...Love...produces an attraction of *unlikes*' (232–3).

134:40   "shining Zeus...Nestis". Burnet 205. Burnet comments: 'Empedokles also called the "four roots" by the names of certain divinities – "shining Zeus, life-bringing Hera, Aidoneus, and Nestis" – though there is some doubt as to how these names are to be apportioned among the elements. Nestis is said to have been a Sicilian water-goddess, and the description of her shows that she stands for Water; but there is a conflict of opinion as to the other three' (229). DHL has incorrectly transcribed 'Vestis' for 'Nestis'.

135:1   the Four also as gods. Burnet writes: 'Empedokles called the elements gods; for all the early thinkers had spoken in this way of whatever they regarded as the primary substance. We must only remember that the word is not used in its religious sense. Empedokles did not pray or sacrifice to the elements' (230).

135:9   Our life...have our being. See Acts xvii. 28. Cf. 'The Four', *Complete Poems* 706.

135:10   the four natures of man. Empedokles was influential in other fields as well. Galen made him the founder of the Italian school of medicine, whose 'fundamental doctrine was the identification of the four elements with the hot and the cold, the moist and the dry' Burnet 201, eventually giving the four natures of man as DHL describes them. The four temperaments are thus related to the elements: air, sanguinary; fire, nervous; water, lymphatic; earth, bilious.

135:15   "the heart...thought of men". Empedokles quoted in Burnet 220.

135:17   the Four Ages. Burnet writes of Hesiod, whose *Theogony* DHL had read: 'In describing the Ages of the World, he inserts a fifth age between those of Bronze and Iron. That is the Age of the Heroes, the age Homer sang of. It was better than the Bronze Age which came before it, and far better than that which followed it, the Age of Iron, in which Hesiod lives' (5–6). See 129:10n.

135:27   as when the dragon...a third part of men. See Revelation xii. 4; viii. 7–12; ix. 17–18.

135:29   a fourth part that is destroyed. See Revelation vi. 1–8.

136:4   The numbers four and three..."the number of the right time". Burnet points out that the Neopythagorean writers created endless analogies between things and numbers and also that Aristotle implies that 'according to them the "right time"...was seven, justice was four, and marriage three"' (107–8). The Pythagoreans also equated the number four with the created world, represented by a square, and three with the deity, represented by a triangle.

136:22   Marduk. The chief god of the Babylonian pantheon.

136:23   magi. The ancient Persian priestly caste, the priests of Zoroastrianism. Hence, in a wider sense, persons skilled in oriental magic and astrology, ancient magicians or sorcerers.

136:24   serious. The *TCC* has 'direct' lightly scored out and 'serious' substituted, but the Orioli edition printed 'direct' by mistake and subsequent editions perpetuated the error.

137:31   *The Golden Ass.* A satire by Apuleius of Madaura in Africa (b. *c.* A.D. 114). It takes the form of the supposed autobiography of the author, who is transformed into an ass by the mistake of the servant of an enchantress. He passes from master to master, observing the vices and follies of men, and finally recovers human form by the intervention of the goddess Isis.

137:39   "time, times and a half". Revelation xii. 14 (AV) ['...a time, and times, and half a time...']. See also Daniel xii. 7.

138:9   a nine-day week. Cf. 'Return of Returns' *Complete Poems* 702. But Gilbert Murray writes: 'Even the way of reckoning time changed under the influence of the Planets. Instead of the old division of the month into three periods of nine days, we find gradually establishing itself the week of seven days with each day named after its planet, Sun, Moon, Ares, Hermes, Zeus, Aphrodite, Kronos...It was the old week of Babylon, the original home of astronomy and planet-worship' (175–6).

139:3   "It is...over again". Burnet writes of Pythagoras: 'we are probably justified in referring to him the conclusion that it is "according to nature" that all Hellenes and barbarians count up to ten and then begin over again' (103).

139:6   "all things are number". It was not the repetition of five but the discovery of the harmonic intervals – the fourth, fifth and octave – 'that led Pythagoras to say all things were numbers...It is enough to suppose that Pythagoras reasoned somewhat as follows: If musical sounds can be reduced to numbers, why not everything else? There are many likenesses to number in things, and it may well be that a lucky experiment, like that by which the octave was discovered, will reveal their true numerical nature.' Burnet 107. Cf. also 'Tortoise Shell', *Complete Poems* 354.

139:10   The Pythagoreans...imagination. Burnet notes that Pythagoras 'used to give the number of all sorts of things, such as horses and men, and...he demonstrated these by arranging pebbles in a certain way....Aristotle compares his procedure to that of those who bring numbers into figures...like the triangle and the square' (100). According to tradition it was Pythagoras who revealed the 'tetrakys of the dekad', a figure which represented the number ten as the triangle of four, thus:
```
    *
   * *
  * * *
 * * * *
```
. It showed immediately that $1+2+3+4 = 10$. See Burnet 102.

139:19   Moses' forehead. Moses is conventionally represented with horns, owing to a blunder in translation. In Exodus xxxiv. 29–30 where we are told that when Moses came down from Mount Sinai 'the skin of his face shone', the Hebrew for this 'shining' may be translated as 'sent forth *beams*' or 'sent forth *horns*', and the Vulgate took the latter as correct.

139:22   ithyphallos. A term often used loosely to mean 'phallic' but specifically meaning the 'erect penis'. Ithyphallic is used of certain images and statues connected with phallic worship, in which the sexual organs are extremely prominent or exaggerated.

139:22   cornucopia. In classical mythology, the horn of abundance, always filled with fruit and self-replenishing according to the wishes of its possessor.

141:7   "And there was war...against the dragon".— Revelation xii. 7 (AV).

141:12   Aphrodite. The goddess of love and beauty who sprang from the foam of the sea near the island of Cythera.

141:27   "and the earth...*Jesus Christ*". Revelation xii. 16–17 (AV) ['the flood which the dragon cast out of his mouth...with the remnant...which keep the commandments of God, and have the testimony of Jesus Christ'].

142:5 **"seven heads...a lion"**— Revelation xiii. 1–2 (AV) ['and upon his horns ten crowns'].

142:7 *explained* **by Daniel.** See Daniel vii.

142:11 **Macedonian.** Macedon was the intermediary between Greek and Hellenistic culture and under Philip and Alexander became a world power but later collapsed before the expanding power of Rome by whom it was annexed as a province in 146 B.C.

142:31 **Frazer's** *Golden Bough.* The Golden Bough is a comparative study of the beliefs and institutions of mankind by Sir J. G. Fraser (1854–1941) in twelve volumes, published between 1890 and 1915.

142:34 **⁊.** This symbol was omitted in the Orioli edition.

143:2 **You can put down the meaning flat.** In the *TCC* DHL has lightly scored out the second half of the sentence: 'plain as two and two make four.' The Orioli edition mistakenly included the deleted words.

143:4 **number 666.** Revelation xiii. 18 (AV) ['...Six hundred threescore and six...']. See Charles, i. 365–8 for interpretations of this number.

143:9 **Simon Magus.** The sorcerer of Samaria referred to in Acts viii. 9–13 as converted by Philip. His attempts to purchase miraculous powers by offering the Apostles money (Acts viii. 18–19) is alluded to in our word *simony.* According to other accounts, he claimed divine attributes and was the founder of an early Christian sect known as the Simonians, regarded as heretical.

143:25 **Revenge Timotheus cries.** Timotheus (447–357 B.C.) of Miletus, a celebrated musician and poet, mentioned by Dryden in his 'Alexander's Feast' where line 131 reads: 'Revenge, Revenge, Timotheus cries,'.

144:1 **"new white garments".** Revelation vi. 11 (AV) ['...white robes...'] and Revelation xix. 14 (AV) ['...clothed in fine linen, white and clean...'].

144:22 **"Babylon...the habitation of devils".** Revelation xviii. 2 (AV).

144:26 **And then all the gold...destroyed in Babylon the great—!** This is a paraphrase of Revelation xviii. 11–13.

145:13 **"To them that have shall be given".** See Matthew xxv. 29.

145:18 **"Render unto Caesar that which is Caesar's".** Matthew xxii. 21; Mark xii. 17; Luke xx. 25.

145:25 **Domitian.** The son of the Roman emperor Vespasian, Domitian (A.D. 51–96) succeeded his brother Titus in A.D. 81. He gradually assumed despotic powers and demanded that public worship should be given him as *Dominus et Deus.* At the end of his reign a persecution of the Christians and Jews broke out. According to a very widespread tradition it was during this persecution that John, in exile at Patmos, received the revelations recorded in the Apocalypse.

145:29   since. The *TCC* has 'for refusal' lightly scored out and 'since' written in, but Orioli printed 'for refusal'.

146:17   **Mussolini.** Benito Mussolini (1883–1945), the leader of Fascism in Italy, became dictator in 1925 with the Fascist party as the sole official instrument of political power. Orioli deleted the references to Mussolini here and in line 19.

147:16   **The modern Christian State.** This is the point at which DHL re-wrote the ending. The original conclusion reads: 'The modern Christian State is a soul-destroying bully, negative. And *every* philanthropist, *every* person who wants the "universal good" of mankind, is a bully. The enforcing of any ideal upon men, is bullying.

　　6. To have an ideal for the individual which regards only his individual self and ignores his collective self is in the long run fatal. To have a creed of love which denies the reality of power makes at last for mere anarchy. Man lives by cohesion and resistance. The greater the resistance the greater the cohesion. Absence of resistance is the breaking down of life itself, for all life depends upon the limits of form, and power sets the limits of form, power and resistance.

　　7. To love your neighbour as yourself means loving him, not as an individual, because he isn't one, but as a fragment of an unformed whole: and then trying to bring to life the organic "whole", which is nation or community or state, wherein the individual fragment can feel itself fulfilled. It needs love and power both, in perpetual interplay.'

147:37   **each man...loves.** Oscar Wilde (1856–1900), 'The Ballad of Reading Gaol' (1898) lines 37 and 53.

148:7   **"caritas".** Latin. Christian charity, the love of God and one's neighbour.

148:14   **Nirvana.** In Buddhist theology, the extinction of individual existence and the absorption of the soul in the supreme spirit.

Appendix I, *Apocalypse*, Fragment 1

153:6   **Thou shalt...thyself.** Matthew xxii. 39; Mark xii. 31.

153:8   **Moffatt's.** See 55:21n. Presumably 'the old Elizabethan language' refers to the Authorised King James Version of the Bible (1611).

153:32   **"Except the Lord...in vain..."** Psalm cxxvii.

154:10   **Babylon.** See 62:23n.

154:11   **Mycenae.** See 90:10n.

154:28   *Credo.* Latin, 'I believe'. A creed, a set of professed opinions, specifically the Nicene Creed said or sung as part of the mass.

154:37   **Love one another!** John xiii. 34 (AV) ['...love...'].

155:19   **Rabelais or *Alice in Wonderland*.** François Rabelais (1494?–1553), the French humanist, satirist and physician. Lewis Carroll's (1832–98) story *Alice's Adventures in Wonderland* was published in 1865.

155:24   **cloacal,** adjective of 'cloaca', an underground conduit for drainage, a sewer, a privy.

156:5   **Baal or Ashtoreth.** For Baal see 51:17n. For Ashtoreth see 53:17n.

156:6   *Wuthering Heights,* Emily Brontë's (1818–48) novel published in 1847.

156:7   **Pluto and the spirit of Hades.** Pluto or Hades in Greek mythology was the god of the nether world. The name 'Hades' was transferred to his kingdom, a gloomy sunless place where, according to Homer, the ghosts of the dead flit about like bats.

156:8   **Saturn.** Originally an ancient Italian god of agriculture, Saturn became identified with the Chronus or Cronos of Greek mythology, one of the Titans, son of Uranus and Gea. See 109:27n and 129:10n.

156:17   **Jahveh.** Jehovah, the name of God; an instance of the extreme sanctity with which the name of God was invested, for this is a disguised form of JHVH, the tetragrammaton which was too sacred to use, so the scribes added the vowels of 'Adonai', thereby indicating that the reader was to say 'Adonai' instead of JHVH. At the time of the Renaissance these vowels and consonants were taken for the sacred name itself and hence 'Jehovah' or 'Jahveh'.

156:20   **Dionysic, Apollo-like.** In Greek mythology Dionysus, the son of Zeus and Semele, was the god of wine; Apollo, son of Zeus and Latona, became identified with the sun. He was also the god of music and poetry.

156:21   **Ra.** In Egyptian mythology, the sun-god and supreme deity, often identified with Horus.

156:23   **Ouranos or Kronos or Saturn.** See 109:27n.

156:23   **Osiris.** The great deity of the ancient Egyptians, the god of the dead whose son Horus was the god of renewed life. The Greeks equated Osiris with Dionysus.

156:24   **Sumerians.** The Sumerian civilisation in southern Mesopotamia flourished during the third millennium B.C.

157:2   **"Shriek...no more.—"** Isaiah xxiii. 1 (Moffatt). See 55:34n.

157:4   **Assyria.** See 55:28n.

157:5   **Moab.** These were inveterate enemies of Israel in the biblical period, specifically excluded from 'the congregation of the Lord' (Deuteronomy xxiii. 3–5).

157:7   **Nineveh.** See 55:34n.

157:9   **Susa.** The Greek 'city of lilies', the capital of Elam, and afterwards of the Achaemenids, where Darius I built his palace.

157:10   **Chaldeans.** See 51:11n.

157:13   **Amalek.** An ancient nomadic people who lived in the Sinai desert between Egypt and the land of Canaan. According to the Bible (Genesis xxxvi. 12) they were of Edomite stock.

157:19   **Herodotus or the Odyssey.** The Greek historian (*c.* 480–425 B.C.) born at Halicarnassus, who travelled widely in Europe, Asia and Africa. The Odyssey is the Greek epic poem attributed to Homer.

159:5   Thou shalt love...your enemies. See Matthew v. 43–4 and John xiii. 34.

159:13   restore the temple. See 67:7n. With the destruction of Jerusalem by the Romans in A.D. 70, however, the Temple worship ceased. The site is now occupied by a Moslem shrine.

159:13   Augustus. Gaius Julius Caesar Octavianus (63 B.C. – A.D. 14), the nephew of Julius Caesar and the first Roman emperor occupying the throne from 27 B.C. till his death. The title of Augustus was conferred on him in 27 B.C. by the senate and the people.

159:20   "How old were...conquered us?" DHL found this expression in Burnet who quotes Xenophanes: 'This is the sort of thing we should say by the fireside in the winter-time, as we lie on soft couches after a good meal, drinking sweet wine and crunching chickpeas: "Of what country are you, and how old are you, good sir? And how old were you when the Mede appeared?"' (114). Cf. pp. 90–1.

160:2   For...the first. Matthew xix. 30 and xx. 16.

160:23   Epicurus (341–270 B.C.), the founder of the school of philosophy that bears his name, was the son of an Athenian father. He was brought up in Samos, and after teaching philosophy in various places finally established his school in Athens. In ethics he regarded the absence of pain or repose as the greatest good. Since virtue produces this repose, it is virtue that we should pursue.

162:27   Render...Caesar's. See Matthew xxii. 21; Mark xii. 17; Luke xx. 25.

163:28   the Borgia popes. Rodrigo Borgia (1431–1503), a Spaniard by birth, the father of Cesare and Lucrezia Borgia, was elected to the pontificate in 1492 and became Pope Alexander VI.

163:29   Mammon. The Aramaic word for 'riches', occurring in the Greek text of Matthew vi. 24 and Luke xvi. 9–13. The name was taken by medieval writers as the proper name of the devil of covetousness.

164:22   "the Fish". See 98:19n.

164:32   Lenin. See 68:23n.

165:2   Nietzsche. Friedrich Nietzsche (1844–1900), the brilliant though erratic German ethical writer and philosopher whose contempt for Christianity's doctrine of compassion for the weak DHL seemed to share. See the last chapter of *Aaron's Rod* (1922) where DHL writes: 'There are only two great dynamic urges in *life*: love and power.' On the distinction between 'power' and 'force', see his 'Epilogue', written in 1924, to the earlier *Movements in European History*.

165:6   Gregory. Gregory I, Saint, 'The Great', Pope (590–604), one of the greatest of the early occupants of the see, a zealous propagator of Christianity and reformer of clerical and monastic discipline.

165:9   Francis of Assisi. See 68:20n.

165:31   "Give us...bread." Matthew vi. 11

166:5   "Our Father...heaven—" Matthew vi. 9–10 (AV) ['Our Father which art in heaven, Hallowed be thy name. Thy kingdom come. Thy will be done in earth, as it is in heaven.'].

166:28   **Kosmokrator.** Cf. p. 75.

167:29   **Caesar.** Caius Julius Caesar (102?–44 B.C.), the great Roman general and statesman, conquerer of Gaul and dictator of Rome until his assassination.

167:29   **Napoleon.** Napoleon Bonaparte (1769–1821), the Corsican general who became First Consul of France in 1799 and who proclaimed himself Emperor in 1804.

168:3   **Orphic mysteries.** See 85:22n.

168:7   **Plato.** See 68:13n.

168:35   **That world where...the death of the gods.** This is a paraphrase of Heraclitus. Burnet quotes him: 'Mortals are immortals and immortals are mortals, the one living the others' death and dying the others' life' (138).

169:4   **Eleusinian mystery.** The religious rites in honour of Demeter or Ceres, originally an agrarian cult, performed at Eleusis in Attica and later taken over by the Athenian state and partly celebrated at Athens. The rites included sea-bathing, processions, religious dramas, etc. and the initiated obtained thereby a happy life beyond the grave.

169:5   **Osiris and Isis.** See 107:10n.

169:5   **Tammuz.** A Babylonian deity, commonly regarded as the equivalent of the Greek Adonis. Originally associated with sun-worship, the deity became the divine personification of the annual decay and revival of vegetation in autumn and spring.

169:6   **Attis.** A Phrygian deity connected with the myth of the 'Great Mother', Rhea, Cybele, etc. The goddess drove him mad because he wished to marry a mortal woman but after his death his spirit passed into a pine tree and violets sprang from his blood. He became a symbol of the death and revival of plant life.

169:6   **Mithras.** See 99:33n.

169:7   **Nirvana.** See 148:14n.

169:20   **Pradhana.** Possibly DHL means 'pranidhana', which is a commitment to gain enlightenment in Buddhist theology, or 'sadhana', a spiritual exercise which is a means of attaining an inner mystical state. Neither of these, however, is equivalent to Nirvana as DHL seems to suggest.

169:24   **Einstein.** Albert Einstein (1879–1955), the discoverer and exponent of the theory of relativity.

169:27   **Thales and Anaximander.** See 87:36n. and 82:25n.

170:15   **a Mithraic fragment.** See 81:33n.

171:6   **Christian gnostics.** 'Gnosticism', derived from the Greek word for 'knowledge', was a complex religious movement which in its Christian form came into prominence in the second century, although many of its beliefs clearly stemmed from trends of thought already present in pagan religions. Gnosticism took many different forms but central importance was attached to the idea of 'gnosis', the supposedly revealed knowledge of God and of the origin and destiny of mankind, by means of which the spiritual element in man could receive redemption. Also characteristic of Gnostic teaching was the distinction between the 'Demiurge' or 'creator god' and the supreme Divine Being. See 83:22n.

172:24   **Pentecost.** The Greek name given to the Feast of Weeks, so called because it fell on the fiftieth day after Passover. At this feast the first-fruits of the corn harvest were presented and, in most later times, the giving of the Law by Moses was commemorated. As the Holy Ghost descended on the Apostles on this day (Acts ii. 1–4) the name was applied by the Church to the feast celebrating this event, popularly called Whitsunday.

172:36   **The Stoics.** A school of Greek philosophers, founded by Zeno of Citium about 310 B.C., whose moral philosophy held that happiness consists in liberation from the bondage of the passions and appetites, and in approximation to God by obeying his will; that virtue is thus the highest good, and suffering a matter of indifference.

173:27   **All of which...if ever there was one.** DHL knew no Greek and derived this argument from Charles's *Commentary*: 'In fact, John the Seer used a unique style, the true character of which no Grammar of the New Testament has as yet recognized. He thought in Hebrew, and he frequently reproduces Hebrew idioms literally in Greek. But his solecistic style cannot be wholly explained from its Hebraistic colouring. The language which he adopted in his old age formed for him no rigid medium of expression. Hence he remodelled its syntax freely, and created a Greek that is absolutely his own' Charles, i. x–xi. See also i. xxi.

173:35   **To him...of God.** Revelation ii. 7. This and subsequent quotations are from the Authorised Version, not from Moffatt, except where DHL indicates to the contrary.

173:36   **He that...second death.** Revelation ii. 11 ['...hurt of...'].

173:39   **To him...receiveth it.** Revelation ii. 17.

174:4   **And he...Morning Star.** Revelation ii. 26–8 ['...morning star...'].

174:7   **He that...angels.** Revelation iii. 5.

174:12   **He that...new name.** Revelation iii. 12 ['Him...'].

174:15   **To him...throne.—** Revelation iii. 21.

174:33   **"He shall...no end.—"** Luke i. 32–3.

174:37   **"And Jesus said unto them...Israel".** Matthew xix. 28 ['...Son of Man...'].

174:39   **"The Lord said...thy footstool".** Psalm cx (AV) ['...Sit thou at my right hand, until I make thine enemies thy footstool...']. See also Acts ii. 35; Mark xii. 36; Luke xx. 41–4.

175:2   **"God hath made...Christ".** Acts ii. 36.

175:6   **"The conqueror...his throne".** Revelation iii. 21.

Appendix II, '*Apocalypse*', Fragment 2

177:7   Epicurus. See 160:23n.

177:18   Isis. See 107:10n.

177:18   Osiris, or Orphic Dionysos, or Mithras. See 156:23n; 85:22n; and 99:33n.

177:25   Stoic. See 172:36n.

178:14   Day of All the Dead. 2 November, All Souls Day. The phrase is a translation of the Italian, 'il giorno dei Morti', which DHL may have picked up in Italy in 1912. He speaks of the 'feast of all the dead' in *Letters*, i. 467.

179:26   Bacchus. A name of the Greek God Dionysus.

181:35   the great history of the gods...Almighty. See 109:27n.

182:2   Nirvana. See 148:14n.

182:5   *samadhi*. The basic term used in both Hindu and Buddhist theology for the state of concentration or higher trance achieved through meditation.

182:7   the three states of man. This is DHL's adaptation of Comte's 'Law of three stages' in human intellectual development. Comte held that human intellectual development has moved from a theological stage, in which the universe was explained in terms of gods and spirits, through a transitional metaphysical stage, in which explanations were in terms of essences, final causes and other abstractions, to the modern positivist stage which recognises the limitations of human knowledge and seeks to discover the laws governing the regular connections among phenomena. Like Comte, DHL was concerned with the question of how our scientific, industrialised civilisation which lacks the beliefs and social institutions of the past, can achieve social stability and provide for the fulfilment of the individual. See letter to Koteliansky, [10? August 1919].

182:21   gaze at the stars. Cf. p. 54.

182:36   Babylonia. See 85:29n.

182:38   Pentateuch. The first five books of the Old Testament (Genesis, Exodus, Leviticus, Numbers and Deuteronomy) taken together as a connected group and traditionally ascribed to Moses.

183:2   Belshazzar's. See 52:14n.

183:3   the "wheels" of Ezekiel. See Ezekiel i. 15–21.

183:6   the year 600 B.C. Anaximander is thought to have lived *c.* 610–540 B.C.

183:26   a city of Stoics. St Paul was a native of the city of Tarsus in Cilicia, which was the seat of a famous Stoic philosophical school.

183:33   apotheosis of the individual. Greek, from θεός 'god'. The pagan custom of regarding as gods emperors or certain other persons, at first only after their death, but from the time of Domitian (A.D. 51–96), who ruled A.D. 81–96, even in their lifetime. This idea of deification has sometimes been thought to be connected with the origins of Christian canonisation. The word is also used in the sense of 'union with God' in eastern Christian mysticism and theology.

184:10   **eastern Fathers.** See 97:38n.

184:21   **John the Baptist...day.** DHL is referring to the Essenes, a Jewish ascetic sect which probably originated in the second century B.C. and came to an end in the second century A.D. but never passed beyond the limits of Palestine. However, the suggestion that John the Baptist had Essene connections is rather improbable.

184:31   **Greek.** See 173:27n.

185:3   **Dispersion.** See 85:29n.

185:21   **Messiah.** From the Hebrew word for 'anointed'. The term denotes a person invested by God with special powers and functions. It was however used more particularly of the king who was conceived as anointed by divine command and his person, as 'the Lord's anointed', was held to be sacrosanct. The appearance of a future king of the house of David whose rule would be glorious, was foretold by Isaiah and Jeremiah. According to the New Testament Gospels Jesus was expressly proclaimed as the Christ or Messiah by angels at his birth (Luke ii. 11). When at his trial Jesus was asked by the High Priest 'Art Thou the Christ?' he replied in the affirmative (Mark xiv. 61ff), and after his resurrection he explicitly taught his own identity with the Messiah of the Old Testament expectation (Luke xxiv. 25–7).

185:29   **Time Spirit and Demiurge and Kosmokrator.** See page 75, 82:23n and 83:22n.

185:36   **Herod Antipas.** DHL is wrong here. The Temple was desecrated by Antiochus Epiphanes in 167 B.C. and ceased as a place of worship when Jerusalem was destroyed by the Romans in A.D. 70. Herod Antipas (4 B.C. – A.D. 39), was the son of Herod the Great who had been appointed King of the Jews by the Romans in 40 B.C. Antipas was the 'Herod the tetrarch' of the Gospels who married Herodias and beheaded John the Baptist, and who ruled at the time of Christ's ministry. See 67:7n and 159:13n.

186:10   **the marriage at Cana.** See John ii. 1–11 for the story of the miracle of turning water into wine.

186:15   **I have not taught in secret...have taught openly.** A paraphrase of John xviii. 20 ['I spake openly to the world; I ever taught in the synagogue, and in the temple, whither the Jews always resort; and in secret have I said nothing.']

186:17   **transmigration.** Transition from one state or condition to another, especially passage from this life by death; passage of the soul at death into another body, metempsychosis.

186:28   **his unknown "editor".** See 81:37n and 86:39n.

187:19   **Even as it is...gods: or heaven.** DHL found this notion in James Pryse's *The Apocalypse Unsealed.* See Introduction, pp. 5–7.

188:15   **seven "stages of the Cross".** Technically, the seven *stations* of the Cross. These stations are also traditionally depicted in a series of fourteen pictures or carvings designed for devotional purposes, which show incidents in the last journey of Christ from Pilate's house to his entombment.

188:37   **anima and animus.** This is DHL's adaptation of various early Greek philosophical accounts of the spirit and soul. However, 'anima' and 'animus' was a distinction made by Jung, who saw them as the female and male part, respectively, of the individual psyche which is in communication with the unconscious.

189:28   **says Thales.** Burnet 47.

189:31   **meant by water.** Burnet writes that according to Thales 'water was the stuff of which all other things were transient forms' (48).

189:32   **All things are full of gods.** Thales, quoted by Burnet 48.

189:36   **what Thales can have meant by "gods".** Burnet explains that a non-religious use of the word 'god' is characteristic in this period of Greek philosophy, and that 'θεός' could be used equally to describe human passions and natural phenomena. See Burnet 14 and 48–9.

190:7   **"All...grow", says Xenophanes.** Burnet 120.

190:8   **"All...Fire", says Herakleitos.** Burnet 135.

190:9   **"Fire...fire".** Burnet 135.

190:22   **"O...rose".** 'A red red Rose' (1794). A poem by Robert Burns (1759–96) [O my Luve's like a red, red rose,] line 1.

190:28   **"Lord...all generations—".** Psalm xc.

191:9   **like a bridegroom...his chamber.** Psalm xix. 5 ['which is as a bridegroom coming out of his chamber,'].

192:35   **Lord Kelvin.** Sir William Thomson, first Baron Kelvin (1824–1907), Professor of natural philosophy at Glasgow University. He advanced the science of thermodynamics and electricity and evolved the theory of electric oscillations, which forms the basis of wireless telegraphy.

192:36   **Darwin.** Charles Robert Darwin (1809–82) whose great works *On the Origin of Species* and *The Descent of Man* appeared in 1859 and 1871.

193:11   **Nirvana or Samadhi.** DHL incorrectly equates these terms. The *OED* defines Nirvana: 'In Buddhist theology, the extinction of individual existence, or the extinction of all desires and passions and attainment of perfect beatitude.' Samadhi, however, is merely a state of higher trance or concentration.

194:3   *ab ovo.* From the egg, i.e. from the beginning.

Appendix III, *Apocalypsis II*

195:33   **A number was once..."natural" number.** See 87:37n and 139:10n; see also Burnet 102–3 and 288–9.

195:34   **"All...again".** Burnet 103. See 139:3n.

196:38   **In some of the dialogues...pure nonsense.** DHL is confusing the Socratic method with that of the Sophists. Socrates inquired into the right conduct of life through the method of cross-questioning the people with whom he came into contact. The Sophists, however, were itinerant teachers who went from city to city giving instruction for a fee. The very nature of their profession tended to place emphasis on material success and on the ability to argue for any point of view irrespective of the truth; hence the undesirable associations which the word came to have and which have passed over into its English derivative.

198:16   **terrible fiasco.** This refers to Plato's friendship with Dion of Syracuse who summoned Plato in 367 B.C. to try to realise the philosopher-king in the person of Dionysius II. Plato felt bound to try, but the new ruler's suspicion of Dion was soon reinforced by his jealousy of his friendship with Plato. He banished Dion and sought to retain Plato, at one point keeping the latter a virtual prisoner. In 357 Dion re-entered Syracuse by force and expelled Dionysius, but was himself assassinated a few years later.

199:29   **Thought is getting out of touch.** Cf. 'Thought', *Complete Poems* 673.

TEXTUAL APPARATUS

TEXTUAL APPARATUS
Introduction to *The Dragon of the Apocalypse*

The following symbols are used:

MS = Manuscript
LM = *London Mercury*
Ed. = Editor
~ = Repeated word in recording an accidental variant.

The accepted reading appears within the square bracket and except where stated to the contrary, this is from the *MS*; the *LM* version follows.

45:7	Señor] Senor	50:12	figures] fitures
45:13	the *Dragon*] *The Dragon*	50:17	correct] Correct
45:15	it? It] ~ ?— ~	50:21	*sanahorias Ed.*] sanahorias MS,
45:17	about?] ~ ?—		LM
45:18	the *Dragon*] *The Dragon*	50:23	*sanahoria Ed.*] sanahoria MS,
45:20	*magic?*] ~ ?—		LM
45:24	used.—] ~ .	51:8	told:] ~ ,
45:25	used!—] ~ .	51:13	god-experience]
45:32	Revelation *Ed.*] *Revelation MS,*		God-experience
	LM	52:11	with spots! he] With spots! He
46:4	zodiac] Zodiac	53:11	carcasses] carcases
46:6	dies,] ~ —	54:1	cosmos] Cosmos
46:37	macrocosm] Macrocosm	54:2	cosmos] Cosmos
47:3	macrocosm] Macrocosm	54:2	magnificent] Magnificent
47:36	Revelation] *Revelation*	54:4	chemical works] chemical-works
48:34	sense-consciousness]	54:23	*Dragon LM*] Dragon MS
	sense—consciousness	54:37	Revelation *Ed.*] *Revelation MS,*
48:35	mental] metal		*LM*
49:7	mental] metal	55:4	Revelation *Ed.*] *Revelation MS,*
49:10	myth] Myth		*LM*
49:16	unconscious"] ~ ",	55:7	the Alpha] Alpha
49:24	the symbol] the Symbol	55:8	Little Bo-Peep] *Little Bo-Peep*
49:35	Christian-allegorical] Christian,	55:39	first century] First Century
	allegorical	56:11	chapel] Chapel

Apocalypse

The following symbols are used to distinguish states of the text:

MS = Manuscript
TCC = Corrected typed carbon copy
O = Orioli, Florence first edition

Whenever the *TCC* reading is adopted, it appears within the square bracket with no symbol. When a reading from a source other than the *TCC* has been preferred, it appears with its source-symbol within the square bracket. Rejected readings follow the square bracket, in chronological sequence, with their first source denoted. In the absence of information to the contrary the reader should assume that this particular variant recurs in all subsequent states.

The following symbols are used editorially:

Ed. = Editor
Om. = Omitted
/ = Line or page break resulting in a punctuation, hyphenation or spelling error
~ = Repeated word in recording an accidental variant

59:6	mystification. On...mystification, and] mystification and *O*	63:14	jasper] Jasper *O*
59:24	or] on *O*	63:16	grand, very grand indeed, once they *MS*] grand. Very grand indeed, since they *TCC*
59:26	Sunday School *Ed.*] Sunday-school MS	63:21	had,] ~ *O*
60:33	that] which *O*	64:3	self-glory] Self-glory *O*
61:6	ever] over *O*	64:18	Primitive Methodist chapel] primitive ~ ~ *O*
61:8	pie-pie, *MS*] ~ /*TCC* ~ *O*	64:19	don't] *Om. O*
61:16	called"—] ~ *O*	64:32	religion of self-glorification *MS*, *O*] religion self-glorification *TCC*
61:23	a Christian, a rider on a white horse must be more than *MS*] *Om. TCC*	65:7	aristocrat] aristocrats *O*
61:32	throne and] ~, and *O*	65:19	In MS, *O*] On *TCC*
61:40	come—".] ~. *O*	65:24	worldly] wordly *O*
62:9	washed] washen *O*	65:28	people] ~, *O*
62:18	kings] Kings *O*	66:25	*creative MS*] creative *TCC*
62:18	waters,] ~ *O*	66:25	nevertheless *MS*] never-the-less *TCC*
62:20	colliers'] collier's *O*	66:31	to *MS*] of
62:21	MYSTERY, BABYLON THE GREAT, ...EARTH *MS*] MYSTERY! BABYLON THE GREAT!...EARTH!. *TCC* MYSTERY BABYLON THE GREAT...EARTH *O*	66:32	second-rate] second rate *O*
		66:33	century. And *MS*] ~, and *TCC*
62:29	Reformation] ~, *O*	66:34	today: *MS*] ~; *TCC*
62:34	bird—"] ~" *O*	67:4	Christianity:] ~, *O*
63:10	Sin] Sion *O*	67:11	saints *MS*] Saints *TCC*

67:18 disguise, and enthroned *MS*]
disguise, enthroned *TCC* disguise enthroned *O*
67:22 O] o *O*
68:5 self-realisation *MS*] self realisation *TCC*
68:9 merely:] ~ ; *O*
68:20 Buddha,] ~ *O*
68:31 forever. Recognise...and] forever. and *O*
68:33 It] it *O*
68:35 happens? *MS*] ~ ! *TCC*
69:16 reversed] reserved *O*
69:19 Tsar *MS*] Tzar *TCC*
69:31 teaching. *MS, O*] ~ : *TCC*
69:35 lord. *Ed.*] ~ : *MS*
69:38 death-kiss *MS*] death kiss
TCC
71:2 saints *MS*] Saints *TCC*
71:12 Tsar *MS*] Tzar *TCC*
71:14 Tsar *MS*] Tzar *TCC*
71:16 Tsar *MS*] Tzar *TCC*
71:20 last] least *O*
71:23 a] *Om. O*
71:29 saint *MS*] Saint *TCC*
71:29 St. *MS, O*] st. *TCC*
73:2 Revelation *Ed.*] *Revelation MS*
73:11 Great War] great war *O*
73:14 only] *Om. O*
73:17 revelation] Revelation *O*
73:22 has] *Om. O*
73:34 the lampstands *MS*] ~ lampstands *TCC*
74:36 dazzler, *MS*] ~ ; *TCC*
74:40 superiority *MS*] Superiority
TCC
75:1 God *Ed.*] god *MS*
76:5 pagans!] ~ *O*
76:26 honoured *Ed.*] honored *MS*
76:28 *somewhere*]somewhere *O*
76:31 astronomists'] astronomist's *O*
77:1 hates] hater of *O*
78:16 *vital MS*] vital *TCC*
78:17 One *MS*] The *TCC*
78:30 katabolism] Katabolism *O*
78:31 same] same with *O*
79:3 Revelation *Ed.*] *Revelation MS*
79:8 anathema *MS*] Anathema *TCC*

79:21 Revelation *Ed.*] *Revelation MS*
79:22 As an *MS*] As *TCC, O*
79:33 destruction of...imagination
ceased] destruction they ceased
O
80:2 *postponed destiny MS*] *postponed-
destiny TCC*
80:29 a simple *MS*] simple *TCC*
81:15 power greater] greater *O*
81:27 book, *MS*] ~ *TCC*
81:39 Old Testament *Ed.*] old ~ *MS*
82:3 God's *Ed.*] god's *MS*
82:8 He *MS*] he *TCC*
82:20 God *MS*] god *TCC*
82:32 scientific *MS*] Scientific *TCC*
83:24 God *Ed.*] god *MS*
83:32 saint *MS*] Saint *TCC*
84:17 star-cults,] starcults *O*
84:26 half-cosmic, half-mechanical]
half-cosmic, half mechanical *O*
84:34 pawns, *MS*] ~ ; *TCC*
85:18 century. Of *MS*] ~ , of *TCC*
85:28 gentiles *MS*] Gentiles *TCC*
85:30 Sunday School *Ed.*] Sunday-
school *MS*
85:31 God *Ed.*] god *MS*
86:1 Gospels] Gospel *O*
86:13 Apocalypse *MS*] apocalypse
TCC
86:25 Revelation *Ed.*] *Revelation
MS*
86:28 them *MS*] then *TCC* that *O*
87:4 been, *MS*] ~ *TCC*
87:7 documents *MS*] document
TCC
87:16 still:] ~ — *O*
87:25 barbarians] barbarian *O*
88:8 stupidity? *MS*] ~ ! *TCC*
88:12 *Neufrecheit*] Neufrecheit *O*
88:33 *of Religion and Ethics Ed.*]
of Religion and Ethics *MS*
90:6 world] *Om. O*
90:7 civilisations *MS*] civilisation
TCC
90:24 inventions; *MS*] ~ : *TCC*
90:25 Christ, *MS*] ~ *TCC*
91:2 great *MS*] *Om.*
92:5 *What MS*] what *TCC*

92:6   rather *MS, O*] ~, *TCC*
93:3   *end MS*] end *TCC*
93:5   full-stop] full stop *O*
93:9   consciousness labours...a goal to] *Om. O*
93:19 depth, *MS*] ~ *TCC*
93:23 appreciate...oracles] appreciate that the oracles *O*
93:31 same, *MS*] ~ *TCC*
95:6   cycle *MS*] circle *TCC*
95:13 conscious-process *MS*] conscious process *TCC*
95:17 A great rock is God.] *Om. O*
95:19 *is* God] ~ god *O*
95:19 is God *Ed.*] ~ god *MS*
95:21 moves: twice *MS*] moves/twice *TCC*] moves: is twice *O*
95:24 God *Ed.*] god *MS*
95:29 god;] ~ : *O*
95:29 or the blue gleam might suddenly occupy your consciousness: then that was god;] *Om. O*
96:11 scientists] philosophers *O*, *see explanatory note*
96:14 translations'] ~ *O*
96:15 script?] ~ ! *O*
96:20 work, which is not its own meaning. It is] *Om. O*
96:23 Professor *Ed.*] Prof. *MS*
96:24 Jowett,] ~ *O*
96:26 Victorian *MS*] victorian *TCC*
97:30 Creatures *MS*] creatures *TCC*
97:31 them] then *O*
97:39 hands *MS*] heads *TCC*
98:4   that *MS*] ~, *TCC*
98:20 star-lore, *MS*] ~ *TCC*
98:28 Lightning *MS*] lightning *TCC*
98:28 Almighty *MS*] ~, *TCC*
98:30 Lightning *MS*] lightning *TCC*
98:33 God *MS*] god *TCC*
98:37 unknown *MS*] ~, *TCC*
99:7   Apocalypse:] ~ —*O*
99:10 has] had *O*
99:19 Lion *MS*] lion *TCC*
99:34 (they...up as...throat) *MS*] (they...up) as they cut his throat, *TCC*

100:16 am—] ~. *O*
101:19 demonstrate. The *MS*] ~ — the *TCC*
101:19 a common...view, *MS*] a common...view *TCC* common ...view *O*
101:26 Far back, *MS*] ~ ~ *TCC*
101:29 potency *MS*] potence *TCC*
102:10 sanguine, *MS, O*] ~ *TCC*
102:17 red!—] ~ ! *O*
102:37 self, *MS*] ~ *TCC*
103:12 is] in *O*
103:13 is] in *O*
103:37 befall *O*] befal *MS*
103:38 hurt.—] ~. *O*
104:16 from the...living "I"] For the soul, the spirit, and the living "I" from the far gate of hell into the new day. *O*
104:20 day, *MS*] ~/*TCC* ~ *O*
104:22 terrestrial *Ed.*] terrestial *MS*
104:27 terrestrial *Ed.*] terrestial *MS*
104:36 "souls"] souls *O*
104:40 I", *MS, O*] ~" *TCC*
105:17 Hades.—] ~. *O*
105:22 six] sin *O*
106:13 God *MS*] god *TCC*
106:22 Amen."—*MS*] ~." *TCC*
106:24 new-born *MS, O*] new born *TCC*
106:32 under-dark] underdark *O*
107:1 the dancing women lift the garlands] dancing women lift their garlands *O*
107:9 on-lookers *MS*] onlookers *TCC*
107:15 Buddhist *MS*] Hindu *TCC*, *see explanatory note*
107:23 ashes: *MS, O*] ~, *TCC*
107:24 body: *MS, O*] ~; *TCC*
108:18 then *MS, O*] there *TCC*
109:14 yet] Yet *O*
109:31 old self, *MS*] ~ ~ *TCC*
109:40 woe, *MS, O*] ~ — *TCC*
110:8 women—] ~ *O*
110:23 old *MS*] *Om. TCC*
111:3 "Loose *Ed.*] Loose *MS*
111:4 Euphrates".—*Ed.*] ~. — *MS*] ~. *O*

111:13 issue *O*] issues *TCC*
111:15 come *Ed.*] comes *TCC*
111:18 symbols,] ~ *O*
111:24 sulphureous] sulphurous *O*
111:26 the sun...the hellish sun.] the hellish sun. *O*
111:26 lions' *Ed.*] lion's *MS*
111:29 horse-bodied] horsebodied *O*
112:20 sulphureous] sulphurous *O*
112:23 were *O*] was *MS*
112:26 sulphureous] sulphurous *O*
112:32 waters] water *O*
112:40 injustice"— *MS*] ~." *TCC*
114:15 to do] do *O*
114:16 new commands, *MS*] commands *TCC*
114:20 gods *MS*] Gods *TCC*
114:20 God *MS*] god *TCC*
115:4 God *MS*] god *TCC*
115:11 Come *MS*] come *TCC*
115:17 Revelation *Ed.*] *Revelation MS*
116:1 The Olympic-heroic period... vision] The Olympic-heroic vision *O*
116:5 The *MS*] the *TCC*
116:6 lords] lord *O*
116:9 Samothracian *MS, O*] samothracian *TCC*
116:24 and, malefic,] ~ ~ *O*
116:31 Babylonian and *MS*] Babylonian, *TCC*
116:35 rain-makers] rainmakers *O*
117:2 self: *MS*] ~ *TCC*
117:8 other, *MS*] ~ / *TCC* ~ *O*
117:33 is, *MS*] ~ *TCC*
118:3 or *MS*] be *TCC*
119:6 unjewish *Ed.*] unJewish *MS*
119:11 heaven; *MS*] ~, *TCC*
119:18 the earth *MS*] earth *TCC*
119:31 the earth] earth *O*
120:6 them,] ~ *O*
120:9 Mother *MS*] mother *TCC*
120:20 queen: *MS, O*] ~ / *TCC*
120:26 Presence *MS*] presence *TCC*
120:32 Woman *MS*] woman *TCC*
120:35 than *MS*] then *TCC*
121:6 winepress *MS*] corepress *TCC* wine-press *O*

121:20 couldn't, *MS*] ~ : *TCC*
121:25 desert,] ~ *O*
121:29 three-and] three and *O*
121:32 Mother *MS*] mother *TCC*
121:34 Woman *MS*] woman *TCC*
121:37 Patmos'] ~ *O*
122:5 jeweller's *MS, O*] Jeweller's *TCC*
122:5 end!] ~ ? *O*
123:6 depths *MS, O*] depth *TCC*
124:6 men *MS*] man *TCC*
124:15 conquest *MS*] Conquest *TCC*
124:16 serpent,] ~ *O*
125:25 a destroyer] or destroyer *O*
125:33 cycle *MS*] Cycle *TCC*
126:16 Laocoön] Laocoon *O*
126:23 coils us] coils in *O*
126:30 significant", *MS*] ~ " *TCC*
127:3 police-woman's *MS*] police woman's *TCC*
127:9 God *MS*] god *TCC*
127:12 old form] cold form *O*
127:16 police-woman *Ed.*] policewoman *MS*
127:17 come, *MS*] ~ *TCC*
127:19 like a spring-time breeze *MS*] like a spring-time; and say nothing. Come in touch, in soft new touch like a spring-time breeze *TCC*, *see explanatory note*
127:28 Europe...with the glorification *MS*| Europe with the glorification *TCC*
127:39 farthest-off *MS*] farthest off *TCC*
128:9 were *MS*] was *TCC*
128:19 old] cold *O*
128:22 silver *MS*] Silver *TCC*
129:1 harlot-woman *MS*] harlot woman *TCC*
129:4 socialists] Socialists *MS*
129:9 white dragon *Ed.*] White Dragon *MS*
129:19 off: *MS*] ~, *TCC*
129:31 still, *MS*] ~ / *TCC* ~ *O*
130:4 seven *MS*] of seven *TCC*
130:12 The number three was three pebbles.] *Om. O*

130:27 God *MS*] god *TCC*
131:7   God *MS*] god *TCC*
131:11 God *Ed.*] god *MS*
131:16 kind] king *O*
131:35 religion] religious *O*
131:38 God *Ed.*] god *MS*
132:2   God-inhabited] god-inhabited *MS*
132:3   God *MS*] god *TCC*
132:5   then, *MS*] ∼ *TCC*
132:6   stars,] ∼ *O*
132:13 cosmic] Cosmic *O*
133:16 Throne] throne *O*
133:30 Maker *MS*] maker *TCC*
133:31 surround] surrounded *O*
134:5   Cherubim, *MS*] ∼ *TCC* ∼ . *O*
134:14 elements] element *O*
134:21 far, far aloft] far aloft *O*
134:27 his: All *MS*] ∼ : all *TCC*
134:28 Fire—, *MS*] Fire-, *TCC* Fire . . *O*
134:36 Love] love *O*
134:40 Nestis *Ed.*] Vestis *TCC*
135:1   gods *Ed.*] Gods *MS*
135:17 brain. *MS*, *O*] ∼ . – *TCC*
135:19 The Golden Age *MS*] the golden age *TCC* The age *O*
135:23 this] ∼ , *O*
135:27 men *MS*] man *TCC*
136:9   Wholeness.] ∼ .—*O*
136:9   no] not *O*
136:13 with sun] with the sun *O*
136:16 men] man *O*
136:24 serious] direct *O*, *see explanatory note*
137:37 conjuring, *MS*] ∼ /*TCC* ∼ *O*
139:8   Pythagoreans,] ∼ *O*
139:12 kings, horns] kings horn *O*
139:19 Uraeus *MS*] uraeus *TCC*
140:15 unchanging, unchanging] unchanging, *O*
141:2   Revelation *Ed.*] *Revelation MS*
141:21 woman, *MS*] ∼ *TCC*
141:31 a new era *MS*] or new era *TCC*
142:3   crowns,] ∼ *O*
142:11 bear,] ∼ *O*
142:30 stands] stand *O*

142:33 shop.—] ∼ .*O*
143:1   something"—*MS*] ∼ "/*TCC* ∼ " *O*
143:2   You can. . .meaning flat.] You can put down the meaning flat plain as two and two make four. *O*, *see explanatory note*
143:7   horns *MS*] ∼ , *TCC*
144:10 been. *MS*] ∼ ! *TCC*
144:26 great—! *MS*] ∼ — *TCC*
144:29 But *MS*] And *TCC*
145:2   matter of fact] matter-of-fact *MS*
145:10 fail,] *fail* O
145:13 etc.—*MS*] ∼ ./*TCC* ∼ . *O*
145:14 is: *MS*] ∼ ; *TCC*
145:15 anything! *MS*] ∼ . *TCC*
145:22 is,] ∼ *O*
145:27 beginning, *MS*] ∼ /*TCC* ∼ *O*
145:28 since] for refusal *O*, *see explanatory note*
146:6   man *MS*] men *TCC*
146:16 Mussolini is also a martyr] others also are martys *O*, *see explanatory note*
146:19 like Mussolini] like those *O*, *see explanatory note*
146:27 so, and] so. And *O*
147:3   Nation *MS*] nation *O*
147:6   so-called *MS*] so called *TCC*
147:18 hierarchy, *MS*] ∼ *TCC*
147:27 mere] more *O*
147:34 man] ∼ , *MS*
147:36 himself, *MS*] ∼ *TCC*
148:4   democrat *cannot* love. Or, *MS*] democrat, *cannot* love, or, *TCC* democrat *cannot* love. Or, *O*
148:16 neighbour, *MS*, *O*] ∼ *TCC*
148:18 State: *MS*] ∼ ; *TCC*
148:18 Gospels *MS*] gospels *TCC*
148:18 Epistles *MS*] epistles *TCC*
148:19 State *MS*] state *TCC*
148:23 simply, *MS*, *O*] ∼ *TCC*
148:25 mercy, *MS*, *O*] ∼ *TCC*
148:28 and *MS*] *Om. TCC*
149:8   gold, *MS*] ∼ *TCC*
149:12 only,] ∼ *MS*

Appendixes

The following editorial changes have been made, signalled by the editorial symbol *Ed.* within a square bracket. The *MS* version appears after the bracket.

Appendix I *Apocalypse*, Fragment 1

155:14 fullness *Ed.*] fulness
156:12 God *Ed.*] god
157:40 Book of Daniel *Ed.*] *Book of Daniel*
158:1 Esther *Ed.*] *Esther*
169:2 god-like *Ed.*] godlike

170:18 revelation *Ed.*] Revelation
170:24 unjewish *Ed.*] unJewish
171:34 fertility-myth *Ed.*] fertility myth
172:36 Stoics *Ed.*] stoics
173:10 Revelation *Ed.*] *Revelation*
176:15 in *Ed.*] on

Appendix II *Apocalypse*, Fragment 2

177:25 Stoic *Ed.*] stoic
179:28 gods *Ed.*] Gods
180:1 [he] *Ed.*] *Om.*
180:37 life *Ed.*] life life
182:37 star-lore *Ed.*] star lore
183:22 that *Ed.*] the
183:26 Stoics *Ed.*] stoics

183:26 Stoic *Ed.*] stoic
184:25 Revelation *Ed.*] *Revelation*
184:26 apocalypses *Ed.*] *Apocalypses*
184:27 revelation *Ed.*] Revelation
184:28 Revelation *Ed.*] *Revelation*
187:21 Revelation *Ed.*] *Revelation*

Appendix III, *Apocalypsis II*

196:21 *volte face Ed.*] *volta face*
197:31 object? *Ed.*] ~.
198:37 Millennium *Ed.*] Millenium

198:38 Millennium *Ed.*] Millenium
199:2 Millennium *Ed.*] Millenium
199:23 God *Ed.*] god

In this edition the following compound words are hyphenated at the end of a line; these hyphenated forms occur in the base-text (*TCC*) and should be retained in quotations:

45:14 post-master
52:14 fortune-telling
52:29 day-school
64:6 mealy-mouthed
69:22 white-feathered
84:2 death-penalties
121:33 half-women

123:28 half-demonish
127:7 police-woman
128:3 hero-kings
144:14 self-righteousness
161:36 group-connection
171:33 fertility-myth